THE GODFATHER OF MODERN HURLING

THE FATHER TOMMY MAHER STORY

ENDA McEVOY

D0840770

Published in 2012 by Ballpoint Press
4 Wyndham Park, Bray, Co Wicklow, Republic of Ireland.
Telephone: 086 8217631
Email: ballpointpress1@gmail.com

ISBN 9780957207202

Cover Photograph: Fr Tommy Maher in typical instructional mode in
Nowlan Park with (left to right) Chunky O'Brien, Tom McCormack, Ger Henderson,
Mick Crotty, Nickey Brennan, Ger Fennelly, Brian Cody, Pat Delaney
and Noel Skehan (facing away from camera). *Photograph by Tom Brett, Kilkenny*

*This book was supported by the Kilkenny GAA Supporters Club
and the St Kieran's College Past Pupils Union*

Book design and production by Elly Design

Printed and bound by GraphyCems

To Dan McEvoy, who saw it all.
Well, nearly all...

CONTENTS

Enda McEvoy was formerly the hurling correspondent of the 'Sunday Tribune'.

He is the author of 'Fennessy's Field' and co-author of 'Triumph and Troubles – The Official Biography of Charlie Carter'.

He is currently a columnist with the 'Irish Examiner'.

PREFACE

On the last evening of June 1957 a 52-year-old man alighted on the platform at Kilkenny railway station and began to make his way home to 92 Patrick Street in the city. He hadn't got very far when he was hailed by an acquaintance coming out of Confraternity in St John's.

"Well, what was it like?" the acquaintance enquired.

The first man, one of the 130 Kilkenny supporters who had travelled on the excursion train to Croke Park for the day's Leinster hurling semi-final against Dublin, shook his head. "No All Ireland for us this year," he replied.

It was little wonder that Jack Leahy was sceptical, for the match he'd made the effort to attend had been an exercise in mediocrity to an almost stupefying degree. Dublin were poor, Kilkenny were no better despite the presence of their new trainer, a young priest from Gowran, and it was the visitors who were hanging on for a draw as the referee, Brian Smith of Meath, blew the final whistle.

It was little wonder either that Leahy was not disposed to expect Kilkenny to improve for the outing and perhaps go on to better things, given that the county hadn't won an All Ireland since 1947, the day Terry Leahy – no relation – elevated himself to hurling immortality with the famous point that won a famous final. Prior to that, moreover, they hadn't won the All Ireland since 1939, the day Croke Park echoed to thunder and lightning and the news that Europe was once more at war.

As it turned out Jack Leahy, by profession a nurse in St Canice's psychiatric hospital and by vocation a hurling fanatic, was wrong. Kilkenny proceeded to beat Dublin in the replay three weeks later before flooring the reigning MacCarthy Cup holders Wexford in the Leinster final and defeating Waterford in a classic All Ireland showdown. Leahy would live until he was 76, witnessing the county win another eight All Irelands along the way.

His inquisitor that far-off summer night, Dan McEvoy from the Hebron Road, opposite Nowlan Park, would also attend the 1957 All Ireland final. Despite the fact that he was 29 years of age, it was only the second All Ireland he had seen Kilkenny win in the flesh. As of the evening of September 4th 2011 he had been present in Croke Park to witness 19 further black and amber-striped autumn triumphs.

As for the young priest from Gowran, this is his story. To some degree it is also the story of the game of hurling since 1957. That is because the story of hurling since 1957 cannot be told without telling the story of Kilkenny hurling since 1957 and because the story of Kilkenny hurling since 1957 cannot be told without telling the story of Tommy Maher. To a large extent it *is* the story of Tommy Maher, and of his works and his deeds and his legacy.

Fr Tommy Maher. Kilkenny's messiah and the godfather of modern hurling.

CHAPTER ONE

Wexford

Wexford are still powerful and must remain favourites to retain their title and thus set a new Leinster record. But I also agree with thousands of hurling supporters who believe that if Wexford are to be beaten this year tomorrow will be the day of their downfall
Pádraig Puirséal, *Irish Press*, August 3rd 1957

It was dry and overcast on Dublin's northside on the afternoon hurling changed forever. De Valera was Taoiseach, Seán T O'Kelly was in the Phoenix Park and Eisenhower in the White House. A sweeping new open-skies plan designed to prevent surprise attack was being presented by the US to the Russian delegates at the London disarmament conference. Up to 10,000 arrests were reported in a crackdown by the regime in Hungary. Tulyar, the 1952 Epsom Derby winner purchased by the Irish state only to prove a notorious disappointment at the National Stud before being sold to an American syndicate, was still making front-page news, fighting intestinal trouble at the Claiborne Stud in Kentucky and reported to be showing improvement. Eddie Keher was playing in the minor match in Croke Park. Brian Cody had just turned three years of age.

Micheál O'Hehir, a racing expert on Saturdays but the voice of the GAA on the Sabbath, came on Radio Éireann at 3.25pm, five minutes before the throw-in and not long after Kilkenny, with a couple of goals from a 15-year-old Keher, had beaten Offaly in the curtainraiser. August 4th 1957. It was just another Sunday. It was just another Leinster final. But by teatime nothing would be quite the same again. This was to be one of those games carved into the granite wall of hurling history.

Wexford were the favourites. That was a given. They were the holders, they were the All Ireland champions of the past two seasons and they were bidding for a record fourth Leinster title in succession. But there was more, much more, to Wexford than that. They weren't simply a team. They weren't simply the most popular team of their era, or the most fondly remembered GAA team of all time, or even one of the few teams in any sport to have succeeded in transcending the confines of their code and crossing the whitewash to be embraced by the public. They were a band of brothers, a collection of unlikely heroes, a bunch of ordinary, painfully humble men who together constituted a cause. Therein was rooted their boundless appeal.

Reviewing a new book called *The Fellowship of the Ring*, the first instalment of a fantasy trilogy, in the autumn of 1954, CS Lewis compared it to "lightning from a clear sky". The Wexford story was the hurling equivalent of JRR Tolkien's epic tale except with stouter protagonists, sterner foes – these orcs were arrayed in red and white or blue and gold – and bolder feats of arms. In a land without hope or heroes, Nicky Rackard and his comrades were giants. Rackard himself, who wore tweed jackets and rode with the hunt, might have been an emissary from a space-age civilisation. "The depression of the decade's economy, the awfulness, the backwardness of agricultural production and management, the unemployment, the listlessness – all were sidetracked while the magic was being produced by twenty-five marvellous performers in an art hitherto believed foreign to them," as Nicky Furlong put it in his delightful memoir *The Greatest Hurling Decade – Wexford and the Epic Teams of the '50s*.

To say Wexford were just what hurling was crying out for is as perfectly accurate as it is cliched. Of the 14 finals immediately prior to their All Ireland triumph in 1955, the county's first since 1910, eight had been won by Cork, a four in a row and a three in a row included, and four by Tipperary, a three in a row included. The game needed something new. From the south east it would get not merely something new but something unprecedented and unimaginable. A century and a half after Wexford erupted in flames, the pikemen marched once more.

Everything about them, these bold Shelmaliers with their long-barrelled hurleys from the sea, was bigger, brighter, different. Books were written about Rackard and his colleagues, a small cottage publishing industry springing up on foot of their gaiscí and still functioning 50 years later. (Billy Rackard's *No Hurling at the Dairy Door* is the most interesting, Nicky Furlong's effort the most stylish, Tom Williams's Nicky Rackard biography essential reading and Dominic Williams's *Wexford Hurling & Football Bible 1887-2008* a monumental reference work, while the autobiographies of Martin Codd and Tim Flood have a charm of their own. These are books every student of hurling should possess.) Songs were composed in their honour. Poems name-checked them: "Insint éachta Wexford, athinsint ar ghníomh dhein Ned, Oliver, nó Jim English ar son an chontae," mar a scríobh Art Ó Maolfabhail in *Inis Córthaidh agus Gné den Stair*.

Their glamour was intoxicating, their perseverance staggering. After emerging almost fully formed in 1950, when they reached the Leinster final for the first time since 1918, Wexford proceeded to contest five national deciders in the next five years and lose them all. Every year they came back for more. Every year they did so with a team that was older than the previous season's edition. Nicky Rackard, for instance, had won a provincial junior medal as far back as 1940. Sisyphus, never mind Oliver, had nothing on them.

Even their defeats had a strange magnificence about them. The 1950 Leinster final saw them beat Kilkenny everywhere but on the Nowlan Park scoreboard before losing by a goal, but a spark had been kindled. The 3-9 they hit against Tipperary in 1951 was an eminently respectable tally for an All Ireland final of the era; a pity about the seven goals poor Ray Brennan, the UCD student touted as "the new Tommy Daly" but hung out to dry by his full-back line, conceded. And with its 17 scores in 60 minutes the 1954 All Ireland final may have been as indifferent a showpiece as was every played, yet no final has been more written about or mulled over. Had Nick O'Donnell not gone off injured and Bobby Rackard filled in at full-back, would Wexford have won on the basis that Rackard's clearances would have been landing 30 yards farther down the field? Or did Rackard's magisterial display on the edge of his own square have in reality the effect of saving the challengers from a heavier defeat, as Christy Ring chose to maintain?

Then there was their sportsmanship, the one word associated more than any other with the Wexford team of the 1950s. Consider the tribute from the *Tipperary Star* after their 1955 All Ireland victory over Galway. "Every match they have played in has left abiding memories. No finer body of men has ever graced Croke Park and no finer body of sportsmen."

The *Star* had seen nothing yet. Moments after paradise was gained against Cork the following year, Nick O'Donnell and Bobby Rackard hoisted Christy Ring, their vanquished opponent but still a hero, onto their shoulders, a gesture without parallel in GAA history. Paddy Downey, who six years later would take over as Gaelic games correspondent of *The Irish Times*, a post he held until 1994, was present and was stunned. "Instead of congratulating themselves they honoured their opponent. I never saw the like of it as a sporting gesture before or since. It was beautiful."

Downey was still hearing encomiums to Slaneyside chivalry two decades later. Willie John Ring told of his brother calling in to see him at home in Cloyne after work one evening a few days before a Wexford/Cork match. On being informed by Willie John that the Wexford lineup had been printed in the paper that day and that he'd be on Bobby Rackard, Christy replied: "That's great. We can play hurling on Sunday." Ollie Walsh recounted to Downey the story of the day he'd spilled the sliotar on his goalline against Wexford. As he scrambled to retrieve it Tim Flood dashed in and, hurley high above his shoulder, prepared to pull on the loose ball, six inches from the goalkeeper's face, before stopping at the last moment, jumping over Ollie and winding up in the rigging. "Why didn't you score it?" Walsh asked Flood afterwards. "There's no game worth that risk," came the reply. Fifteen great sportsmen. Or near enough.

Wexford. They were the hope of the neutrals, the refuge of the romantics, Ireland's team. Would they win the All Ireland they so richly deserved while they still had life in them? Would Rackard reach the Promised Land before he got too old? And would they ever find a half-decent goalkeeper?

The hope of seeing the answers to such questions put feet on terraces like never before. Prior to the redevelopment of Croke Park the three biggest attendances at an All Ireland hurling final all involved Wexford: 77,854 in 1955 against Galway, 83,096 in 1956 versus Cork and 84,856 in 1954 against the same opponents. For the 1955 All Ireland semi-final with Limerick, Mackey's Greyhounds, they attracted 51,000 spectators, 12,000 more than the previous best for a semi-final. For the final of the 1956 Oireachtas tournament, that autumnal afterthought of a competition, they drew 37,172 spectators.

And it was Wexford who turned the Leinster final from a fixture into an event. When they drew 41,226 to the 1955 decider, which ended in stalemate with Kilkenny, it was a record. When they drew 52,077 to the 1956 renewal it was a record too. But even the latter figure would be surpassed when 52,272 spectators descended on Croke Park a year later. Among the attendance was the new American ambassador, Scott McLeod, with his wife and family. Only a month in Ireland at the time, Robert Walter Scott McLeod, a former journalist and FBI agent, had been the US's first assistant secretary of state for security and consular affairs, in which capacity he fired some 300 State Department employees on suspicion of Communist sympathies at the height of the Red Scare in the early 1950s. Amid the subsequent backlash against McCarthyism his star fell, and President Eisenhower deemed it politic to pack him off to Dublin.

Also in the crowd was the future Wexford GAA historian Dominic Williams.

And: a 13-year-old boy from Kilkenny city and future brother in law of Ollie Walsh's, Jim 'Galtee' Murphy, who so idolised Tullaroan's Seán Clohosey as to have been accused of imitating his walk and who 54 years later on a Kilkenny street could instantly recite the afternoon's scoreline and relive Johnny McGovern's run for the opening goal.

And: 11-year-old Matt Ruth, who'd paid 6/8 on the train on the old railway line from Ballyragget in the company of a group of neighbours of all ages who looked after him when they arrived in Dublin. Ruth had attended the 1954 All Ireland final with his father but, squashed amid the press of humanity on Hill

16, didn't see any of it. Three years older and a few inches taller, today he'd have a better view.

And: 11-year-old Liam Griffin from Rosslare Harbour, who was agog with excitement. His first visit to Croke Park, his first Leinster final.

And: a teenage Dubliner called Eamon Dunphy, who along with his father Paddy, the son of a man from near Lisdowney, spent Sunday after Sunday during the 1950s making the ten-minute trek from home in Richmond Road to Croke Park to watch Kilkenny, usually to see them lose to Wexford or Tipp. The young Dunphy was yet another member of the Seán Clohosey fanclub. "Oh, a beautiful hurler, so stylish." Much to his gratification, he would discover in later life that the two of them were distantly related.

Not present was Dan Butler, an aspiring young teacher from near Piltown who stayed away because he feared for Kilkenny's chances. He would not make many similar errors of judgment during the course of the next 50 years and more.

The team McLeod et al had come to see had won every competition they'd contested in 1956. The National League, the Oireachtas, the Walsh Cup, the Leinster championship and the All Ireland. To all intents and purposes they'd won the Railway Cup as well, given that nine Wexford men featured on the Leinster combination that laid waste to Munster, 5-11 to 1-7, at Croke Park on St Patrick's Day. Two months later at the same venue the MacCarthy Cup holders entered the realm of high baroque in the most extraordinary National League final ever played.

Tipperary led by 2-10 to 0-1 at half-time. Wexford stormed back in the second half and caught them in the closing stages to win by four points. Phil Purcell, the Tipperary county secretary, had declared publicly beforehand that he would believe Wexford could beat Tipp in a national final when he saw it on the scoreboard after the match. This was the day he did. Wexford 5-9 Tipperary 2-14. Incredible. Phil Purcell could have been forgiven for doubting the evidence of his own eyes. Having nearly stayed at home because of a severe dose of the flu, Nicky Furlong travelled, watched the game from the upper deck of the Cusack Stand, became enraptured in the mayhem of the second half and on the final whistle found himself a new man, all symptoms of illness quite banished by the tumult.

Wexford's year of liberty was their year of fulfilment. By defeating Cork, Munster opponents, in the All Ireland final – a 'proper' All Ireland triumph, as it were – any asterisks that had hovered over the defeat of Galway in 1955 disappeared. Had Nicky Rackard sat down and shed a tear in some quiet corner during the winter of 1956-57 it would have been understandable.

Like Alexander, there were no lands left for him and his colleagues to conquer.

The sweets of '56 lasted well into the following year. In late May the All Ireland champions travelled to New York and beat Cork in front of more than 30,000 spectators at the Polo Grounds. Vividly recorded by Martin Codd in his memoir *The Way I Saw It*, it was the holiday of a lifetime in an era when that phrase contained genuine meaning. The Wexford players visited Niagara Falls, went racing at Belmont Park, watched the golf in New Rochelle and the boxing at Madison Square Garden. Codd, who was accustomed to spending his winters cutting bits out of his boots to ease the pain of his chilblains and getting up in the middle of the night to lamp rabbits for the English market, goggled at escalators and elevators, freezers and fridges.

On their return home Bobby Rackard's career was ended by a farming accident he suffered on the eve of the championship. His brother Nicky was back on the beer following his decision to have a bottle of Schlitz in New York. And Wexford did not impress when beating Offaly by 5-10 to 3-3 at Nowlan Park in the provincial semi-final. In every way – physically, mentally, emotionally – they had tested and tasted too much.

If they were entitled to start as favourites against Kilkenny, who were trained by a young priest and maths teacher called Tommy Maher, they were not entitled to start as unbackable favourites. On that point the formbook was insistent, at least when inspected closely, for Wexford had been fortunate against their neighbours in both the 1955 and '56 provincial deciders. The 1955 showdown went to a replay that was decided by one of the most freakish goals ever scored at Croke Park. Nicky Rackard gained possession from the throw-in at the start of the second half and sent in a ball from 60 yards that hopped on the sunbaked sod, reared up in front of the Kilkenny netminder Dick Dunphy – no defenders in front of the goalkeeper at the throw-in to clear an incoming ball in those days – and bellyflopped over the line. Wexford ended up winning by 5-6 to 3-9.

The following year's renewal had the most dramatic denouement imaginable. Wexford, now the All Ireland champions, led by 2-2 to no score after ten minutes but were hanging on by two points in added time when the referee, Mick Spain of Offaly, awarded Kilkenny a close-range free. Bill Walsh stood over what would be the last puck of the game and went, as he had to, for a goal. The sliotar struck a Wexford stick and skewed over the bar. John D Hickey in the *Irish Independent* called it "a game that had everything". The *Kilkenny People* dubbed it the county's best performance at Croke Park since the 1947 All Ireland final.

But fine words butter no silverware, and when the teams renewed acquaintance in 1957 Wexford were going for the first four in a row in the history of the Leinster championship, a feat Kilkenny had never managed in spite of their 33 titles to date.

The holders lined out as follows. In goal Art Foley, who the previous September had brought off the most storied save in the annals of Gaelic games.

In front of him Mick Morrissey from St Mullins in Carlow, a sleek brylcreemed stylist who left for America shortly afterwards; Nick O'Donnell from Graignamanagh, full-back on both the Team of the Century and the Team of the Millennium, a sub for Kilkenny in 1947 but subsequently lost to the county in messy circumstances; and Ted Morrissey, the hurler and footballer brother of Jim's.

On the half-back line the human spinning top Jim English, the team's sole right-hand-under and a man whose immense strength and unorthodox grip had long been a source of perplexed respect from none other than Christy Ring; Billy Rackard, the thinking man's hurler; and Jim Morrissey, a fine overhead and ground striker who seldom took the ball into his hand.

At midfield the blond Greek god better known as Ned Wheeler and the stocky, no-nonsense Seamus Hearne, man of the match in the 1956 All Ireland final.

On the half-forward line Oliver Gough, whose brother Claude had won an All Ireland minor medal with Kilkenny in 1950; Martin Codd, who liked to compare himself to a card player who'd been dealt a reasonably good hand that he proceeded to play well; and Padge Kehoe, crewcut, bulletheaded and dangerous, the son of an Enniscorthy senator.

And on the inside line Tom Ryan, the team's other Kilkenny refusenik and resident scamp, who'd driven Fr Tommy Maher to his first posting in Dublin as a young priest nine years earlier; Nicky Rackard, enough said; and Tim Flood, who scored in no fewer than 33 of his 38 championship outings and who was so fast and stylish that the sight of him in possession always struck terror into the heart of Seán Clohosey down the far end of the field.

Man for man they may not – Billy Rackard, Wheeler, Kehoe and Flood apart – have quite measured up to Kilkenny in terms of pure and absolute skill. But they were bigger, they were stronger and they were packed with, in the words of Clohosey, "guys who'd knock you over". Going in the gate at Croke Park before the game, Clohosey looked around and saw the Wexford players filing in a few yards away. "The size of them. My stomach nearly went on me."

Paddy Buggy: "They were all big men bar Tim Flood and Jim English. The rest of them were mighty men. And they were able to stand over the ball and rise it in spite of you. You couldn't shift them."

Mick Kelly: "The Wexford backs, they were brilliant. With Bobby Rackard, your hurl wouldn't reach his hand when he was catching the ball. He'd stretch to 12 foot high, double his length. It was hard to get enough scores to beat Wexford. And Nicky was always able to register one at the other end."

The challengers, each of whom held his hurley in orthodox fashion, lined out thus. In goal Ollie Walsh, hitherto an exciting young custodian who this afternoon would take the first step on the road to beatification and who by year's end would be a credible candidate for canonisation on foot of the numerous miracles, attested to by thousands of witnesses, he'd performed throughout the summer.

In front of him the brothers Tom and the beefy Jim "the Link" Walsh from Dunnamaggin, the latter three years younger and the bigger of the pair, and John Maher from Freshford, a third sound man in a line of sound men.

On the half-back line Paddy Buggy, GAA president during the centenary of the organisation in 1984; Mickey Walsh, also from Slieverue, not an overly big centre-back but a long striker off both sides and a man whose claims for the position had been championed during the spring by Peter Holohan of the *Kilkenny People*; and Johnny McGovern, five feet eight inches of Bennettsbridge terrier.

In the centre of the field Mullinavat's John Sutton, a noted overhead hurler, and the wiry Mick Brophy from Danesfort.

On the half-forward line Denis Heaslip, slick and slight, could only have been a Kilkenny forward; Mick Kenny, the bustling Callan man who had captained the county in the 1950 All Ireland final and later hurled for Tipperary; and 28-year-old Mick Kelly, the captain, blocky but injury-prone and consequently on and off the Kilkenny team since Bennettsbridge won their first county title in 1952. "Faith, don't forget the 'off' part..."

Inside them Slieverue's Dick Rockett, a goalkeeper in his younger days and according to himself a better footballer than a hurler; Billy Dwyer, the sawn-off shotgun of an attacker from Foulkstown outside Kilkenny city who in his first Leinster final the previous season had given Nick O'Donnell plenty of it; and Seán Clohosey, the team's talisman, satin-smooth and fluid, a classic Tullaroan ballplayer in the mould of Lory Meagher.

It was a team that has been largely overlooked by posterity, not only outside Kilkenny but within the county borders also. Few people have ever felt impelled to dispute Paddy Buggy's description of them as "a reasonable side, nothing more". In the pantheon of successful Noreside outfits they figure closer to the bottom than the top. Yet what they achieved was something much more profound and far-reaching than a mere provincial or All Ireland triumph. Partly by good luck, partly by good leadership, they found their way onto an unmapped yellow brick road and suddenly the drab, monochrome world the county had inhabited for the previous ten years turned to gorgeous technicolour. Modern hurling begins with the 1957 Leinster final.

Prior to throw-in there was not a more famous hurling man in Ireland than Nicky Rackard. There was scarcely a less famous or celebrated one than his old classmate and friend Fr Tommy Maher. But Fr Maher had not been idle for the fortnight after Kilkenny's win against Dublin in the replayed provincial semi-final. The intervening period was spent productively in Nowlan Park. Fr Maher knew what he wanted his players to do against Wexford. By the end of the fortnight they knew also.

Do not let the Wexford players stand over the ball. Do not hit the ball in the air, not even if your name is John Sutton. Keep it on the ground and keep it moving because – and this was one of the stone-chiselled lines in the trainer's profession of faith, espoused hundreds of times over the years to hurlers of all ages and abilities – "the ball travels faster than any player".

Recent Leinster finals had been fought on Wexford's terms. The Leinster final of 1957 would be fought on terrain of Kilkenny's choosing. Terrain of Fr Maher's choosing. And Fr Maher hadn't just trained his players for the game. He'd *coached* them.

It was an afternoon when everything that could go wrong for the champions, and one or two things that couldn't go wrong, did go wrong. Playing into the Canal End with the wind behind them, they had the first chance when Seamus Hearne attempted a point from out the field but was inches wide. Straight from the puckout one of the game's critical moments occurred. As the sliotar dropped in the middle of the field and the ash whirled, Ned Wheeler went down injured. Paddy Buggy was near him, could hear Wheeler groaning ("he dropped like a stone") and ran over.

It was so severe a belt that Wheeler was stretchered off unconscious, to be replaced by John Redmond, and by the following Thursday he was still in the Mater Hospital, albeit sufficiently recovered to be able to talk to his father on the phone. Ever afterwards it was John Sutton who was cited as the Kilkennyman whose hurley had connected with Wheeler's head, a charge which so disturbed Sutton that decades later he felt it necessary to make contact with the Wexford midfielder and swear he wasn't the player involved. Wheeler was happy to accept the assurance.

With Wheeler's departure the pendulum swung a little Kilkenny's way – and swung their way a little more when Sutton opened the scoring after a minute and a half, this after Ollie Walsh had saved a shot from Tim Flood and cleared it. Walsh had been criticised for being unnecessarily flashy, to the point of rashness, in the replay against Dublin. There would be no criticism of him in Monday's papers, just choruses of hosannas from on high.

How the challengers' goal remained intact for the next few minutes was a small miracle. Hearne levelled matters from a 35-yard sideline cut in the fourth minute, the trigger for a burst of sustained Wexford pressure. Nicky Rackard had a wide, then evaded the Link Walsh and let rip with a piledriver from 20 yards; Ollie Walsh saved it brilliantly and the sliotar was muddled clear. Wexford pressed again and won a 21-yard free. Up stepped Rackard to uncork one of his specials; it was deflected out for a 70. Jim Morrissey took it and dropped it in the square; Tom Walsh cleared the danger but he didn't clear it very far and Hearne, swooping, sent the loose ball wide with a snap shot. Somehow it was still 0-1 apiece. Somehow Wexford hadn't scored a goal. Nobody could have known that their moment had come and gone and that the momentum was about to pass to their opponents.

The champions did take the lead in the tenth minute, the one and only time they led, when Hearne pounced on a loose clearance by Ollie Walsh and found the range. Mick Kenny levelled almost immediately from a close-range free at the other end. The levee was about to break.

Up to this Johnny McGovern had had his hands full with Padge Kehoe. "Very skilful and accurate. Well built and strong. For his size he had a bit of speed and was able to move fairly well. You had to be watching him the whole time." Now the sliotar came McGovern's way and off he went on a solo run, Kehoe in pursuit. He dropped the ball, retrieved it, saw space in front of him and kept on. Ten yards, 20 yards, 30 yards. "He was waiting to crook me from behind so I stayed going as long as I could."

At last McGovern, shortening his grip, hit the sliotar high in the direction of the Wexford square, hoping to God that it wouldn't be caught by a defender who'd clear it back down the field and catch him out of position. It wasn't. Someone got a touch and diverted the ball in the direction of Dick Rockett, drifting in from his corner to the edge of the square with one of the trainer's catchphrases – "Fill all gaps" – ringing in his ears. When the sliotar fell to Rockett there was nobody but Art Foley within an ass's roar of him. He couldn't miss and he didn't.

That the initial incision was made by Johnny McGovern was apt. The greatest Kilkenny defender of his generation and the holder of a record 11 county senior championship medals, his attributes were summed up by one scribe in this fashion: "He doesn't delight you with the sweetly doubled overhead ball or the well timed drop-puck, but his virtues are solid and substantial. He is first of all a worker, a dogged and determined bulldog type, active and tireless. In physique he is stocky, but with strength and solidity of chest and shoulders. A quick and decisive tackler, he clears without hesitation, seldom venturing to lift and strike unless he has ample time to do so."

Now his upfield foray against Wexford brought the purplest of prose from another reporter. "Suddenly, over from his post on the left wing swooped Johnny McGovern. He checked the Wexford raid, got the leather into his hand and, hopping the sliotar on his hurley, started diagonally upfield. Evading tackle after tackle he broke out of Kilkenny territory and as he approached midfield he found himself in the clear. There he balanced ball on stick in the best egg-and-spoon style and went speeding on. It was an inspired moment which placed the Wexford defence in a nasty dilemma: should they go to meet McGovern or let him come to meet them, or fall back to guard the goal; and it was while they momentarily hesitated that the stocky Bennettsbridge star reached the 50-yard line and thence sent the leather sailing into the Wexford goalmouth. From that centre came Kilkenny's first goal, and so began the landslide of scoring which engulfed the champions' hopes in such spectacular fashion." Truly they don't write 'em like that any more.

A minute later Seán Clohosey was fouled for a 21-yard free. Kenny went for a goal, Billy Rackard blocked it but failed to clear and Billy Dwyer was in to flash the sliotar to the net. Two goals in the space of a minute. The hunter had become the hunted. This was a new game.

Kilkenny pressed on. Dwyer added a point. Clohosey had a shot saved by Foley. The first Wexford sally in a while saw Flood's stinging drive force a fine save from Ollie Walsh. It was a rare moment of respite for the champions and a fleeting one, for the 20th minute brought the underdogs' third goal. Kenny, hard against the sideline, lobbed a free goalwards, the defenders hesitated and Clohosey – "brilliant" for the 30 minutes he was on the field, according to the *Wexford People* – ran in unhindered to scoop the ball to the net. Mick Brophy landed a point moments later from all of 80 yards to stretch the gap to 11 points. Kilkenny 3-4 Wexford 0-2.

Seán Clohosey had fancied his chances on Mick Morrissey from the moment he took up position on him. In the 1956 Leinster final the pair had faced each other on the wing, with Morrissey having the better of the battle. "He was strong, he was fit, he always got the ball out quickly," Clohosey acknowledges. "But I didn't do myself justice that day." At the next opportunity he would. "I'd been thinking about the previous year. I saw the Wexford team. There he was at right-corner back. 'Here,' says I, 'this is my chance.' It was a pudding. Every time the ball came down I ran around him."

The Wexford selectors did what they could, first switching Jim Morrissey and John Redmond, then moving Tim Flood to centre-forward and Martin Codd to top of the left. It made not a whit of difference. Clohosey had a point in the 23rd minute and two minutes later Denis Heaslip ran through to ram in the challengers' fourth goal. The fifth arrived within 60 seconds: a McGovern clearance, Clohosey slipping Mick Morrissey and cutting in from the Hogan Stand side to beat Foley just as Nick O'Donnell charged out to meet him. "He put his big shoulder and hip in my way. Whatever way he did it, my knee went. That was that for me."

The last two scores of the half went Wexford's way, a Rackard point from a 21 and a Tom Ryan goal from a goalmouth tussle, and reduced the arrears from 18 points to 14 (5-5 to 1-3). From an impossible situation to a merely hopeless one.

The opening exchanges of the new half predictably saw Wexford pressing and Kilkenny resisting. The problem for the former was that, contrary to cliché, the harder they tried the unluckier they got. Tim Flood, who had proved a handful for Tom Walsh while in the corner ("a real hurler, very fast," says Walsh, "and a great friend afterwards"), raced through but saw his effort deflected out for a 70. Billy Rackard took it but the ball dropped well short and was cleared. Martin Codd shot narrowly wide. Seamus Hearne's sideline cut was – anathema to Tommy Maher, this – allowed go wide with no Wexford player getting on the end of it. Nicky Rackard tried again from another 21 but this, it was rapidly becoming apparent, wasn't his day and Ollie Walsh did the needful. Almost inevitably after the creation and squandering of such a host of chances, the first score of the new half came at the other end via a Mick Kenny free from 30 yards.

Wexford continued to make chances and to waste them, Codd and Oliver Gough being the next culprits; their opponents continued to maximise what possession they had, as was illustrated by a neat point by Dwyer and another Kenny free, this one won by Heaslip. By a bitter twist of fate the king of the close-in free would depart the championship arena for the last time without a goal to his name. And even when they breached the Kilkenny full-back line there was one last obstacle to pass. Of one of Ollie Walsh's saves from Tim Flood, the latter asserted many years later: "I couldn't believe that Ollie had saved the shot. He appeared out of nowhere to block the shot and clear the ball down the field. When I was striking the ball the goal was empty."

Rain began to fall in the closing stages. Students of English literature present may have appreciated the pathetic fallacy. PJ Garvan, who'd replaced Seán Clohosey at half-time, scored the winners' sixth goal in the last minute. He may well have been inside the square. It made no difference. Kilkenny 6-9 Wexford 1-5. And lo, the earth shook and the sun was obscured and the veil of the temple was rent in twain.

True to form and reputation, the Wexford players congratulated their opponents generously at the final whistle. That made no difference to young Liam Griffin, who didn't stop crying on the way back to Rosslare in the family Morris Minor, registration number ZR 338, until Arklow. Only when he was much older did the situation's symmetry strike him. How fitting, Griffin decided, that it was not Cork or Tipperary who had put an end to the Rackard era but rather Kilkenny, the county of the great man's education, and by way of a masterplan dreamed up and brought into being by one of his oldest friends. The ultimate hurling romantic had been trumped by the ultimate hurling rationalist.

When great teams fall they tend to do so not in silence but with a crash. The best explanation for Wexford's demise was the most obvious one. Too old, too successful, too sated, too much mileage on the clock. In tipping them in the *Irish Press* the day beforehand, Pádraig Puirséal had been careful to add a considered caveat. "I do not expect these Wexford lads to be quite the irresistible force now that they were last September. In the first place they are, if a year wiser also a year older, and will not be getting any faster." The champions, as Seán Clohosey points out, "couldn't keep winning", while their opponents were younger, faster and hungrier, as well they might have been.

But Puirséal, as befitted one of the great GAA writers, went deeper than that when anatomising the game the following Tuesday. Some of the winners' cleverest hurling he avowed to have been played *before* they scored their opening goal, adding: "The most interesting feature of this Kilkenny display was the marked success with which they incorporated fast ground striking into their customary 'pick and puck' game, while their wing-to-wing tactics had the Wexford defence in trouble right from the start. It was a marked improvement on Kilkenny's previous championship outings and showed that their course in 'tactics' at the training sessions had been very well learned." In other words, some guiding spirit had planned and overseen the enterprise. It would not be apparent to the public for some time precisely who that guiding spirit was.

From the remove of a new century, Puirséal's decision to place inverted commas around the word 'tactics' is striking. One can almost hear the faint accompanying sniff. It was as though tactics were not entirely to be trusted. A bit newfangled, vaguely redolent of other codes, bearing implications of dark plans and deeply laid stratagems, not quite behoving the manly, uncomplicated Gael. To Pádraig Puirséal and his generation they were 'tactics'. To Tommy Maher, who'd attended St Kieran's College a decade after Puirséal, they were tactics.

Defeat did not spell the end for Wexford, although the *Irish Press* saw fit to give a young John Healy, the future *Irish Times* columnist and author of *No One Shouted Stop*, the acclaimed account of the death by neglect of his native Charlestown, a slot on the bottom of Monday's front page speculating that it might be. Wexford's demise was more just than a sports story because Wexford were more than just a sports team.

It did not spell even the beginning of the end. Three years later they would return with a new team to shock Tipperary on the first Sunday of September. For the next two decades they would continue to contest All Ireland finals. For the next decade they would continue to win them. And in a sense the Wexford team of the 1950s would never die.

Because hurling is circular, moreover, 19 years later the county would enact a precise and perfect revenge for 1957. As Wexford had done back then, Kilkenny went into the 1976 Leinster final as the All Ireland champions of the previous two seasons. As Wexford had perished horribly back then, so too would Kilkenny perish horribly. Fittingly, the man coaching Kilkenny was the same man who had coached them in 1957, this time an older Prospero, his staff soon to be consigned to the ocean's depths but his wisdom imparted and his legacy long since enshrined. And the boy who cried all the way to Gorey would eventually bring about his own day of atonement. One of the first things Liam Griffin mentioned when buttonholed by the media after his Wexford team beat Kilkenny in the first round of the 1996 Leinster championship at Croke Park was the provincial final of 39 years earlier. Some scars never quite heal.

It was not the end for Wexford, but it was the beginning for Kilkenny and their trainer. The beginning of the modern game's empire of empires on the day of the most significant hurling match of the second half of the 20th century.

CHAPTER 2

Whitepark

*It is no exaggeration to say that the main interest of the average student of St Kieran's, outside his work, **is** hurling: he plays it, if he can; and, in any case, he thinks about it, talks about it, reads about it, dreams about it. Almost standard equipment for the new boy entering the college is a hurley, and almost his first act after arriving is to get on the playing field to try his skill with the other newcomers*
St Kieran's College Record 1958

Tommy Maher barely knew his father. He didn't know his mother all that much better. Four of his siblings had died before he was born, two of them in the one week in 1912. One of his brothers died at the age of two months, one of his sisters when she was a year old, another sister at the age of four and a third at the age of eight. Compare and contrast with Tommy, the youngest of the 11 children, who lived to see his 90th birthday.

He sprang from generations of Kilkenny soil, a land of limestone fields and Norman ruins, of mild autumns and frigid winters. The Mahers and the Fowlers had lived in Whitepark, four miles from the village of Gowran, for time out of mind. Maher and Fowler headstones in the cemetery in the nearby hamlet of Dungarvan date back to the early 1800s. Various Fowlers emigrated to Australia in the middle of the 19th century, one of their descendants going on to become the mayor of Geelong in Victoria. Another of their descendants was Annie Fowler.

John Maher of Whitepark didn't go far when he decided to look for a wife. Annie Fowler hailed from the next house up the lane. The 13-year gap between the pair was no obstacle. They married in April 1904. It wasn't long before the children began to arrive.

Willie was born in 1905, Tim the following year, Denis in 1907, Anastasia in 1908, Johnny in 1909, Catherine in 1910, Mary in 1911, Din (another Denis) in 1913, Dan in 1916, Mary Kate in 1919 and Tommy on April 25th 1922 – the same age as the new state. He was not yet a year old when his father died the following February. By then John and Annie Maher had already buried four of their children. The first Denis only lived for a couple of months. The whooping cough carried off both Anastasia and Mary in the space of three days in December 1912. The Spanish flu pandemic that was to claim more victims than the First World War took Catherine in 1918. The oral history of the family spoke of a 12th child, a girl, who died young but whose demise was not recorded.

Four years after John's death one last hammer blow fell. Annie Maher felt unwell one day. The children – and this was Tommy's last memory of his mother – were at the dinner table when Uncle Thomas, their father's brother, came in to say that the hackney car had arrived to bring her in to the hospital in Kilkenny. Annie collapsed on the steps leading into the old Auxiliary Hospital in Wolfe Tone Street and died shortly afterwards. It may have been a heart attack. The only other memory Tommy had of her was when she carried him out one time to see a foal being born on the farm.

Whooping cough. Spanish flu. Dead siblings. Dead parents. Misery upon misery. Not the typical Irish family life of the early 20th century. But not wildly atypical either.

One can only speculate how the surviving children were affected. Johnny, who became a teacher, never said much about his childhood in later life, but to his children "there was a lot of emotion buried there". Tommy himself consistently maintained that while he had grown up to all intents and purposes an orphan, the loss of his parents had had no discernible effect on him because he'd hardly known them to begin with. Uncle Thomas, who was tall and stern and had a moustache, stepped into the breach after Annie's death and acted in loco parentis. It wasn't his fault that the younger children would grow up without the benefit of a woman's touch in this – Tommy's words – "house full of men": himself, his five brothers and Uncle Thomas. Mary Kate was gone after primary school, sent into Kilkenny to live with an aunt in Green Street and attend secondary school in the Presentation Convent.

The Maher homestead in Whitepark was long and thatched and had four rooms, with a farm of 37 acres attached. There were pigs and chickens and a few cattle. The family grew potatoes and made butter, which was sold in Walsh's shop in Gowran. And of course there was always a sliotar and a few hurleys around the place; one of the earliest photos of Tommy shows him, aged five, with his camán. And of course he banged the ball against the wall of the barn and broke slates and got into trouble for it. And he learned Irish dancing as well. "Oh, a good little stepdancer," his first cousin Bridget Brennan, neé Fowler, who lived in the next house, recalls. "Light on the feet."

That was Tommy Maher's childhood. The kind of childhood which is idyllic exclusively in retrospect. Usually someone else's retrospect.

He started school at the age of seven. The three-teacher school in Dungarvan was three miles away. He walked across the fields – Fowlers', Quirkes' and Dreas' – to reach it. On a wet day he might get a lift in the family horse and cart. The school was a stone building with a slate roof and separate entrances for boys and girls. One of the teachers was May O'Neill from nearby Neigham, whose grandson Pat was centre-back on Kilkenny's All Ireland-winning teams of 1992-93. Another was a man from Carlow, a strong nationalist, who Tommy was to remember as "very knowledgeable and an admirable teacher" and who imbued him with a love of the Irish language. Although there were about 60 children enrolled in Dungarvan school, full attendance was rare, what between the demands of farm work and the limited *meas* that local families placed on education.

With Tommy Maher it was different. He was there to learn. He was there to learn because he would eventually have to go out into the world and make a career for himself. "Education was not appreciated by most because they knew they had somewhere to go afterwards," he explained many years later to June Grennan, one of his parishioners in Mullinavat, for an award-winning college project she did on his life and times. "I didn't. The farm could not provide a livelihood for us all."

The annual school fee equating broadly to the annual income of the Maher farm, in the normal course of events Tommy would not have gone to secondary school in St Kieran's College. In which case Ted Carroll would never have become as solid in the tackle as he did, while Eddie Keher's freetaking technique would have been rather more hit (literally) and miss (far too often) than it was. In which case Cork might have been out of sight by half-time in 1969, while Waterford would not have been taken for 14 points from 14 shots by one man in 1963. But sometimes it happens that a butterfly flaps its wings in Gowran.

By 1936 Johnny Maher was teaching in Kilmacow and Dan, the second-youngest of the brothers, had joined the civil service in Dublin. Between them they were able to scrape the money together to send the baby of the family to the diocesan college.

Tommy started in St Kieran's in September 1936, just another schoolboy and knowing only one other pupil among the 200 or so there, his neighbour Mikey Brennan, later a Kiltegan priest who spent most of his life on the missions in Kenya. A month later, delayed by a bout of typhoid which had affected his whole family, there started someone who was not merely another schoolboy and who would grow up to be far more than merely another hurler.

It may be overdoing matters, albeit only slightly, to state that Nicky Rackard's arrival on the College Road was the equivalent of a god come down among mortals, but certainly no first year ever created anything like the sensation the boy from Killanne did during his first week in the school. There was his surname: to the ears of his contemporaries, odd. There was his provenance: odder, because he was the only Wexford boy there. There was his hair, blond and crewcut as a result of the typhoid treatment. There was his hurley, cut from a holly bough and almost unbreakable, with its purple and gold favours. There was his strapping physique, which had the older boys coming along to gawk at him and which soon yielded the unflattering nickname The Sow. To add to all of this there was his confidence and self-possession, astonishing in one so young. Tommy Maher could scarcely believe what he was witnessing.

"In those days the first years were timid and didn't know where to go whereas the second years would assemble where the Tech building is now, a field with a big oak tree at the side of it. Straightaway Rackard was in the middle of the second years, fighting for every ball and having a go at everyone. He made his mark on his very first day." Rackard and Maher: it was, in the words of Ned Kavanagh from Urlingford, who was a year behind the two of them, "an important year".

Sent to St Kieran's by his father "to do some work", Rackard soon discovered his true vocation. Hurling. Not that he was the most gifted hurler in the house; that honour fell to Kevin Brennan from Tullaroan, later a priest in Liverpool, to whom Tommy Maher paid the following tribute. "I have no hesitation in saying that Kevin Brennan was the greatest hurler I ever saw. He had magnificent ball control. I would rate him higher than Christy Ring or anyone else. When he got the ball no one could touch him. He would weave and dodge, appear to go one way, then suddenly change direction and go another and strike the ball."

Brennan was left-corner forward, Maher right-half forward and Rackard centre-forward on the St Kieran's team that won the 1939 Leinster colleges title, defeating O'Connell Schools from Dublin in the final in Athy by 2-8 to 0-3. They were champions again the following year, atomising Knockbeg by 10-4 to 0-1 in the final on February 15th with what the *Irish Press* hailed as "this brilliant team of coming hurlers". The side were captained from centre-back by another future priest, Mick Holden from Mullinavat, the toughest opponent the schoolboy Maher ever marked and a dab hand at hooking Rackard during practice matches in Fennessy's field. Rackard's main weakness, and the primary reason he never graces lists of the game's all-time stylists, was his wide swing, which rendered him vulnerable to being hooked and blocked. A secondary weakness was what Tommy Maher termed his "bad leg action". But Nicky Rackard, as the GAA world would gradually discover, was far more than the sum of his parts.

Maher was, according to Ned Kavanagh, "very fast, very clean, very difficult to mark – a completely different style to Rackard". And very versatile; right-half forward in 1939 and midfield in 1940, he was the goalkeeper for the 1941 provincial colleges decider, a 4-3 to 2-1 success against O'Connell Schools at Dr Cullen Park. Kavanagh was right-corner back and Liam Reidy from Bennettsbridge the left-half back.

It wasn't only the combined talents of Maher, Rackard et al that served to make this a golden era for the college. As the junior dean on the layside for 16 years, Fr Dickie Lowry was, in the vernacular, "the man over the hurling" in St Kieran's. Like subsequent deans such as Fr John Joe Reidy, who as manager of the college teams of the late 1940s employed tactics he'd witnessed at Roker Park during his days as a curate in Sunderland and who as parish priest guided Camross from Laois to the 1977 All Ireland club final, he was a visionary. "He did an awful lot for hurling in the school," Ned Kavanagh recalls. "He made us hurl every afternoon, he picked the teams, he was the manager. A good man."

Speaking seven decades later in San Francisco, having ministered in nearby Sacramento since his ordination in 1948, Monsignor Kavanagh reflected on the regime in St Kieran's during his day. An austere establishment, yes, as befitted the times, but a tolerable one nonetheless. "Not a bad place – I enjoyed every minute there." The same went for Tommy Maher, who loved his new home and had no objections to being immured in its grey stone bulk each year from September to Christmas, Christmas to Easter and Easter to summer.

He excelled at maths and was friendly with Charles Sandvoss, the gentle, kindly maths professor. He was good at English and attributed his fine prose style to the influence of his teacher, Fr Peter Birch, the future Bishop of Ossory. (Theme of Peter Birch's MA thesis: 'The Revolutionary Element in the Poetry of Shelley.' Subject of essay he once set his students in St Kieran's: 'The Phantasmagorical World of Novels and Opium.' But Birch was a hurling man too, attending every All Ireland final from 1932 to 1980 bar two: 1937 in Killarney and 1962, when he was appointed coadjutor bishop.) And as a Latin student, the adolescent Maher soon graduated from *Amo amas amat* to being able to translate the college motto *Hiems transiit* – "Winter has passed", reflecting its status as the first Catholic secondary school to be opened in Ireland after the passing of the Relief Act of 1782.

It was Fr Lowry who chose the Leinster team for the annual colleges interprovincial game with Munster – the All Ireland colleges championship had yet to be established – in 1940. The side featured seven Kieran's men, among them Ned Kavanagh in goal, Mick Holden at centre-back, Tommy Maher at midfield where he was partnered by Cork's Eamon Young, a student at Good Counsel in New Ross, and Nicky Rackard and Kevin Brennan up front. Munster were favourites for the game; Munster always were, and this year's model from the south included Harry Gouldsboro from Thurles CBS and a future GAA president Con Murphy, who would mark Rackard, from North Mon.

The 1940 colleges interprovincial decider remained seared ever afterwards into the memory of the spectators – one report put the attendance at 7,000, another at 10,000 – at Nowlan Park. Munster led by ten points at one stage in the second half before Maher and Young gained control at midfield. Leinster had cut the gap to three points with time almost up when Rackard rose like a steeplejack on the edge of the square, caught the sliotar and palmed it to the net. Munster 4-4 Leinster 3-7. The latter maintained their momentum in extra time to win by 6-11 to 4-4.

Rackard hurled senior for Wexford before he finished in St Kieran's. "That's some honour, me man," an uncharacteristically complimentary Fr Paddy Dunphy, the senior dean who patrolled the refectory and gave out the post and whose brother Watty had captained Kilkenny to beat Tipperary in the 1922 All Ireland final, observed as he handed him his call-up letter from the Wexford county board one lunchtime. (Clearly the college authorities were not above opening the students' post.) But the hurling field was not the only place where Nicky Rackard would make his mark in 1940. Bogskar was the reason why.

Bogskar wasn't a hurler, he was a horse. And he wasn't any old horse, he was one of the contenders for the Grand National at Aintree. Rackard, who was racy of the soil, fancied Bogskar no end and Rackard, whose father had a farm and a pub, had the money to follow his fancy – unlike cronies such as Tommy Maher, Seán Breen and Seán McDonald, who didn't. Nevertheless by hook and by crook a few of the gang managed to scrape some modest pennies together to put on Bogskar. Rackard, naturally, had his tonsils on.

There was khaki in the stands and air-raid instructions in the racecard for the 1940 Grand National, the last renewal of the event for six years. It was a dry afternoon in Liverpool but a wet one in Kilkenny, and most of the school were parading up and down the glasshall when a mighty cheer went up. Bogksar had come late under Flight Sergeant Mervyn Jones, who would perish over Europe two years afterwards, to win by four lengths at – *mirabile dictu*! – 25/1. Unfortunately Dickie Lowry was on the premises and heard the commotion. At study that night the head prefect was despatched to announce that everyone who had backed a horse in the National was to proceed at once to the junior dean's room. The fact that the staff had had their own sweep on the race was conveniently ignored. Nobody moved a muscle, which led the authorities to issue a last-chance summons at suppertime.

When Fr Lowry came in at the beginning of second study the entire room, with a few exceptions, rose and followed him upstairs: one in, all in. A vast scrum formed at the dean's door and the culprits, all guilty with no hope of acquittal, were admitted one by one. Fr Lowry snapped the same three questions at each of them. "What's your name? What horse did you back? How much did you win?" Outside in the corridor Leo Holohan, son of the Mount Juliet electrician and one of the most brilliant intellects of his generation in St Kieran's (he would write the obituary of his great friend Patrick Kavanagh in *The Irish Times*), piously suggested reciting a decade of the rosary in honour of the dean. In the end all winnings were confiscated, the malefactors fined three times their stake and the money given to the missions.

Rackard, livid, had his revenge on college sports day a couple of months later. He trained hard for the 440 yards race, the showpiece event which had a beautiful silver tea set as a prize, and made it clear to all and sundry for weeks beforehand that he was determined to win it. Bad leg action or not, this he did to great rejoicing. Fr Lowry could only grit his teeth and smile as he handed over the tea set. Bogskar had been avenged.

Tommy Maher's friendship with Nicky Rackard would last for the rest of the latter's life. The pair were not long departed St Kieran's when Maher went down to Killanne for a weekend visit. Rathnure were playing a match in New Ross next day and the Rackards plus house guest travelled in by horse and trap. The competition, the opposition and the result have all been lost to history, but not so the detail that Tommy Maher lined out, illegally, for Rathnure. "Nicky had a terrific opinion of Tommy," Billy Rackard revealed years later. "He was very impressed with his speed and ball control. He thought he was a flier."

Another contemporary on whom the teenage Maher made an impression was John Kevin Keogh from Callan. Interviewed in the *Kilkenny People* on the occasion of his 90th birthday in April 2011, John Kevin, who hurled on the St Kieran's junior team in 1937, recounted the story of a long-puck competition which was held in the school and commenced on the 70-yard mark. "We didn't even have a decent, never mind a new, sliotar. There were 19 lads who reached the final stages of the competition. Then it was eventually whittled down to two, Tommy and myself. We both shot two points with our first efforts. Tommy made it three in a row with his third shot. My third effort went just wide, so Tommy was declared the winner. He was a class act. He was more than a deserving winner."

Tommy Maher sat his Leaving Cert in 1941. He came through with banners flying, obtaining honours in Irish, English, Greek, Latin, history and maths, and was one of Bishop Collier's two nominees from the diocese to go to the national seminary in Maynooth. The next seven years would be about study, about prayer, about BAs and H Dips and preparation for life as a man of the cloth.

Hurling? That would be, as it had to be, an afterthought.

CHAPTER 3

1945

*I must heap on the scales in Tipperary's favour a will to win, a determination to
stave off defeat, a psychological factor of immense importance when pressure is
greatest, a something hard to define, but a something that makes all the difference
between victory and defeat*
Winter Green of the *Tipperary Star* previewing the 1945 All Ireland final

The greatest or most fascinating GAA book never written? A full-length Christy
Ring biography, warts and all, is one obvious contender for the title. The story
of the 1947 All Ireland football final at the Polo Grounds is another, that of the
Cork/Kilkenny trilogy of 1931 yet another. On foot of a visit to the Lory Meagher
Museum in Tullaroan prior to the 2004 All Ireland final, Seán Moran suggested
in *The Irish Times* that every county board be required to appoint a heritage officer
tasked with the job of interviewing the hurlers and footballers of yesteryear.
Would that some predecessor of Mr Moran's had made the same excellent
proposal half a century earlier. Would that it had been acted on by the GAA. Would
that so many tales of great games and fabled personalities had not been lost
forever.

The greatest extended GAA monograph never written? The tale of Corrigan
Park in 1943 springs readily to mind. How exactly did Kilkenny – Kilkenny! – end
up losing to Antrim – Antrim! – in the All Ireland semi-final? What factors led
to the biggest shock in hurling history? Overconfidence? Naivety? Or the most
popular and predictable of the conspiracy theories that did the rounds
afterwards, drunkenness?

The truth was more prosaic. Kilkenny were knackered.

The train to Belfast left Amiens Street in Dublin at around three o'clock on
the Saturday afternoon. The Kilkenny players queued from 10am on a hot day,
the last day of July, and were then forced to stand all the way to Belfast. On arrival
there they were met by a detachment of British soldiers with lorries, who
accompanied them to their hotel. That night the Antrim county board put on
a céilí for their guests. Marching behind the band next day, Glenmore's Mick
Heffernan, one of the visiting players, found he couldn't rise his feet. The
queuing, the standing, the dancing: it had all caught up with him. "That's the way
I was. I had to shuffle."

Antrim won by 3-3 to 1-6 and their opponents, accompanied back to the station by the soldiers, slunk home in ignominy. "We were the disgrace of the county," Heffernan says with some understatement.

When sorrows come they come not as single spies. The following year Kilkenny went to New Ross for the Leinster semi-final and lost by 6-6 to 4-6. It was the first time Wexford had knocked them out of the provincial championship since 1901 and it was almost as big a sensation as Corrigan Park had been. While a lull was to be expected after the county's glories of the 1930s, this was getting ridiculous. Mick Heffernan was again an onlooker at the scene of the crime, this time clad in a purple and gold jersey because he was working in New Ross and had, from necessity, joined the Geraldine O'Hanrahans club. Among his opponents in stripes was his brother Jimmy.

Mick scored two points, Nicky Rackard – lining out at midfield, his customary position for most of his intercounty career – hit 1-2 but the real hero of the hour for Wexford was Patsy Boggan of St Fintan's who rattled in four goals. Corrigan Park 1943 and New Ross '44: they were, in a minor key, Kilkenny's version of Stalingrad and the Kursk, twin disasters from which all of the participants made it home but few lived to see a brighter tomorrow.

The brighter tomorrow began in 1945. The New Ross disaster was avenged when Wexford came to Nowlan Park for the first round of the Leinster championship and were defeated by seven points. Offaly suffered a 4-15 to 2-1 cuffing at the same venue in the semi-final and Dublin were seen off by 5-12 to 3-4 in the provincial decider at Croke Park. This put Kilkenny into an All Ireland semi-final against Galway in Birr.

Not for the last time in the era, the westerners proved doughty opponents. They led by eight points at half-time and were seven ahead entering the last quarter before the Leinster champions rallied and Jim Langton won it, 5-3 to 2-11, with a late point. Victory came at a cost, however. Liam Reidy broke an ankle.

There was an obvious replacement on the panel in Shem Downey from Ballyragget. There was a less obvious replacement who wasn't on the panel at all in Tommy Maher. He was home from St Patrick's College, Maynooth for the summer and hurling away – hurling very well too, as he'd demonstrated both for Castle Rovers, a club formed in the parish of Gowran in January 1944, and with a fine performance for the northern junior selection against Éire Óg in the senior championship. Partnered by Dick McEvoy at midfield he got the better of a variety of opponents, among them Tommy Murphy and Jack Gargan, Kilkenny regulars both. The display earned him a call-up to training for the All Ireland final against Tipperary.

The clerical student had little doubt he'd be able to cope if called on. After all, he'd been in St Kieran's with Liam Reidy and reckoned he was as good as him. And Reidy fitted in well for Kilkenny alongside Langton and Gargan and Jack Mulcahy, so why shouldn't Maher do likewise? To ready himself for the big day he did "a good bit of preparation" at home in Whitepark.

It was as well that he did so because Kilkenny's training for the All Ireland final was notable for two features. The first was the training itself – or, rather, the lack of proper training, specifically the lack of coaching. It was all a blur of trudge and toil, of laps of the field and practice matches and the steam rising off the players afterwards. Brief though it was, his time as an intercounty panellist made a profound impression on Tommy Maher. Surely, he concluded, there had to be more to training than this delirium of effort for its own sake. Surely there had to be room for thought, for logic, for imagination, for the cultivation of science, for the identification of problems, for the improvement of weaknesses and for the coaching of skills. "Teams preparing for games in the past just pucked the ball around and I never saw anybody making an effort to coordinate the efforts of the players on the field," was how he put it to Paddy Downey in an interview in *The Irish Times* 30 years later.

He had an anxious moment the week of the final when Bishop Patrick Collier turned up at the last training session in Nowlan Park to impart his blessing to the players. Maher may have been studying for the priesthood in Maynooth rather than in the Ossory equivalent, the St Kieran's College seminary, but the princely Collier, whose native Camross instincts and early enthusiasm for hurling had long since been mislaid somewhere in the velvety depths of his chauffeur-driven episcopal Dodge, was his bishop all the same, and this was an era when collar and camán did not rhyme and were definitely not supposed to.

"We have one of your students playing on Sunday," Tom Walsh, the county chairman, said to his visitor. "Oh yes," declared Dr Collier, "I want to see him." Tommy Maher was sent for and turned up.

"You are playing on Sunday, I see, and you have not your bishop's permission," quoth the great man in forbidding tones.

"I didn't know I needed your permission," Maher replied nervously (and completely untruthfully).

"Oh yes, you do. But" – a gracious smile flickering across the bishop's features – "I suppose I can't stop you now. You may play."

Recounting the episode four decades later in the Mullinavat club history published for the GAA's Centenary Year, the now Monsignor Maher opined that bishops and even cardinals were content to turn a blind eye to the rules where their own counties were concerned. Catholicism clearly had its share of judicious hypocrisies, blatant among them the one pertaining to the ban on clerical students playing for their county – a ban that was unnecessary, impractical and unenforceable. It was a lesson that would help inform Tommy Maher's life as a priest. Some rules had to be obeyed. Other rules were too silly or petty to get worked up about. Common sense would always be common sense.

The first post-war All Ireland final drew a monster crowd of 69,459 to Croke Park, 18,000 up on the previous record of 51,235 from 1935. Among the spectators were a group who'd assembled at 2.30am on the Parade in Kilkenny to be sure of catching the 9.30 bus. The gates were closed hours before throw-in and an estimated 5,000 would-be spectators locked out. It wasn't until the teams took the field that the Kilkenny XV was known. Tommy Maher was making his championship debut on the biggest stage of all. As befits a student who'd studied hard for an exam and knew it, he had no nerves beforehand. Anyway, nothing would be quite as queasy again as his encounter with Bishop Collier.

The debutant scored the opening point of the game after two minutes, whereupon things rapidly began to go downhill for Kilkenny. They couldn't stop conceding goals – four in the first half – while at the other end they couldn't get the ball past Jimmy Maher. Singling out "the redoubtable little goalie and his stonewall resistance", the *Kilkenny People* deemed the Tipp custodian's heroics to be responsible "more than anything" for his side's victory. While the winners merited their success, the *People* conceded, "it will be admitted by every impartial observer that they had more than their share of luck and their goalie saved many shots that normally would have beaten any goalie".

Following a defensive meltdown triggered partly by bad goalkeeping and partly by the loss of centre-back Billy Bourke through injury, Kilkenny trailed by 4-3 to 0-3 at the break. They rallied in the second half, with Dan Kennedy and Tom Murphy dominant at midfield, and goals by Maher and Seánie O'Brien reduced the gap to four points. The *Kilkenny People* criticised the forwards for concentrating on goals in the second half when points were there for the taking. It was surely a harsh complaint given that points alone were not going to retrieve this particular situation. What happened next would irritate, if not downright haunt, Tommy Maher for years to come.

Tipperary had a puckout. He drifted back from left-half forward to try and win it. The sliotar eluded him initially but he snapped up the break and headed for goal. He had just decided to take his point when the Tipperary right-half back, Michael Murphy of Thurles Sarsfields, tripped him. He fell, his elbow on the ground but the sliotar still in his hand, palm upwards. Maher was back up and about to continue on when the referee, Vin Baston from Waterford, blew the whistle. Maher assumed it was for a free in. It wasn't; Baston had penalised him for handling the sliotar on the ground. Maher, furious, told him he hadn't and pointed out that Baston, who was following the play from behind, couldn't have seen whether he'd handled it or not anyway.

Worse was to follow. Tipperary took the free and moments later the ball was in the Kilkenny net. That was that. Out, brief candle. Momentum lost, game over. It ended 5-6 to 3-6 in Tipp's favour, an honourable defeat in view of the losers' disastrous first half but a defeat nonetheless – and a defeat that Tommy Maher, to whom the *People* afforded "great credit for giving a fine display in his first intercounty game", would never have the opportunity to rectify on the field of play. One can only idly wonder whether matters might have been different for Kilkenny in the 1946 All Ireland final, and whether that of 1947 would have turned out to be a classic at all, had his clerical obligations not intervened.

The Baston episode had a postscript many years later. During one of the New York trips in the 1960s Fr Maher and Paddy Leahy, the chairman of the Tipperary selectors, were having a late-night cup of tea. That was no surprise, for if their players abhorred one another at the time, Maher and Leahy were kindred spirits: both of a green hue in political terms, both farsighted in hurling terms. John Doyle, not one to throw compliments around like snuff at a wake, decreed Paddy Leahy to be "50 years ahead of his time".

Apropos of nothing Leahy said, "Do you remember the day in Croke Park you were blown for a foul you never committed? I was only a few yards away from you and you never fouled it." Fr Maher was surprised and flattered. "How good out of Paddy Leahy to say it," he told people afterwards. Sometimes simple love of the game and the strictures of sportsmanship transcend petty rivalry.

The 1945 All Ireland final was Tommy Maher's first and last match for Kilkenny. He was a panel member for the 1946 decider against Cork but didn't feature in the game. He hurled that same summer with Thomastown, the eventual county champions. En route to glory they beat James Stephens by 4-8 to 4-4 in the second round on September 8th, the week after the All Ireland final. Club lore in the Village had it for years afterwards of how Bobby Brannigan, who'd come on as a sub for Kilkenny in the Thunder and Lightning final, was "hurled out of it" by a young clerical student.

Said clerical student was back in Maynooth for the final, which took place on October 11th and resulted in a 5-4 to 4-5 victory for Thomastown against

Carrickshock. He played with the club again the following summer. The last competitive game he ever hurled, the 1947 county semi-final at Nowlan Park on August 17th, ended ingloriously. Thomastown went down by 6-8 to 1-6 to Eire Óg, who went on to see off Tullaroan in the final seven days later, and *The Post* reported that "Dan Kennedy, though mainly responsible for the Thomastown scores, did not strike his usual form at centrefield, where his partner, Tommy Maher, was also off colour."

One story survives from his time with Thomastown. Among his teammates was Ned Ryan, an army man. In the dressing room before one of the matches – presumably in Nowlan Park, given that dressing rooms were few and far between in Kilkenny in the 1940s – Ryan pulled on a pair of splendid new white shorts with pockets in them. Another Thomastown player threw him a pair of faded togs in the club's blue colours and told him to give the white shorts to Tommy Maher, their resident clerical student. Ryan, whose respect for the priesthood didn't extend to sacrificing his new shorts, declined the suggestion.

Maher had been in St Kieran's when he told his sister Mary Kate one day at home in Whitepark that he was considering the priesthood. The decision was his and his alone. Any question of his family pressurising him into it did not arise, and he did not have parents to please by becoming a priest.

Life in Maynooth was monastic, the day beginning with Mass at 6.30am, but he made the best of it. He played hurling and football. He developed a taste for tennis (and, typically, sourced from somewhere an 18-page A4 instructional manual to assist in improving his game). He helped out on the school farm. And he was involved in drama. For Shrove 1948 the clerical students staged *Hamlet*, complete with backing from an orchestra that supplied selections from Beethoven, Mozart and Handel. Tommy Maher was a member of the eight-man organising committee and oversaw the props, which he listed down on paper: "letter for Polonius", "book for Hamlet" and so forth.

Among his contemporaries were Ray McAnally, later to find fame on stage and screen, and John Wilson from Cavan, presently a St Kieran's teacher and later a government minister. At one stage he did make what he termed "a feeble attempt to leave", but his moment of personal crisis soon passed.

To be or not to be a priest? That, in the end, was a question with only one answer. A resounding yes.

CHAPTER 4

Curate

Crumlin was a completely different world
Tommy Maher

Tommy Maher was ordained in St Patrick's College, Maynooth, by the Archbishop of Dublin, John Charles McQuaid, on June 20th 1948. He was one of 53 men raised to the priesthood in the national seminary that year. A further seven were ordained outside the college. He celebrated his first Mass in Maynooth the following day, a Monday. He said his second Mass the day after that at home in the church in Dungarvan. Among the congregation was his cousin Bridget Fowler, whose parents Willie and Anne, Tommy's godparents, had travelled to Maynooth for his ordination two days earlier.

With no idea of what either the Lord or the Bishop of Ossory had in mind for him, the young priest wrote to the latter, being the more easily contactable, applying to go on temporary missionary work in San Diego. Bishop Collier replied telling him not to arrange any temporary work.

All through the month of July, as the Russians tightened their blockade on Berlin and Britain's national health service came into being, the new priest wondered what the immediate future held for him. On August 15th, the Feast of the Assumption, he received a letter from Archbishop McQuaid appointing him as chaplain in Sion Hill convent in Blackrock, Dublin. As clerical postings went he could have done worse; with its school of domestic science as well as its large secondary school for girls run by the Dominican nuns, Sion Hill had a certain name and prestige to it.

He travelled up to the capital with three companions: Tom Ryan, Fr Ned Dowling and a greyhound. Ryan, a native of Maddoxtown, a few miles from Whitepark but in the parish of Clara, was in his pre-Wexford incarnation as a garda in the capital and volunteered to do the driving as he "knew Dublin". Fr Dowling was a priest in the diocese of Kildare and Leighlin. History does not record what became of the greyhound, which belonged to Ryan and was bound for a trial at Shelbourne Park.

On the way up Fr Maher suggested stopping "to get a bit of grub somewhere". Not at all, Tom Ryan reassured him, there'd be plenty of grub waiting for him where he was going – the domestic science school, remember. The car drew up at the gates of Sion Hill and Fr Maher was about to bring in his bags when he decided he'd better check to see he was in the right place first. He went to the front door. A small lay nun opened it.

"I'm your new chaplain," he announced. "Ah, you're not!" she retorted, upon which she turned around and left him standing gobsmacked on the doorstep while she went in search of the authorities.

The head nun eventually came out. A new chaplain? This was news to them, she informed him. Nobody had told them they were getting a new chaplain. They already had a chaplain in Fr Rogers as it was. There was no job for Tommy Maher, it appeared, and there was certainly no room at the inn. The nun told him he'd have to get his own digs and gave him the addresses of a few boarding houses nearby.

With Tom Ryan, Fr Dowling and the greyhound still in tow, he tried them all without success. At one establishment he was told to call down to the parochial house in Blackrock where the priest was a Kilkenny man, a Fr Brophy. He knocked and was received by the housekeeper. On hearing the new curate's tale of woe she went in to talk to Fr Brophy and returned speedily. "He doesn't know any place," she declared firmly. Not even a fellow priest from home would come out to greet him. Charming.

Thoroughly fed up at this stage, he tried a place in Booterstown Avenue, an impressive house with a flight of seven or eight steps up to the hall door. The lady was a Miss Osborne. She had taken in chaplains before but had given it up on the basis that she was rarely around; her brother was a racehorse trainer and she went to the races most days. "I won't take you," she said. "But you look so miserable I'll take you for the night or for a couple of days until you get somewhere else."

All was well that eventually ended well. After a couple of nights with Miss Osborne, and then a spell lodging with an English lady who had three daughters permanently on the phone to their boyfriends (most distracting for a priest trying to prepare a sermon!), he finally found a suitable abode owned by a Kilkenny woman who had a maid from Ballyragget. He stayed there for a year. The only downside was the location in the main street in Blackrock. A tram stop was situated right outside and the house rattled all day long.

Shared interest in the national games has a habit of bringing people together in unlikely circumstances. So it was with Fr Maher and a young lady who was to become a lifelong friend. Word soon got around the domestic science school in Sion Hill that the new chaplain had played in an All Ireland final. One student whose interest was piqued was 18-year-old Christina Brennan from Cloonacoole near Tubbercurry. Her father Jack was chairman of the Sligo GAA county board and later the Connacht Council.

Officially Christina was in Sion Hill to learn the finer points of cookery, needlework, crafts, the methodology of teaching and the like. In practice she felt much more at home playing camogie in the Phoenix Park, unsurprising for a girl described by a classmate as "perhaps the most Irish of us". The student and the chaplain were kindred spirits. What's more, though she wouldn't have dreamed of saying it to him, deep down Christina felt a little sorry for Fr Maher.

"He'd spent his time in Maynooth thinking of all the good he was going to do when he became a priest – and now here he was thrown into a gaggle of nuns and girleens in gymslips and very sophisticated young ladies in the domestic science school. It must have been a blow to him to be appointed to Sion Hill. It was easy to be intimidated by the posh girls. It used be drummed into us that we were going out into the world and would be one of a kind. If you were daft enough to believe them you'd regard yourself as being a cut above the rest – and there were a lot of girls daft enough."

It was Christina who got Fr Maher a ticket for the 1950 All Ireland final, Kilkenny versus Tipperary. By now a curate at St Agnes's in Crumlin, he'd had his appendix out that summer and wasn't able to stand up for any lengthy period of time. Christina had a word with her father and the ticket materialised late in the week. "I took the bus out to Crumlin on the Saturday afternoon. He'd given up hope because the last post had come and gone with no ticket. It was a Hogan Stand ticket costing 7/6. He gave me a cheque. I never cashed it."

The parish priest in Crumlin was a Tipperary man who went to all the Tipp matches. The pair of them didn't get on well, and not for hurling reasons, but it didn't stop the older man making Fr Maher chauffeur him around when necessary and it didn't stop him importuning him for a ticket for the big match. "Sure you have your own way of getting tickets," the young curate replied. The PP punished him for his effrontery by putting him down to say 12 o'clock Mass on the day of the All Ireland.

When Mass was over Fr Maher cycled to Croke Park, arriving not long after the minor match, in which Dublin caused a mild sensation by beating Tipperary. Who was sitting a few seats away from him but the parish priest. "Who said 12 o'clock Mass?" the PP frowned. "Nobody – there's no 12 Mass today," Fr Maher retorted.

Crumlin was an eyeopener for a country lad. Large families, urban squalor, social deprivation, bolder and more knowing children. One incident from his time there has the power to disconcert today.

A local man was neglecting his family in favour of his local. After all manner of intercession had been tried and failed, Fr Maher went for the nuclear option and arranged to have him sent to prison. The shock therapy worked. The man went on the dry and rebuilt his life. To the end of his days he had nothing but gratitude for Fr Maher and his intervention. But for him, he said, he would have lost his home, his family and himself.

Yet there was more to Crumlin than social problems. The area also had a hurling tradition, one that went back as far as the 1740s when Crumlin Common hosted a game between the hurlers of Leinster and Munster. Local legend had it that Leinster won with a late goal. Two centuries later the boys of Crumlin were winning Dublin primary schools championships on a regular basis, even though most of the players gave up the game after that. In order to staunch the bleed, St Columba's Hurling Club was established in 1945, the prime mover a local Christian Brother, Brother McCormack, a native of Cavan.

Tommy Maher became involved almost despite himself. Before he was ordained he'd decided that the only place in Croke Park for priests was in the stand. "I made up my mind that priests should have nothing to do with games at all, except perhaps back in their own parishes." For his first year or two in Dublin he went to Croke Park, Lansdowne Road and Dalymount Park on a regular basis. "I simply wanted to enjoy watching games."

By degrees, however, he came to the conclusion that hurling and his ministry need not be mutually exclusive, and in Crumlin he saw so much potential for the game's development that he broke his resolution and helped out. Long before the term became popular, it struck him that Gaelic games could possess social capital. Even in a working-class Dublin suburb. Especially in a working-class Dublin suburb.

This new course of true love did not run entirely smooth. One year he helped organise a street league in conjunction with the Crumlin-Kimmage civic week. All went swimmingly until the final, which attracted a huge crowd. Ten minutes from the end the game had to be abandoned following a controversial free and a sit-down by the penalised party. "That was a black day for me in Crumlin," he acknowledged.

Life was continuing all the while back home in Whitepark, where in the summer of 1949 a near-catastrophe befell the Mahers. The Fowlers had just finished their dinner one day when Willie, Tommy's uncle, noticed smoke billowing from the thatched roof of Mahers' next door. Willie Maher, Din and Uncle Thomas were inside at their own dinner, oblivious. Bridget Fowler jumped into her family's Ford Prefect and made her way in to the post office in Gowran to raise the alarm. The fire brigade were summoned from Kilkenny, but amid the panic the details were lost in translation and they rushed to Whitehall, Paulstown instead of Whitepark, Gowran.

By the time they realised their error and reached the scene of the fire the house was destroyed, despite the best efforts of a number of local farmers who attempted to fight it with buckets they filled from a nearby pond. "To look at the flames and feel the heat in the yard was the most frightening thing about the day," Bridget remembers. Some furniture was saved.

In the summer of 1953 her cousin had an altogether more pleasant duty, officiating at the wedding of his old pal Nicky Rackard to Miss Ailish Pierce of Tinahely in University Church, Dublin. The groom's brother Billy was best man and the reception was held in the Shelbourne Hotel. The honeymoon was spent in Jersey, from where a postcard with a two-penny stamp was sent to St Agnes's presbytery, Crumlin, on June 12th.

"Dear T," it began, "Having a glorious time. Weather simply beautiful. We got an awful dose of sun on Tuesday and we are both suffering still. In fact my legs are so swollen I am hardly able to walk. They are better to-day but I am afraid I won't be able to play on Sunday. [Against Laois in the Leinster semi-final. In the event Rackard did line out and scored a goal in Wexford's win.] We hired a car for our stay and have seen the whole island. It is really wonderful. Will see you when I get back. Best wishes and thanks for everything. Ailish and Nickey."

The same year saw a GAA-sanctioned hurling coaching course, one of the first of its kind, held in Croke Park. A certain Kilkenny-born curate was invited to take charge of a group of 30 and help coach the coaches of the future. Around the same time he was involved with a Dublin minor team that beat Kilkenny in the Leinster championship in Nowlan Park and was working with Tony Herbert, who'd won an All Ireland medal with Limerick in 1940, on the under-age side in St Columba's.

But home was calling. Much to Herbert's angst ("I was left holding the baby"), Tommy Maher was summoned back to St Kieran's for the second half of the 1953-54 school year to replace his old teacher Peter Birch, who had been appointed professor of education and lecturer in catechetics in Maynooth, as professor of English. In September 1955 he returned there full-time as professor of his beloved mathematics, having reacquainted himself with the subject by doing a refresher course during the summer.

Teacher, junior dean, president and hurling guru, it would be his home for the next 28 years.

CHAPTER 5

Fennessy's Field

In my time, when the college opened in September, the newcomers usually assembled in the junior field, there to indulge in very earnest puck-abouts and generally display their prowess to their elders. Soon the whole talent of the college would be formed into teams in three grades, senior, intermediate and junior, with usually three teams in each grade, and these teams met each other in a whole series of epic struggles based on the league system.

Each league lasted a term, and I sometimes wonder if we then rather blotted our copybook as amateurs. Because, in my day, each man playing in the league subscribed a shilling, and the winning side collected three shillings a man at the end of the competition!

However, the rewards of victory we reckoned as nothing in comparison with victory itself, and there were epic battles in league finals in St Kieran's that would not have disgraced an All Ireland field, and this even in the junior grade. In those days the senior cup side was the only team which went out to do battle for honours, and rarely had it to go into action until after Christmas. Then a panel of players would be picked out and training commenced.

In my early years at St Kieran's such training was only very loosely organised and was usually left to the initiative of the players themselves under the captain regnant of the year. But later on Rev Richard Lowry took over the training of the cup teams and under his tutelage the efficiency of Kieran's teams increased by leaps and bounds.

Father Lowry had himself been a distinguished colleges hurler, and during the late '30s he turned out a whole series of wonderful teams that never tasted defeat. Stars on those teams included the one and only Nicky Rackard and Tom Maher, who, now Fr Tom Maher, trains not only St Kieran's but the Kilkenny senior hurling teams today. Since then Kieran's have seen good years and lean, but since Father Maher's return to the college the black and white jersies have been very much in the limelight again.

Nowadays I note, when I go to see St Kieran's play, that most of the students seem to come along to cheer their team to victory. That was not the case in my day. Then only the team travelled to a match, and as the evening of the game wore on we, back in the college, grew more and more fretful as we waited for news. There would be speculation and whispering through the study hall as time wore on and no news came. And then, suddenly, there would be the sound of hurleys clattering

in the tiled glasshall outside, and a wild yell of victory, and only then did we know
that the Leinster cup had come home to St Kieran's once more.
Pádraig Puirséal, *Our Games Annual 1958*

Ned Costello was a gadgets man before gadgets men were heard of. He owned
a Grundig tape recorder, an immense beast with magnetic tape reels he used
for taping Irish music or Irish language programmes off the radio. When he wasn't
teaching Irish in St Kieran's College he liked to turn his hand to fixing watches
and engraving charms and medals in PT Murphy's of High Street, the Kilkenny
jewellers he'd married into. And sometime in the winter of the 1956-57 school
year Ned Costello invested in a second-hand Kodak 8mm cine camera, complete
with cast-iron projector and silver screen. For many years the cine camera, which
took films lasting four minutes or so, was to be a staple at Costello family
gatherings. Holidays in Tramore or Dunmore East, the aftermath of First
Communions and Confirmations in the garden at home in New Street, that sort
of thing.

Ned Costello also brought the camera to colleges matches. One such match
was the 1957 All Ireland final between St Kieran's and St Flannan's of Ennis in
Semple Stadium. Some of the footage, which was extracted by his son Martin
in 2009 and transferred to DVD, can be seen on the school's website. It is
tremendously evocative material, all the more so when one realises that not every
young man pictured would live to watch it half a century later. Here, all fresh
face and black curls, is the adolescent Eddie Keher; it could not be anyone else.
There is Dick Walsh, the number 11 in the black socks, scoring the goal that ignited
the St Kieran's comeback the same day. At the end of the game Ted Carroll, the
boy captain who would grow up to be a Kilkenny defensive stalwart of the 1960s
and the Texaco Hurler of the Year in 1969, is pictured with the Croke Cup. And
seen in glimpses, but never at the centre of the shot, is the man who *was* at the
centre of it all. Fr Tommy Maher.

Later the same year, 1957, he would come to national prominence as the trainer
of the Kilkenny team that won the All Ireland. But this overcast late-April
afternoon in Thurles was the day he established himself as a coach. The day he
demonstrated that the small things were the big things, that success in hurling
was about mastery of the basic skills, that practising the skills was not only
desirable but crucial and that practice – proper practice – could mean the
difference between victory and defeat.

St Kieran's were in one of their regular phases of mediocrity when Fr
Maher returned to his alma mater in 1955. They'd won only one of the previous

five provincial titles, the other four having been shared by Patrician of Ballyfin (two), O'Connell Schools from Dublin and Knockbeg College. By way of indicating how far off the pace the school had fallen, the 1955 championship brought a 6-7 to 1-6 trimming at the hands of Knockbeg and the 1956 renewal a 7-2 to 3-3 reverse against Ballyfin, who had Seán Buckley from Freshford making midfield hay for them.

These were dark days for the college and its tradition, but out of the darkness a glimmer of light emerged in the spring of 1956. A junior team that featured Ted Carroll at centre-back and someone named in the newspapers as "Ted Kerr" among the forwards won the Leinster title in style. It was enough to kindle hope in the breast of Con Kenealy, the *Irish Independent*'s colleges correspondent, that St Kieran's would shortly emerge "out of the doldrums in which they have been for the past few years". Writing in the first issue of the *St Kieran's College Record*, the Patrick Street native and past pupil mused: "Some time ago I wrote that the success of the college has always come in spells; and if history does repeat itself, another run of victories is just about due. And there is absolutely no reason for not believing that next year should start the College off again."

Kenealy knew whereof he spoke. He'd seen Ted Carroll and his twin brother Mick in action. He rated Har Hickey of Johnstown the closest marking colleges defender in the province. And if he'd talked to Fr Maher he might have discovered the latter's opinion of one of the younger members of the team, an Inter Cert student from Inistioge. Eddie Keher was little more than a kid, but in terms of physique he was way ahead of his contemporaries. In many ways, in fact, he was a mini Rackard. Not quite as big, certainly not nearly as bulky, but as fast as Rackard (like Rackard he was a regular contender in the athletics events on college sports day), more skilful and possessed of a far wristier and tighter swing. No modern-day Mick Holden would be hooking Keher in Fennessy's.

While all this was happening Fr Maher had not been idle, not even during the unsuccessful 1956 campaign. To him every game was not just a game but a forensic sample, not simply to be watched in real time but to be brought home, placed under the microscope and analysed. Where were players going wrong? What facets of their game could be improved? None other than Ted Carroll, formidable as he was, was singled out for special attention. Ted's weakness was that he was holding back when blocking, thus leaving himself open to getting hit. Fr Maher showed him the proper way to block – "stand in close: that way you can't get hit" – and went through it with him over and over again, each of them taking it in turn to block the other. "It became a real strong point in Ted's game afterwards. When he was hurling with Kilkenny he was regarded as hard to get through."

The 1957 colleges campaign began with a comfortable if unimpressive win against St Peter's in Carlow and continued with a hard fought victory over Mount St Joseph's, Roscrea. The provincial final in Athy was a repeat of the previous season's decider, St Kieran's versus Ballyfin. It may have looked a fifty-fifty game. It turned out to be anything but.

The challengers played ground hurling and they played it crisply, stringently and effectively. Ted Carroll and his wing men in the half-back line first-timed ball after ball away to safety. At midfield, where Fr Maher had instructed his charges to keep the ball wide in order to minimise the influence of Seán Buckley, Kevin Mahony shone in the first half and Ollie Harrington did likewise in the second period. Dick Dowling from Glenmore, who'd begun the season at full-back before being converted to full-forward, scored three goals in a 6-3 to 3-0 triumph and Tom White bagged two more, the finishing touches to creative work by the half-forward line, notably Eddie Keher. Con Kenealy, ecstatic in the *Indo* the next day, reported that the winners "showed that the almost forgotten art of ground hurling has not been neglected and also proved that much can be done by a player who though beaten for the ball can effectively 'hook' his opponent to turn defence into attack". As would be the case with Kilkenny against Wexford at Croke Park a few months later, St Kieran's hadn't merely been trained for the game. They'd been *coached*.

The players were thrilled with themselves. All winter they'd regarded Ballyfin as the team to beat. Their coach moved quickly to prevent heads swelling ahead of the All Ireland with St Flannan's. This, he told them, was where it only began. Now they'd be meeting hurlers for the first time.

Keher and Dowling, later a TD for Carlow-Kilkenny, became a special project for the coach as the big day in Thurles drew close. All year they'd been rehearsing a move from the Maher playbook: Keher soloed in from the half-forward line, Dowling waited on the edge of the square, the full-back charged out to meet Keher, the latter tossed the ball over the full-back's head and the now unmarked Dowling buried it. It was as if Fr Maher had taken a theorem out of one of his maths classes and plonked it down right in the middle of Fennessy's field for the pair of them to mull over.

Given: Two boys, two hurleys and a sliotar.

To Prove: The creation of a goal through coordination and practice.

Construction: Keher on the run, handpass to Dowling, shot, goal.

Proof: Hmmm...

Aye, there was the rub. The theory was fine; the reality had been less productive, the tactic yielding no more than a point or two during the Leinster championship. But Fr Maher kept them at it. Each training session would be followed by ten minutes of practice in a deserted Fennessy's, solo-handpass-shoot, Keher to Dowling, over and over again. Come the last training session, Dowling found the net twice. *It works*, he told himself, half in disbelief.

As though to emphasise the importance of the occasion, Fr Maher's old acquaintance Bishop Collier materialised in the college on the morning of the All Ireland final to impart his blessing to the team. (He somehow refrained from interrogating them as to whether they had his permission to play.) When the sliotar was thrown in at Semple Stadium a few hours later, it soon became apparent they needed all the divine assistance going. Perhaps unsettled by the early departure of Ollie Harrington with a cut over one eye, the Leinster champions raised barely a gallop in the first half and at the interval trailed by 2-3 to 0-1.

Back in the sanctuary of the dressing room, silence reigned. The players half-expected Fr Maher to denounce them from a height. After all, many another trainer would have – and, what's more, would have been well entitled to do so in the circumstances. But Fr Maher wasn't many another trainer. He wasn't any other trainer. No ash plants were splintered, no bottles fired at walls. In truth he barely uttered a word. His voice was ever soft, gentle and low, an excellent thing in a coach. "I've trained ye to hurl a certain way – now do it," was about as much as he said.

The recess brought no respite even though Harrington, now patched up, resumed at midfield. The Harty Cup champions restarted with two points. With a quarter of an hour to go St Kieran's trailed by 2-5 to 0-1. Martin Walsh from Thomastown, who'd hit their point in the first half, then doubled his and the team's account to leave nine points in it. Only nine.

It was all over bar the shouting and the final whistle. Then St Kieran's went mad. Utterly, totally, unrepeatably mad. Transfiguration in Thurles.

Why did it happen? Who knows. Why did it take so long to happen? The disruption that resulted from Harrington's injury may have played some part, although the *Kilkenny People* advanced another theory. St Kieran's, it surmised, were "obviously cowed to some extent by the high rating given to the opposition and took time to overcome the disadvantage in height and weight". But Fr Maher may have come closest of all in his diagnosis. Sometimes, he frequently pointed out, these things just happen: as simple, or as simplistic, as that. "People think you can give a message from the sideline, but you can't. It just works out so that a team which hasn't been playing well gets a break – and that lifts them completely." Further enquiries to the Offaly and Limerick teams of 1994.

It was the 15-year-old Keher who was the man, as he would so often be as an adult in black and amber. Off he went on a run. Pass to Dick Walsh, the centre-forward. Goal. A couple of minutes later Keher went through again and, eschewing the option to lay the ball off, lifted the net out of it. Now there were only three points in it, 2-5 to 2-2, and a wealth of ball being channelled through to the forwards from Harrington and Kevin Mahony at midfield.

St Flannan's had a breakaway point, no more than a lull in the storm that was breaking all over them. Mick Carroll sent Keher through for another terrific goal only for the referee, Galway's Inky Flaherty, to call back the play and award a free following the throwing of a Flannan's hurley. Bizarrely, Keher made a hash of his lift, but the ball was only half-cleared, he returned it with alacrity and there was Tom White to score another goal.

A point between them now and the black and white hoops rampant. What happened next was, sadly, not captured on Ned Costello's cine camera for posterity. But let us pretend that it was, let us imagine that some Hollywood director remastered the footage 50 years later and let us picture Keher gossamering his way through, the full-back charging out to meet him and Dick Dowling loitering with intent on the edge of the square.

This was the moment. The moment Fr Maher had prepared them for. The moment they'd rehearsed half a thousand times in Fennessy's.

The action slows. Portentous music rolls. The audience waits breathlessly.

The dark-haired youth continues his run before releasing the sliotar at the optimum moment. The thundering full-back descends on him a heartbeat too late. The sliotar describes a perfect arc. Dowling waits, his left hand twitching. And catches. And strikes. And buries it.

Quod Erat Demonstrandum.

To Fr Maher's eyes the sliotar took an age to loop from Keher to Dowling. The latter, who didn't see his shot hit the net, endured a horrid moment of uncertainty: might the goalie have saved it? The thunderclap of cheering told him he hadn't, and everyone he asked afterwards confirmed that there had been no stopping the shot. Mick Carroll glanced over towards the St Kieran's supporters jumping around on Semple Stadium's old cinder bank and saw a vast cloud of dust rising. (Among the jubilants was Liam Hinphey, whose father had come to Kilkenny from Derry in 1938 to work as a garda and settled on the College Road, whereupon he fell entirely in love with hurling and used to go to matches just to see Paddy Phelan play.) The game's last reel really would have been a moviemaker's dream.

To a young Fergus Farrell, the future St Kieran's historian who had travelled from Johnstown with his father to support their neighbour Har Hickey, it was the strangest of afternoons. "Everyone was quiet for most of the game, then everyone was cheering, then the game was over. Then we went home."

Telegrams flooded in to Fr Maher next day. Congratulations from St Joseph's of Fairview, from Rockwell College, from Ballyfin, from Nicky Rackard and from former St Kieran's students now studying in Kiltegan or ministering in England. Another was addressed to Canon Loughrey, the president of the college. "Heartiest congratulations to you, Fr Meagher [sic] and the team. Stop. They have earned a free week." It came from Dublin and was signed Paddy Purcell – better known to his readers as Pádraig Puirséal.

A couple of mornings after the match, Fr Maher collared Dick Dowling in the refectory and asked him to describe his goal again. "He was still thinking about it," Dowling recalls. "A marvellous trainer and such a patient and understanding man. Even if you played badly he still said 'Well done.' There was something about the man that made you give 150 per cent to the cause. And he believed in us. That day he should have made two or three changes when we were going badly – and had he done so we would have lost. He had faith in the team."

It was now official. The Maher credo worked. It was about coaching, about rehearsing the skills over and over again and rehearsing them correctly, about practice making perfect, about good habits becoming good instincts. It was about the handpass, although the handpass wasn't a weapon to be sprayed around indiscriminately, as the man himself was careful to emphasise. "In order that the handpass works effectively the man passing the ball must judge the distance accurately so that the player to whom it is passed can catch it on the run. Otherwise it either goes astray or the player to whom it is passed must stop. This, naturally, limits its effectiveness."

Having been a forward himself, moreover, Tommy Maher's coaching embraced the creative impulsive. To build rather than destroy, to open up rather than close down.

There was more. Martin Walsh learned from him that it was not feats of genius that counted but the little things. "Walsh, if you beat your man by six inches and move the ball on, you've won. If you beat your man by six inches and move the ball on, then it's up to somebody else to take care of it." Dick Walsh discovered the importance of using one's body. "In training he'd put his big backside around the ball and wouldn't let you at it. There was specific training. How to hit fellas with your hip. You'd learn fast how to take a tackle."

To Martin Walsh the man was "full of innovations". One winter's day, with snow on the ground outside, they were ambling around the glasshall when Fr Maher told them to tog out. Astonished expressions all round. Once they were togged out he had them line up and put Walsh and Har Hickey, the two slowest members of the team, in front. The speed merchants – Ollie Harrington, Dick Walsh, Eddie Keher et al – he placed five yards behind them. Walsh and Hickey were told to run while the others chased and pelted them with snowballs. It didn't turn the duo into reincarnations of Jesse Owens, but it didn't do any harm for morale.

He wasn't above the occasional sally into psychological warfare. Martin Walsh was under age for junior in 1958 but couldn't face St Peter's in Carlow as a result of a recent appendix operation. Fr Maher ordered him to tog out anyway and make himself visible pucking around beforehand right in front of the St Peter's lads. It was designed to impress and it did. A member of the previous year's All Ireland-winning team who couldn't make the junior side now..?!

If perfection was impossible, the pursuit of it was not. Eliminating the variables was ever the quest. Visitors to Fr Maher's room in the college would often find him measuring hurleys or weighing wet balls and throwing them against the wall. The ridges on the sliotar, bigger then than now, were a source of particular angst to him. Why not get rid of them altogether?

"Say when Eddie Keher was taking the frees, there was always one that would go astray. I got a new hurling ball one time and went to a hard wall and just threw it up at the wall. One in ten I was not able to catch coming back. What was making it go astray? The ridge. So Eddie puts one wide, there mightn't be an ounce of fault on his part, he might have hit it the very same as the previous one."

It is tempting to imagine a young Tommy Maher today opting for a career in medicine, higher mathematics or forensic science. (Or possibly, in view of his fondness for the game, as a professional tennis player: the ultimate pull-first-time sport.) What one can be sure of is that his vision of coaching was anchored in his maths background. Many a maths problem can be solved more than one way, but the quickest and simplest way is always the best way. So it was for him with the skills of hurling, a series of small knots to be unravelled and retied. The quickest and simplest way was always the best way.

The qualities that made Tommy Maher a nonpareil trainer of St Kieran's teams did not contrive to make him the type of junior dean beloved of the college authorities. Being a coach entailed working with the young men under him; being a dean emphatically did not. In an era and an establishment where overt religiosity and strict discipline were norms to be enforced at the end of a cane or the swing of a strap, Fr Maher was rather too easygoing and laissez faire for the powers that were.

In Crumlin, he often pointed out, teachers wouldn't dare slap the students. In St Kieran's they were expected to slap, which he didn't approve of. And whatever about slapping for wrongdoing, slapping for poor exam results was anathema to him. "There was a conservative element in the college which didn't approve of me as dean on that account." When Tommy Maher slapped, he didn't slap hard or slap out of malice or slap to make a point. The same could not be said of every priest in the house.

He once let Ted and Mick Carroll out to play for Lisdowney in a minor match against Ballyragget with instructions to come back immediately afterwards. The curate in Ballyragget saw them playing and, in the college for dinner next day, eyes brimming with crocodile tears, raised the subject with the president. "What is the college coming to, letting two students out to play for Lisdowney yesterday?" The president buttonholed Fr Maher and asked him was this true. "Yes," Fr Maher said. "I didn't see anything wrong with it. They were back for study."

That was Tommy Maher. He was a coach, not a manager. A mentor, not a martinet. He instructed and demonstrated, not screamed blue murder or barked orders. He led, not drove. Kicking posteriors wasn't his style. Life was far too unimportant to be getting tied up in rules and regulations. Still, none of this meant he was incapable of seeing quite through the deeds of men and boys. Around the time of the Beatles' first LP or a little later, one of his students, a young man from John Street called Eamon Langton, took to promoting local pop groups and arranging concerts. For some reason this proved a source of considerable mirth to certain of his contemporaries. Tommy Maher was having none of it. "That lad will be a millionaire before the rest of ye even have jobs," he informed the sceptics one day. Ah, the prescience!

The Monday after a St Kieran's or Kilkenny match, his maths students would try to get him talking about it in the hope he'd spend the whole class replaying the game. He frequently did. The Monday after a televised rugby international, Ireland versus one of the other four nations, he could with a little subtlety be inveigled into fulminating about what a waste of time – literally – rugby was, how long the ball had been dead on Saturday and how little play there had really been. A "foreign game"? Not to Tommy Maher, to whom games were first and foremost games, regardless of their provenance. He'd have watched the rugby alright, and watched it with the eye of a mathematician.

It was this mathematician's eye that allowed him to make sense of the 1958 All Ireland colleges final, a repeat of the previous year's decider. For 50 minutes the match was a precise replica of the 1957 edition. Same teams, same venue, same St Flannan's dominance, same miserable St Kieran's tally of 0-2. This time there would be no dramatic comeback. The final score was 3-10 to 0-2 in favour of Flannan's.

The outcome was all the more shocking in view of the consensus that this was a better St Kieran's team than that of 1957, with most of the players on the age. They'd suggested as much by putting ten goals past Mount St Joseph's in the Leinster final. To Dick Walsh, as anonymous on the big day as any of the other forwards, Keher included, they were overcooked. "We'd been on the go for two years with the college and, some of us, with the county." To Keher the problem was complacency. "We trained hard, came through Leinster in style. There was no reason why we shouldn't have won. But on the day we just weren't fired up. Afterwards you recognised what overconfidence was and what it did to you. Fr Maher probably learned a little bit from it as well."

The remorseless nature of the vagaries of chance was one lesson the defeat brought home to the coach. "Everything went wrong on the day that day. Balls were hit at the Flannan's goalie, at least three, that were scrambled away. Any other day they would have gone in. The thing about hurling is that it's not a mathematical business where there's an answer to everything. Games have a certain element of chance. The aim is to try and minimise the chance factor, the possibility of things going wrong." The 1958 colleges final was a day things went woefully wrong.

The late Martin Lanigan from Thomastown was one of the younger team members. He couldn't decide afterwards whether the occasion had been more painful for the likes of Eddie Keher and Dick Walsh, with their big reputations, or for an unknown like himself. Probably for himself, he concluded wistfully, because at least Keher and Walsh and the rest of the established players had All Ireland medals. Lanigan felt awful because he was sure his chance of glory was gone. "Now we'd had a lot of county minors on that team, a lot of stars. Anybody would have said that we had a far better side in 1958 than '59. That was the general view. But the 1959 team would prove itself to be better balanced."

Tipperary CBS, the sensational winners of the Harty Cup, provided the opposition in the 1959 All Ireland final. Four special trains brought 1,500 supporters from Tipp town to Thurles. Lurking on the sideline when the sliotar was thrown in was the Rattler Byrne, right-corner back on Tipperary's three in a row 1949-51 team, the winner of a record 14 county senior medals with Thurles

Sarsfields and now making a good deal of noise trying to direct the referee's attention to what he viewed as the no-prisoners approach of one of the St Kieran's corner-backs.

Pots and kettles? That was certainly the thought that struck Tommy Maher as he happened by. "Don't mind him at all," he called soothingly to his defender. "Yer man was an awful fella in his day." The Rattler, a famous character and raconteur, chortled. It was hard to know which of the pair enjoyed the encounter more.

If to the *Tipperary Star* this wasn't as good a St Kieran's side as the 1957 equivalent, the trio of the captain Keher, John Alley from Durrow and Martin Walsh excepted, they were the classier hurlers and, crucially, knew what kind of game they were trying to play. The *Star* criticised the CBS lads for attempting "to hurl the Kilkenny boys at their own skilful type of game and [they] were robbed of possession or found themselves unable to do the fancy things they tried to accomplish. Tipperary CBS should have maintained the first-time ground hurling that tied down Kieran's so effectively in the opening quarter. They were unable to match skill with skill."

St Kieran's led by 1-6 to 1-1 at the break, conceded three goals in a wretched third quarter – their goalkeeper Pat Duggan, a converted forward Fr Maher had prepared for his new role by taking him down to Fennessy's a couple of evenings and letting fly at him with ball after ball from all sides for half an hour, was left helpless on each occasion – but came with a wet sail in the closing stages to win by 2-13 to 4-2. The points count told its own story.

The late John Nyhan, who hailed from around the corner from St Kieran's on the Circular Road and was subsequently a priest in South Korea, was full-forward and the scorer of the winners' first goal. Paschal McCann, who had been a student for two years in O'Connell Schools in Dublin before his family returned to Kilkenny and who went on to be a lieutenant colonel in the army, was the left corner-back. Both had their own memories of Fr Maher and his ways.

"He was always on to the corner-forwards," Nyhan recalled. "Every time you allowed the sliotar to cross the endline it was as though you'd stopped it and pucked it 70 yards back the other way, he kept saying. And he drummed it into the forwards to always face the opposition puckout. Now that might seem unimportant, but when you're playing game after game there's bound to be a bad puckout somewhere along the line – and if you're waiting for it you've an almost certain score. Or when a half-forward was soloing through, the inside forwards would always get out of the square in the hope that our markers would follow us and so open it up for the lad coming in. Most of the students in St Kieran's were boarders, and what else had they to do at the weekends but hurl? The basic skills were being practised day in day out, often almost unconsciously. Because there was so much ability already present, therefore, Fr Maher was able to concentrate on his little details."

Paschal McCann: "He brought a real breath of fresh air with him. Not just to the hurling but to the whole scene in the college. He was firm but fair. Even-handed. Would have done well in the army. He never had to lift his hand or bawl anyone out. And he was very well respected, even by the hardest guy in the school.

"His theory was that every position on the field had its own requirements. The corner-backs were to be close and tight, the corner-forwards to hug the endline and hold up the ball and feed it back for someone else to shoot. Everyone would wait with bated breath for the senior panel to go up on the board in the autumn. Fr Maher would have been spotting talent in the house matches. He never missed a game. He'd bring in one or two springers, lads who weren't rated but who would be taken by him from oblivion to stardom, almost. I was one of those in 1959. I'd been nothing extraordinary all along when suddenly my name was on the board. The spirit in the team that year was top class and Keher was excellent at geeing up the younger players before a match. Going out onto the pitch you felt pretty confident. We knew we had the skills."

Fr Maher would be hands-on for one more national colleges triumph. Fittingly it fell to his favourite side to wear the black and white, the all-singing, all-dancing outfit of 1961. "The greatest machine to ever represent St Kieran's," he wrote, "from big Patsy Foley in goal to the even bigger Rory O'Moore at full-forward."

Eddie Keher was gone but not missed, for the team also contained the freescoring Pierce Freaney from Inistioge, later the Leinster Council's refereeing coordinator, who naturally drew comparisons with Keher, and Tom Forristal from Dunnamaggin, a chap whose first touch was so sleekly perfect that he was one of very few St Kieran's players ever to be told by Fr Maher to do more or less what he wanted. "If the ball doesn't come up the first time, let it go on the ground," was the coach's mantra, pragmatic in view of the state of the pitches in springtime: muck everywhere apart from the sideline areas, which made it extremely difficult to jab-lift on the run. Keher was one of the exalted handful to whom the let-it-go watchword did not apply. Tom Forristal was another.

The All Ireland final brought Forristal and co up against the reigning champions North Mon, who had the support of their old boy Jack Lynch, the Minister for Education. In front of 7,000 spectators in Semple Stadium the Mon were eaten alive, 8-8 to 1-4, with Forristal and Freaney unstoppable. Maurice Aylward scored one of the goals but was perhaps more chuffed to get a lift back into Thurles in the ministerial car, courtesy of the fact that both his father Bob, the former Kilkenny county chairman, and Jack Lynch lined out for those other kingpins of the national scene, Fianna Fáil. The *Waterford News & Star* went into rhapsodies over "a perfectly trained hurling unit which found plenty of opportunities to display exceptional ability and natural craft". The *Tipperary Star*, who didn't have quite as far to travel, predicted that Kilkenny "need have no worries" about retaining the *Irish Press* Cup if the formline held true at minor level later in the year. The formline did.

Ollie Ryan from Inistioge, the St Kieran's centre-back, had often watched Fr Maher pucking around with the clerical students and concluded he'd been a far more gifted player than was realised. "You'd see him between a couple of the cleesies, in between them, striking overhead. The ball would never hit the ground. Having been a forward himself he was probably a better trainer of forwards than backs. Keep the ball moving, he emphasised. He was always talking about Hopper McGrath of Wexford, what a good player the Hopper was because he was always moving and how he never stood still. Frees, 70s, sideline cuts, puckouts – he was a great man on these. He wanted puckouts like Nick O'Donnell's, deliveries that would land in the middle of the field and carry on low into the forwards instead of ones that dropped like a stone for the opposition defenders. He rarely said much about a match until the night before, when he'd tell you who you were playing on, what he was like, what side he hit with. He'd done his homework and had gone to see the opposition. And he never made noise in the dressing room. Always only a few quiet words."

Fr Maher's active missionary work in the school was done by 1961. Thereafter he was happy to take a back seat and leave most of the training to seminarians. Tom Murphy, for example, oversaw the team that won the 1965 All Ireland. But his presiding genius endured. Many a drizzly evening in training the players would look up to find his familiar black Volkswagen Beetle parked at the edge of Fennessy's, the field marshal come to inspect his troops, and hear him issue a couple of instructions before departing.

After the 1965 team had drawn with a Belcamp outfit inspired by a human whirlwind called Frank Cummins from Knocktopher, Fr Maher had the goalposts in Fennessy's dug up and temporarily replanted in the middle of the field, with the forwards made to run round and round the uprights in an effort to improve their concentration on their objective. Whether because of this or despite it, St Kieran's won the replay and went on to win the All Ireland. They were champions again in 1971 with a team that included Brian Cody, Billy Fitzpatrick and Nickey Brennan and that was coached by Dermot Healy. Brennan was "awestruck" on first encountering Fr Maher. If this man's coaching had been good enough for Eddie Keher...

Odd as the question sounds now, both before and during his college presidency Fr Maher was regularly asked why the school hadn't had a bigger influence on Kilkenny hurling. "Considering the fame of St Kieran's on the hurling field down through the years it is surprising at first sight that so few of its former stars have won All Ireland medals with Kilkenny," he acknowledged in 1982. But he had a simple answer. "St Kieran's is first and foremost a seminary."

No longer. Much has changed since 1982 both inside and outside the colleges arena. Some schools have ceased to exist as hurling powers (St Peter's, North Mon) or, in the case of St Finbarr's of Farranferris, the Black and White's great rivals in the early 1970s, have ceased to exist altogether. Not St Kieran's, whose relevance continued after the school's boarding arm was closed, and not only continued but intensified. Following a hiatus between 1975 and '88 they returned to win three All Ireland titles in a row, the first of them with an outfit featuring DJ Carey, Adrian Ronan and Pat O'Neill. Further triumphs followed in 1992-93, in 1996 with a side that numbered Henry Shefflin, in 2000 with Tommy Walsh, Brian Hogan and Jackie Tyrrell, in 2003-04 with Richie Power and in 2010-11.

The explanation for the relative paucity of alumni who progressed to All Ireland senior glory became obsolete quite some time ago. While it may be pushing it to say that a good Kieran's team means a good Kilkenny minor team, although there are worse rules of thumb, it is a simple and inarguable fact that the college has been one of the engines of Kilkenny hurling since the late 1980s. That the county won four All Irelands in a row under Brian Cody made Tommy Maher a proud and happy man. That no fewer than 15 of the 24 players who saw action in the four finals were St Kieran's men, and the manager another, made him prouder and happier still.

CHAPTER 6

Darkness

One Glorious Triumph in Isolation
Title of chapter on 1939-57 period in *Kilkenny: The GAA Story 1884-1984* by Tom Ryall

They came from near and far to Dublin the day the skies opened and the world turned to night. Tommy Cummins, son of Kilkenny city's Town Sergeant, on his 15th birthday with his brother Jimmy and father Paddy. Tony O'Malley from Monaghan, where the young Callan man was a reluctant clerk in the Munster and Leinster Bank. A 17-year-old Nicky Rackard from Killanne, cheering for Kilkenny and his hero Paddy Phelan. Tom Cuddihy and Tommy Cody from Tullaroan, who arose in darkness, cycled into Kilkenny and attended early Mass in the Friary before catching the train to Dublin.

As the 39,302 spectators descended on Croke Park, the chimes of doom were sounding afar. At 11.15am Neville Chamberlain announced from 10 Downing Street that, following Hitler's invasion of Poland, Britain was at war with Germany. During the afternoon in the House of Commons, watched from the visitors gallery by a young Bostonian called John Fitzgerald Kennedy, Winston Churchill, the new First Lord of the Admiralty, declared that it was not a question of fighting for Danzig or fighting for Poland but of saving "the whole world from the pestilence of Nazi Germany".

At Croke Park thunder rumbled and lightning cracked, leading some in the crowd to believe that the Luftwaffe were attacking Dublin. The rain came down like a waterfall, the colours in Nicky Rackard's black and amber paper hat soaking into his hair and skin. Standing on the Canal End, Paddy Cummins clutched his sons' hands tight. It was only the roar of the crowd that told them the winning point had been scored through the curtain of rain at the far end of the field and it was only on the trek back to Kingsbridge that they learned Jimmy Kelly had scored it. The newspaper reporters themselves had to check the identity of the scorer afterwards, so blinding was the downpour.

By the time the train pulled into Kilkenny railway station that night, the lights of the city had been quenched. The Cumminses made their way home in darkness. Tom Cuddihy and Tommy Cody collected their bikes and headed for Tullaroan in the small hours with sugáns, normally used to tie cocks of hay, inside their tyres substituting for tubes. Tony O'Malley and his travelling companion embarked on an eerie journey north, scoured dark Dundalk for a pub and celebrated victory by guttering candlelight, "contented Kilkenny hurling men although the shadow of a world war hung about us everywhere".

O'Malley went on to become one of the most acclaimed Irish artists of the second half of the century. Cummins ended up as head barman in Langton's, scarcely a lesser achievement. Tom Cuddihy and Tommy Cody spent the years left to them recalling the wonders they'd witnessed amid the Croke Park tempest. Well might all of them have looked back on the Thunder and Lightning final with fondness. It was the day the second golden era of Kilkenny hurling ended.

Eight years separated Kilkenny's 12th All Ireland title from their 13th. Ten years separated Kilkenny's 13th All Ireland title from their 14th. One glorious triumph in isolation indeed. Tom Ryall couldn't have nutshelled it more precisely. For the Black and Amber, the 1940s ended not in 1949 but in '57.

The best of times, the 1930s, gave way to the worst of times. Defeat was piled on defeat, with the occasional embarrassment thrown in for good measure and a stifling despondency and general aimlessness shot through it all. After the humiliations of Corrigan Park and New Ross the county stirred from slumber in 1945, winning the first of three consecutive Leinster titles, but the 1947 All Ireland triumph was followed by defeat to Laois, among whose stars was another future government minister, Paddy Lalor from Abbeyleix, in three of the next four seasons. Nemesis then changed her colours from blue and white to purple and gold: four times in the five seasons from 1952 to '56 Kilkenny had their championship interest ended by Wexford.

Quite how Wexford came to have Nick O'Donnell, a Graignamanagh man, wearing the number three jersey is a footnote that has never been fully amplified. It is a fact that he was the third of the six Kilkenny substitutes listed on the match programme for the 1947 All Ireland final. Also on the bench was Ned Kavanagh, who after showing up well for Tullaroan against Éire Óg in the county final a fortnight beforehand was on holidays in Tramore when he received the call. Kavanagh was about to enter his last year in the seminary in St Kieran's, upon which he would be ordained for the diocese of Sacramento. Combining hurling and his clerical studies was, he says, "kind of an issue, but I never paid it any attention – I was going to America."

Kilkenny were well in command in the final against Cork when Peter Prendergast, their centre-back, went off injured during the second half. The selectors might have brought in Nick O'Donnell at full-back and sent Diamond Hayden out to centre-back. They might even have sent in Ned Kavanagh as a direct replacement for Prendergast. Instead they fell between two stools. "You go in and tell Diamond to go out and mark Ring," Tom Walsh, the county chairman, told Kavanagh. The latter was flabbergasted. "I didn't expect it. I didn't want it either. Diamond didn't like it but he went out to centre-back. They should have left me off completely."

The reshaping of the defence unsettled Kilkenny, Cork pounced for two quick goals and instead of cruising to victory the Noresiders had to come from behind to win the day, 0-14 to 2-7, via Terry Leahy's immortal injury-time point. One teenage Kilkenny supporter became so caught up in the late frenzy that he did his sums wrong ("14 points – and two sevens are 14...") and was under the impression for a few minutes afterwards that the game had ended in a draw.

What is also a fact is that Nick O'Donnell did not receive a winner's medal, Paddy Grace's explanation in his capacity as county secretary being that O'Donnell was not an official sub and there were only so many medals to go around. O'Donnell, who went on to make 35 championship appearances for Wexford, the first of them versus Dublin in the 1951 Leinster semi-final at Nowlan Park, was a quiet man. But he never made any secret of his displeasure, and he made his feelings abundantly clear to Grace in that great Kilkenny house, Hanrahans' of New Ross, after a match years later.

It may not have seemed that way at the time, but the health and future prosperity of hurling in the county now teetered on the edge of a knife. The success story that is modern Kilkenny hurling began in the mid-1950s. In different circumstances, or had the people who mattered been content to allow the drift to continue, it might never have begun at all.

How did it get to that stage in the first place after the four All Ireland triumphs of the 1930s? Dermot Kavanagh, whose oeuvre includes an Ollie Walsh biography and a history of Kilkenny county senior finals, has cited a variety of theories for Noreside's post-1939 travails. Inexplicable selections made on the eve of important games which saw regular players dropped in favour of championship debutants; players being called out of retirement for big matches; the chronic inability of the county board to finish its championships within the year, and this at a time when there were no intermediate or under-21 competitions to worry about.

"Clearly something was very amiss both on and off the field," Kavanagh argues. "The gospel of the GAA was not being spread effectively. The junior championship was strangled of its best players, who once they'd made their name there usually succumbed to the charms of the high-profile senior clubs. One example: the Rower won the junior championship in 1944, lost seven of their best players to senior clubs in the space of the next year and ended up worse off for their success. It took 12 years for them to be competitive again.

"You'd wonder that had hurling received serious competition around then from soccer, rugby or even Gaelic football, would it have attained the heights it eventually did? The irony was that during those fallow years Kilkenny were served by some of the most committed GAA men the county ever produced. It seems that nobody ever complained. It was, simply, just how things were."

A shaft of light split the gloom in 1954. On foot of a proposal by Slieverue, seconded by Tullaroan, the parish rule was introduced following a one-year experiment with a three-parish rule. It is no exaggeration to say that the move transformed hurling in the county. All changed utterly, and utterly for the better. Nor was it that Paddy Buggy, who moved the motion, was acting out of self-interest; Slieverue actually ended up losing four first-choice players who lived just the wrong side of the parish boundary.

No longer would the Kilkenny senior championship be the preserve of a handful of superclubs as it had been for the previous 30 years, a period in which Carrickshock won seven titles, Tullaroan six, Mooncoin five and Éire Óg four. To take one team at random: had the members of the victorious Éire Óg outfit of 1947 been alive 50 years later and performing with their home clubs, Jim Langton would have been lining out for Clara, Jack Mulcahy for O'Loughlins, Diamond Hayden for Barrow Rangers, Nick O'Donnell for Graignamanagh, Ramie Dowling for Kilmacow, Mick Neary for Dicksboro and Liam Reidy for Bennettsbridge.

The prevailing dispensation served the few rather than the many. That was inarguable. "Tullaroan had the pick of the north of the county," Paddy Buggy explains. "Carrickshock had them from Thomastown, Slieverue, Glenmore. The introduction of the parish rule meant the big teams were not as strong as they had been. Things became more balanced. It was for the betterment of hurling. It spread it all over the county. There were no more good players going away to a strong senior club and leaving a weak junior team, or no junior team, behind them."

On top of that, according to Dermot Kavanagh, the fixtures themselves became more attractive. "Men on the Kilkenny team who had played for Tullaroan or Carrickshock or Éire Óg were now playing for their parish. This brought a glamour to junior matches that hadn't been there before."

The introduction of the parish rule was accompanied by the establishment of a slew of new clubs. Young Irelands, the team a young Tommy Maher would have played for had they existed, were formed in Gowran in late 1952, St Vincent's – now Graignamanagh – in early 1953 as an offshoot of Brandon Rovers, Clara and Windgap in 1954. O'Loughlin Gaels and Ballyhale Shamrocks, two of the latterday dynamos of the local club scene, would follow in 1972. Power and players were no longer centralised. As the tide gradually rose a flotilla of boats were lifted, self-sustaining hurling communities emerging all over the county.

In time all the roots would receive water and most of them would produce blooms. St Lachtain's of Freshford won two senior titles in the early 1960s. Eddie Keher's Rower-Inistioge struck gold in 1968. James Stephens won their first title in 32 years in 1969 and were a power ever afterwards. The early 1970s brought the rise of the Fenians from Johnstown and the late '70s that of Ballyhale Shamrocks. St Martin's, Clara and Glenmore added their names to the roll of honour in the 1980s. Young Irelands and Graigue-Ballycallan did likewise in the 1990s, a decade in which Dicksboro were crowned champions for the first time since 1950. And when Richie Mulrooney managed Kilkenny to three successive All Ireland minor final appearances in 2008-10, he did so with a group composed mainly of players from intermediate and junior clubs: Tullogher-Rosbercon, Lisdowney, Blacks and Whites from Skeoghvosteen, St Patrick's of Ballyragget and so on. Nobody wins unless everybody wins.

The numbers do not lie. Kilkenny won 13 All Ireland senior titles in the first 70 years of the GAA, the period preceding the introduction of the parish rule, and 20 in the next 57. One National League title in the 28 years of the competition before 1954 and 13 in the next 57. Four All Ireland minor titles in the 26 years of the competition before 1954 and 16 in the next 57. Yet the point cannot be stressed often enough: there was no element of manifest destiny about any of this.

The implications of the paradigm shift took time to ramify downwards, understandably. Defeat would be Kilkenny's lot at the hands of Wexford in 1954, a game that marked the end of Jim Langton's storied career, and again in '55 and '56. The county continued to wander through the wilderness without a sight of water. Paddy Grace had wiseacres telling him he should give Nowlan Park over to pasture for cattle. It was into this hurling Narnia, where it was always winter and never Christmas, that Fr Tommy Maher ventured at the invitation of Grace, supported by the Bennettsbridge club.

Kilkenny had a new trainer. It was not front-page news. There was no obvious reason why it should have been.

Not only in hurling terms was Kilkenny an impoverished county. The first month of 1957 saw over 550 people without work, 100 employees let go from the Padmore and Barnes boot factory in the city and a reduction in staff at the St Francis Abbey brewery. A sawmills in Freshford closed temporarily following petrol rationing. A steady stream of emigrants, estimated at 20 per month over the previous 12 months, was reported leaving for England from the city's railway station. There was flooding in Threecastles, the Waterbarrack, Graignamanagh and Thomastown. At least the nation's cattle and sheep population was rising. So too were clerical numbers at St Kieran's College, where a new wing was being built to cater for the increased number of young men going for the priesthood.

Such a different Kilkenny in so many ways to the Kilkenny of 2012. Such a similar Kilkenny in so many others.

The hurlers began their season on February 24th with a 2-5 to 0-5 win against Dublin in the National League. It was unimpressive stuff, the *Kilkenny People* deploring their "pick and poke methods", but they looked a different team when racking up 7-11 against Waterford in a mudbath at the Gaelic Field, now Walsh Park, on the last day of March. Let it never be said that media pressure is a new phenomenon; the season may have been only two games old, but Peter Holohan in the *People* was busy championing the claims of Mickey Walsh, "a fine hurler and has speed and youth as well as a very courageous determination", for a defensive berth. This was the natural habitat, he argued, of the Slieverue man, who had hitherto been employed up front.

Finishing top of their section of Division One brought Kilkenny face to face with Tipperary in the National League final in front of 43,721 spectators at Croke Park on May 12th. Those supporters who trembled at the thought of the blue and gold jersey had their worst fears justified. Tipp led by 1-7 to 0-1 after 22 minutes and, as if lulled into a not particularly false sense of security by this patent paucity of opposition, fell asleep and found themselves a point behind, 2-5 to the same 1-7, five minutes into the second half following a goal by Denis Heaslip. Once they woke from their stupor there was only one team in it, Tipperary kicking on for a 3-11 to 2-7 victory. Self-evidently the winners were the better team. In addition they were stronger, mentally as well as physically, and while Kilkenny may not have been seven points inferior – Seán Clohosey hit the woodwork three times – they were in trouble in the half-back and full-forward lines and had no answer to the crispness of Tipp's ground hurling.

Given the fact that Kilkenny hadn't beaten Tipperary in a big match since the 1922 All Ireland final, a record of failure that had by now been officially acknowledged on Noreside as "a bogey", this might have been acceptable. What was not acceptable was what happened next. On the eve of the championship a full-strength Kilkenny were beaten 4-10 to 2-9 in Ballyragget by a Tipperary team containing only five regulars. The *People* reported that no more than four of the losers' players – Clohosey, Mick Brophy, Paddy Buggy and Tom Walsh – "could be said to have come through the game with unblemished reputations". If a big improvement wasn't forthcoming against Dublin, the paper predicted, an early championship exit was a certainty. As nerves continued to jangle, a reader wrote to the *People* with his suggested championship XV in the hope that it would "stop the rot that has set it", even if, he conceded, "we have not a great deal of material at our disposal".

The natives were right to be restless. Nothing about the Leinster semi-final at Croke Park on June 30th turned out to be good. Dublin were bad, Kilkenny equally so and the standard was dire. The visitors were on top for most of the game but their opponents, four points down with two minutes left, rallied for a goal by Paddy McGuirk and a point by Kevin Heffernan to earn a draw, 1-11 (K) to 2-8. It could have been worse; Heffernan had the sliotar in his hand on the call of time with a chance of the winner beckoning, but he dallied and the referee Brian Smith, who had captained Meath to their breakthrough All Ireland football title in 1949, blew the final whistle.

To Paddy Buggy it was a case of the St Vincent's man trying to make assurance doubly sure. "He took too long to hit the ball. He steadied himself to make absolutely certain. And as he did, Brian Smith blew full time." Speaking 54 years later, Heffernan remembered the incident but not the apparent hesitation. "I was playing on Tom Walsh. A high ball coming. Hurleys in the air, fencing. The ball broke. I grabbed it. I stepped outside to shoot – and heard the feckin' whistle. Looking at it at the time, what we'd have perceived was that this was a Meath man determined to do Dublin down. Very unfair to Brian Smith, of course! But whether I hesitated or not, I couldn't tell you."

At this point we pause for a moment, suspend the players in freeze frame and invite the reader to construct his or her own counterfactual in the fashion of a certain branch of modern historiography. What if the weather had enabled the Spanish Armada to effect a landing in England? What if Hugh O'Neill had won at Kinsale? What if Dev had gone to London, Kennedy not gone to Dallas or Hitler decided against invading Russia? And what if Kevin Heffernan had been half a second quicker, let fly and with the last puck of the game put the sliotar between the uprights?

Let us assume for the moment that he did. The history of hurling, if we ever pause to think about it, may appear to run in straight lines, but there was nothing preordained about Kilkenny's return to glory. It only seems inevitable here and now because it happened. It was anything but inevitable there and then.

So let us pretend that Kevin Heffernan was half a second quicker. Dublin win by a point. Another barren season has elapsed for the once-mighty Black and Amber. The services of Fr Maher, with his newfangled ideas about how the backs should place the ball to the advantage of the forwards, are summarily dispensed with. Granted, Paddy Grace would surely have fought hard to retain him and Grace, as we will see, had a habit of getting his way in such situations. But let that pass. This is alternative history, remember.

The pubs of the city and county resound to bar-stool sages decrying his success with St Kieran's – only a bunch of young lads, after all – and announcing wittily that wasn't "a coach" a vehicle used for transporting teams to matches anyway? Now everything changes. The story of modern Kilkenny hurling is different. The story of modern hurling is different.

Extend the conceit. Without Fr Maher, without 1957, what would have become of Kilkenny? What, come to think of it, would have become of Dublin, who in five championship meetings with the Noresiders between 1957 and '59 drew two of them and lost another, the 1959 Leinster final, by a point following Seán Clohosey's goal with the last puck of the game? Might Kevin Heffernan have given up on football to concentrate on hurling as opposed to the other way around? Might Dublin rather than Kilkenny have vied for provincial supremacy with Wexford throughout the 1960s? Might fortune have smiled on them in the 1961 All Ireland final and helped them – with Heffernan in tow – beat Tipperary by a point rather than lose to them by a point? Might Heffernan's second coming have occurred as manager of the all-conquering Dublin *hurlers* of the 1970s? What then of Dublin and Kerry, Heffo and Micko, Jimmy Keaveney and Pat Spillane, Mikey Sheehy and Paddy Cullen? Butterflies flap their wings on Dublin's northside as well as in Gowran.

Under such a dispensation would Kilkenny now be the equivalent of, say, Limerick, a county with a fabled hurling tradition long behind them? With – a worst-case scenario, this, and shades also of Limerick – a solitary All Ireland triumph to their name since the 1940s? Or, at best, with an average of one All Ireland victory per decade to their name since the 1960s, which they sneaked in for on the blind side while Cork and Tipperary were recuperating and rebuilding after compiling sequences of success with great teams? In allowing Kilkenny to remain at the top table, had the legendary triumphs of 1939 and '47 and their contingent drama disguised the reality that the county were no longer able to consistently beat the best but simply ambush them occasionally?

In 1934, the GAA's golden jubilee year, Cork and Tipperary headed the roll of honour on 11 titles each with Kilkenny one behind on ten. By 1959, the next milestone year, Cork were out in front with 19 to Tipperary's 17 and Kilkenny's 14. Wexford had met Munster's finest in the league and All Ireland showdowns of 1956 and sent them hameward tae think again; Kilkenny hadn't beaten Munster opponents in a national final since 1947. Glory in isolation? Absolutely.

Speculate as we may, and there's no reason why we shouldn't, not least because it's fun, of this much we can be sure. There was not a second Tommy Maher out there who would have saved the county.

The Kilkenny of early 1957 was a land of ice and snow, with no indication of any imminent thaw. The Kilkenny of late 2007 was a land of milk and honey, the county having recently joined Cork at the top of the championship roll of honour on 30 titles apiece and standing poised to outstrip them. In the space of 50 years, everything had changed.

Hiems transiit alright. Winter had long passed.

CHAPTER 7

Daybreak

Entities must not be multiplied beyond necessity
Definition of Occam's Razor
(Alternative definition: Other things being equal, a simple explanation is better than a more complex one)

The 1957 Leinster semi-final replay at Nowlan Park attracted 18,000 spectators who paid gate receipts of £2,500. To say they witnessed a new and vastly improved Kilkenny would be overdoing it. The standard was better than it had been at Croke Park. On the other hand it could scarcely have been worse. Though Dublin were the speedier team, the hosts muddled through by 4-8 to 2-8. "Tantalising mediocrity" was the phrase the *Kilkenny Journal* reached for to describe their form over the life of the two games.

Still, some pennies were beginning to drop. The more Kilkenny trained under Fr Maher, the more familiar – if not always comfortable – they became with what he wanted of them. Handpassing practice was a staple, the players being drawn up in lines and instructed to palm the sliotar to one another. Older hands like Paddy Buggy never got into it. Too new, too unfamiliar, too difficult to get the hang of. "We had our own ways to move the ball. Move back a couple of steps or move to the side to make room to clear."

Tom Walsh, in his second coming after failing to make the grade in trials for the county in 1951, was staggered on being told by the trainer that his left wasn't as good as his right and that he should improve it against a gable end at home or in a ball alley somewhere. Being advised to go off and work on a particular skill? This was novel. "There was never anyone to tell you anything," remembers Walsh. "You just went out and hurled. Did the best you could."

Fr Maher's initial and unsurprising discovery on taking the team was that nobody had ever put any effort into coaching them in skills or methods or combination play. "They were just put out on the field and they pucked around or played backs and forwards." At the first training session he outlined to the players what he was going to do. He put them in lanes and had them hit the ball first time. No little touches to tee it up; hit the moving sliotar each time and all the time. Like the boys in St Kieran's College a few months earlier, they gradually discovered that this man wasn't training them: he was *coaching* them. Even more remarkably, the players found they were enjoying it.

"Thou shalt not hit a thoughtless ball," was the first of the commandments handed down from Mount Maher. There were more commandments and more stone tablets to follow.

Long before Jack Charlton was heard of, the importance of putting opponents under pressure was emphasised. Chase everything. Never give anyone a loose puck. Giving away soft frees, or any free, was anathema to Fr Maher because conceding a free meant you weren't using the skills of the game to dispossess your opponent. Only when an opponent was bearing down on goal and certain to score was a foul agreed to be understandable.

For a corner-forward to let the sliotar out over the endline was a court-martial offence. "If you didn't bust a gut to keep it in you were bad news," Paddy Buggy recalls. The trainer was always on to Dick Rockett – stocky and blocky and nobody's idea of a handy corner-forward – to keep the ball in play. One evening he even went in to demonstrate how it should be done. Rockett, in the role of corner-back, promptly hit Fr Maher a belt on the hand. "Now you know what it's like for me!"

To Rockett, Fr Maher was – in the phrase most commonly used of him by the members of his first All Ireland-winning team – a man before his time. "He was always giving out to the backs for hitting in this big high ball to the forwards. He wanted them to play it into open spaces to give the forwards a chance, being a forward himself. He'd give out to the backs on match day. 'I'm after preaching to ye what way to hit the ball in. And ye still won't do it..?'"

To Ned Fenlon from obscure Graignamanagh, 21 years old and the substitute corner-back, the trainer "was magic". At home in Graig the players trained themselves, doing sprints and laps of the field. Now here he was, not only inside in Nowlan Park, that holy of holies, but – amazingly – being directed by someone as to what to do. Fenlon's job was to clear his lines not by belting the ball away as hard as he could but by handpassing it to a loose man who'd take it from there. Different, yes, yet logical and sensible and effective. Better still, while Fr Maher was nominally the boss, to Fenlon he "wasn't a real boss. He was kind. I wasn't a first-choice player but he gave me his full attention."

Denis Heaslip's main memory was of the importance Fr Maher attached to proper communication. One evening he cited the case of a world-famous coach who, asked at a coaching seminar to identify the greatest attribute an athlete could have, paused and responded, "His voice." The Kilkenny players were encouraged to talk to one another on the pitch. "On your own! "Left!" "Right!" Encourage a player taking a free. Warn one who was being pursued.

World-famous coaches. Seminars. Communication. New words, new concepts, new thinking. Here was a hurling man of the 1950s whose casement window looked out onto strange and exotic lands. He acknowledged the existence of other sports and was prepared to learn from them. He had a vision for his own sport and was determined to propagate it.

The trainer wanted teamwork, the lack of which he believed had been the primary cause of Kilkenny's barren run since 1947. He wanted coordination. He wanted structure. He wanted players to think their way around the field as opposed to getting the ball, hitting it mindlessly and leaving it to someone else to retrieve the situation. He wanted each ball struck with a purpose behind it and a recipient in mind for it. He wanted the simple things done well, the easy frees scored. He wanted hard won possession to be protected, particularly at sideline cuts. He wanted every yard of the pitch employed and he wanted every gap filled – space, after all, was friend to the skilful player and the enlightened coach – and as a general rule he preferred a short pass to a long pass. The 1957 Leinster final was the game that delivered the first intercounty fruits of the Maher philosophy.

In retrospect Kilkenny's defeat of Wexford, whatever about its margin, should not have been greeted with the surprise it generated. After losing to their neighbours for three years in succession it would have been a stain on the Noreside escutcheon – and, less loftily, an indictment of their hurling savvy – had the challengers not been able to draft and execute a cunning plan. Action and reaction, reformation and counter-reformation, point and counterpoint, the hunter becoming the hunted. Five years of Offaly, Clare and Wexford giving way to a decade and more of Cork, Kilkenny and Tipperary. Kilkenny in 2006 decoding Cork's Enigma possession machine. Tipperary in 2010 storming Kilkenny's fortress by blowing holes in the walls and pouring through. Kilkenny returning the compliment in 2011 by demonstrating that the whirl of Tipp's attacking carousel could be jammed by nothing more complicated than good old-fashioned man to man marking. The wheel always takes a new turn.

As well as providing them with a passport for Croke Park on the first Sunday of September, the defenestration of Wexford marked a milepost that would be encountered by the county time and again in the coming years, under both Fr Maher and his successors. Poor form early in the championship, such as that shown against Dublin, was no guarantee of ultimate failure. Kilkenny had improved as the summer of 1957 went on. They would improve as future summers went on too.

Happily for their peace of mind, the blue and gold ghost of Septembers past would not return to haunt them. Tipperary had been beaten in the Munster semi-final by Cork, who in turn succumbed by five points to Waterford in the provincial decider. A unique All Ireland final pairing was the upshot. Kilkenny versus Waterford, neighbours but until now never championship opponents. From such a local row was forged an epic that spanned four enthralling finals over the course of the next seven seasons. Patrick Kavanagh should have written verses about it.

One evening in Fraher Field early that year, the Waterford players had been addressed by the new county chairman Pat Fanning, a man destined for greater things in the GAA. "As God is my judge," Fanning declared, "I believe there's the winning of an All Ireland for Waterford in this team. It will take a great effort. You will have to give a great commitment. You will have to give until it hurts and then give more. Everything possible will be done by the county board. But lads, it's a matter of pride in the Waterford jersey. Cork and Tipperary and Kilkenny have their tradition. But we have our tradition too. It's easy to come back when you're winning. But picking yourself up and coming back for more – that's the Waterford tradition."

If Fanning, an orator so gifted that in the words of the full-back Austin Flynn "you were ready to break down the door for Waterford or die in the attempt", was the group's inspiration, John Keane, an All Ireland winner in 1948 and centre-back on the Team of the Century, was their trainer and unofficial psychologist. Not unlike Tommy Maher, Keane's specialty was the quiet word in a player's ear when he felt the occasion required it.

There were other commonalities. Dick Rockett had been two years ahead of John Barron at school in De La Salle in Waterford. Paddy Buggy had gone to Mount Sion. A bunch that included Martin Óg Morrissey, Larry Guinan and Frankie Walsh worked in Clover Meats, that great melting pot of hurling men and methods, on the Kilkenny side of the Suir. Bennettsbridge had regularly encountered Mount Sion, who supplied six members of the Waterford team, in tournaments in Dunhill and Cahir during the preceding seasons and usually, according to Mick Kelly, came out on top. "Bennettsbridge and Mount Sion were two teams to have in tournaments. We knew the Waterford lads well and felt we were in with a big chance."

In addition, by now Kelly and his colleagues were more familiar with Fr Maher, with his theories and with how to apply them. "Although it was only his first year in charge he was someone to look up to. He was very determined, very serious, which was a big help. Most of the players understood him and what he wanted of us."

It was not a clash of like versus like in physical terms. Terry O'Sullivan, the social diarist of the *Evening Press*, visited the hotels of both teams on the night of the All Ireland final. "The Kilkenny men and their supporters are the largest number of tall men we have ever seen," he wrote. "By contrast, the Waterford men remind us of the Welsh men who turn up here for the occasional rugby internationals... small, lean, wiry."

Seán Clohosey, whose knee hadn't recovered from the attentions of Nick O'Donnell in the Leinster final, was Kilkenny's big worry beforehand. That same last week of August 1957, the renowned English batsman Denis Compton was also attempting to shake off a serious knee injury. The papers were full of it. Would Compton's knee hold out? Would Buckingham Palace fall down if it didn't? Dr Kieran Cuddihy, the Kilkenny team doctor who'd come to town from his native Dublin in 1952 and later became the regional pathologist, affected chagrin. What was far more important than Compton's knee in his eyes was whether *Clohosey's* knee would hold out. Before the match Dr Cuddihy brought in an anaesthetist to give the Tullaroan man an injection. The good knee was then painted with a red antiseptic to give the impression it was the bad knee. The bad knee was cleaned up with Dettol.

The final attracted an attendance of 70,594. Following early Masses in the Friary and St John's at 6.30am, four special trains brought 1,951 supporters from Kilkenny railway station to Kingsbridge, the first of them leaving at 7.25am and reaching Dublin at 9.05, the fare priced 14/6. Others specials went from Thomastown (240 passengers), Ballyhale (116), Bennettsbridge (111), Attanagh (84), Mullinavat (164) and Kilmacow (178). The Waterford trains went to Westland Row.

It cost six shillings into the Cusack Stand. The sharper eyed there and elsewhere in the stadium noticed something amiss during the pre-match parade. Kilkenny had *16* men marching. What eejit, some wag wondered loudly, was in charge of them at all?

The presence of a 16th man was no accident. He was later revealed to be the English actor John Gregson, who was playing the lead in *Rooney*, a film about a hurling-loving Dublin rubbish collector based on a Catherine Cookson novel. Gregson had originally been due to march with Waterford, the favourites, a plan shot down on the grounds that it might distract the players. Paddy Grace was implored to save the day and agreed. To be fair to Gregson, the magnitude of the occasion was not lost on him. He was white as a sheet in the dressing room beforehand and it was with some difficulty that he managed to overcome his nerves and lace his boots.

Between them the small and lean Déise men and the large, hornyhanded sons of the Kilkenny soil, *sans* their 16th man, produced a game to remember. The referee was Stephen Gleeson from Limerick, one of the umpires was Nicky Rackard and so gripping was the ebb and flow that John D Hickey of the *Irish Independent* was left "groping for words". Judging by the tsunami of prose that followed, he recovered fairly quickly.

Now that the frenzy had died down, Hickey wrote, "I still feel a thrilling glow of satisfaction that I was privileged to see it. While a few days hence when I am more composed I may think differently, I now without reserve assert that my predominant feeling is one of regret that it was not a draw.

"Many great finals I have seen. Many more I was not lucky enough to see – I was born too late as far as my hurling desires are concerned – but never, I feel, can there have been a more pulsating All Ireland final than we saw yesterday. It was a match that one dreams about and then awakes feeling cheated that it was a myth. What a pity that two sides cannot win!"

One word stands out from Hickey's report. Their stickwork polished, buffed and lacquered by Fr Maher's coaching, the play of the Kilkenny attack was, he asseverated, at times "bamboozling". "Their forwards were experts at finding the unmarked man as they switched the direction of the attack in most baffling fashion." Frequently, Hickey went on, the man who received the final pass had too much time on his hands and tried to be over-careful – hence the Leinster champions' six wides in the space of eight minutes in the first half.

Bamboozling. It was a striking use of language and an adjective that had not been employed in the reportage of recent All Ireland finals. Not about Cork and their beloved ground hurling, not about Wexford's aerial power play, not about Tipperary's hip-to-hip stuff. The *Kilkenny Journal* ("in the concluding stages the combination of the Kilkenny forwards was the telling factor in their great recovery from what seemed to spectators an almost hopeless position") agreed with Hickey, as did the *Kilkenny People*, who rated the game below the 1947 final in classical terms but acknowledged it as a thriller nonetheless. The Leinster champions won, wrote An Camán – Peter Holohan – because they played Kilkenny hurling as it should be played.

"The sides were evenly matched and if Waterford were slightly faster at some sectors Kilkenny's traditional craft was an important advantage and in the final analysis it was that superior craft that had a very important bearing on the result. Kilkenny packed more finesse into their work and when the need came for that vital rally on which so much depended their forwards worked through so cleverly that the best that the Waterford defence had to offer could not prevail."

Likewise Pádraig Puirséal in the *Irish Press*: Kilkenny won "because they were the craftier side".

A number of inferences flow from the observations of the fourth estate. Firstly, this was new, thinking man's hurling, bracing and imaginative. Secondly, it was, as it had to be, the product of enlightened coaching. Thirdly, the Kilkenny forwards were not quite talented enough to exploit it to the full. But the day might come when they would be.

Waterford led by 1-6 to 1-5 at the end of the first half, the highlight of which had been an extraordinary triple save by Ollie Walsh in the 18th minute. All three stops came from point-blank range, two of them when he was off balance. The Munster champions' goal was scored by Phil Grimes from a free, the Kilkenny one by Billy Dwyer and it was Dick Rockett who was the creator of their second goal early in the second half, chasing down a ball on the endline, keeping it in play and flicking it back for Dwyer to apply the finishing touch. A corner-forward preventing the sliotar dribbling out for a puckout: Rockett had been listening.

The switch of Seamus Power to midfield, where John Sutton had lorded it in the first half, gave Waterford a platform on which to build a 3-10 to 2-7 lead at the three-quarter stage following two goals by Donal Whelan. Enter Mick Kenny, who was using Ned Fenlon's spare hurley, a home-made effort ("and he never gave it back to me either," Fenlon, a carpenter and the grandson of a cooper, reports wryly), to send the green flag flying twice in the space of five minutes, the second time with a soft goal from 30 yards that went through the fingers of Dickie Roche on the line. How much more might Waterford have won in that era had they been blessed with an Ollie Walsh? It is a question not confined to the 1957-63 period.

The momentum had swung Kilkenny's way and they held it to the finish. Seán Clohosey, "quite patently" always fearful of a charge, according to John D Hickey, danced through for the equalising point – kudos to Dr Cuddihy and his subterfuge, for the good knee shipped a few clatters that the bad knee would not have withstood. The winning score arrived four minutes from time from the stick of the captain Mick Kelly after John Maher hit a long clearance down the left flank. He was about 50 yards out and the angle was acute, but Kelly judged his shot beautifully and it just cleared Roche's upraised stick before falling over the crossbar. It was the first time Kilkenny had led in the second half.

Kelly's account of the winning point went thus. "Back then when a fella had a ball in the backline you'd anticipate where it would land. You'd know the strength and the length of it. Whatever way John Maher was facing, I anticipated the pitch of the drop. When he struck it I knew immediately it was on the way towards me." An anonymous bard of the day commemorated the score rather more colourfully in suitably heroic rhyming couplets:

"But the game's not o'er, we've a minute more of this titanic fray,

Whose will be the lot of a lucky shot to carry off the day,

Maher's mighty stroke 'mid the forwards broke, then Mick Kelly, brightest star,

Collects a pass and in a flash the ball soars o'er the bar."

Contrary to subsequent popular Noreside belief, Kelly was not on his knees when he scored. He did score such a point the same afternoon – but that was his *first* point, early in the second half. One can only speculate as to how many other hurling myths have endured and been nourished down the decades by dint of the lack of unassailable evidence to the contrary.

The scoreboard read 4-10 to 3-12 in Kilkenny's favour at the long whistle. As with 1939 and 1947, the county's two most recent All Ireland successes, it was a victory by the minimum margin – "the usual point", as Jack Lynch doubtless put it afterwards to anyone who'd listen. The ability to do the right thing in tight corners had outlasted the vicissitudes of the previous two decades: call it race memory. And no fewer than seven members of the team hailed from junior clubs, vindication for nobody more so than for Paddy Buggy, the right-half back and the man who'd moved the parish-rule motion.

If every man in stripes played his part on the day, some played a bigger part than others. Mick Kelly: "Ollie was brilliant. Some outstanding saves. The forwards would be standing in the square alongside him when he was trying to stop the ball and he was so good, so agile. And Mick Kenny beside me was a great man to have at centre-forward. Always available. Very reliable."

The winning trainer was not lost for words either. "I think it was a really great game, ranking with the best I have ever seen," Fr Maher enthused. "Waterford played brilliant, brainy and forceful hurling. Midway through the first half I considered we had the game safe and had our forwards taken the chances that came their way the game would have been as good as over at half-time. Waterford definitely got the breaks that gave them a point lead at the interval and we got the breaks that gave us the same margin at the final whistle."

Loud were the cheers and the tobacco spits. Eighty-one-year-old John Grogan of Ballyhendricken, Ballycallan, had seen every one of Kilkenny's All Ireland victories since their first in 1904 and rated the latest "as good as the best of them". The reception for the winning team was held that night in the Hollybrook Hotel in Clontarf with Martin White, the county's two-goal hero against Clare 25 years earlier, the master of ceremonies. Seamus McFerran, the president of the GAA, hailed the game as one of the greatest in the Association's history. Pádraig Ó Caoimh, the general-secretary, revealed that it was the 57th final he had seen and added that he'd never witnessed a better one. Mick McGuinness, in the first of his seven terms as mayor of Kilkenny, toasted the defeated minors as well as the victorious seniors and paid tribute to Bill Walsh, who had been picked for the 1947 All Ireland final but missed out due to a hand injury and, having laboured for little reward during the intervening decade, had come on for John Sutton midway through the second half.

There was a story to that one. PJ Garvan, Seán Clohosey's replacement in the Leinster final, was the appointed substitute and was in the process of taking off his coat to replace Sutton when Bob Aylward, the county chairman, barked at his fellow Carrickshock clubman Walsh to "go in there". Aylward in his own speech sympathised with Waterford, who unlike his own county "had to put up with foreign elements and foreign games", and thanked the man "without whom Kilkenny would not have won", Fr Maher.

The following day's *Evening Herald* carried a front-page photograph of Fr Maher, the physical trainer Syd Bluett and a number of players, among them Dick Rockett and Paddy Buggy, reading the *Irish Independent*'s report of the game. In the afternoon they listened to a recording of Mícheál O'Hehir's commentary before leaving Kingsbridge at 6.15pm. They received rousing welcomes in Carlow, Milford, Bagenalstown and Gowran, the first station in Kilkenny, arriving at the city railway station at 9.20pm. Over 20,000 people flooded onto the streets to greet them, with four bands – St Patrick's Brass Band, Graignamanagh Brass Band, James Stephens Pipers Band and the St John's Boys Flageolet Band – accompanying them on their triumphal procession to the Parade. On a night that, as Mick McGuinness said, "had been awaited for ten years", among the worthies on the platform were Ollie Walsh's parents.

The comments of the man without whom the festivities would not have been taking place deserve to be recorded in full. Fr Maher claimed he happened "by mere chance" to have charge of the training arrangements for the year, the county board and Bennettsbridge having asked him to come on board. He had to admit that he had "been rather lucky" in his association with teams even if not always successful.

"Yesterday's was a thrilling battle. We know that we caused you many anxious moments. We know too that many of you panicked when the outlook was dimmest, but we are glad that in those anxious moments we had full confidence in the team's ability to come through. We knew they were capable of doing the job. We believed that our light training methods would carry us to victory, which if it came only at the eleventh hour made it all the sweeter."

In training, he continued, his object was to get every player to play for the other 14 and the 15 to play for the county. In their many defeats in recent years, as he saw them, what Kilkenny had lacked was teamwork and coordination in their efforts. He set out to give this to the team and in doing so his labour became a pleasure as he found the 15 players and the six substitutes most willing to cooperate in every detail. There was nothing which they failed to do when asked. "You do not know that there are men on the platform who have given up smoking and drinking for the past three weeks [!] to bring this victory to you. You will, I am sure then, pardon them if they exceed the limits of moderation in their joyous celebrations this evening."

The team, he went on, exemplified the doctrine of all for one and one for all. There was no distinction between one player and another. It mattered not from what corner of the county a player came. It mattered not from what club he came. All were united in a common bond of friendship and one common object of attainment.

Teamwork, coordination, light training methods. Out of the mouths of babes and seers.

Afterwards the conquering heroes were entertained to supper in the Metropole Hotel, with 160 guests attending and the menu card in the county colours festooned with a black and amber ribbon. The night ended with a céilí in the Mayfair Ballroom in the company of the Ormonde céilí band and 800 camp followers. The following night the Kells Pipe Band led Tom and Jim Walsh through the village of Dunnamaggin. Later in the week Mick Kenny, the top scorer with 2-5, was presented with a wristwatch by his colleagues in the 13th Battalion at Kickham Barracks in Clonmel and received a vote of congratulations from the members of the town's corporation. Heroes all for the week that was in it, even if few of their names would echo down the decades.

"An average team overall," says Dick Rockett, "but then we had a great goalkeeper, and that counted for a lot. If Ollie was playing today, nothing would pass him."

Listening to Johnny Barry's late-night music show on KCLR 96FM, Rockett occasionally hears a song about Kilkenny's hurling triumphs that for some reason omits mention of 1957. It is an oversight and a bad one. Few Kilkenny teams have won a worthier All Ireland. None have won a more important All Ireland.

A hurling decade like none before or since, the 1950s yielded three in a rows for Cork and Tipperary, successive titles for Wexford and a second and to date last MacCarthy Cup victory for Waterford. All of these were headline-making achievements. But none was ultimately as significant as Kilkenny's lone title would prove to be.

The Roman historians had a phrase for it. *Ab urbe condita.* From the foundation of the city. In the case of the Eternal City it was 753 BC. In the case of modern Kilkenny hurling it is 1957. Everything starts from there.

CHAPTER 8

Waterford

They think it's all over... It isn't now!
**Kenneth Wolstenholme (in a parallel universe) commenting on the
closing moments of the 1959 drawn All Ireland final**

Kilkenny had not won consecutive All Irelands since 1932-33. Irrespective of the
presence of Fr Maher, this state of affairs was not about to change any time soon.
Nonetheless, 1958 saw the county make a creditable attempt to retain the
MacCarthy Cup, even if they again required two games to dispose of Dublin in
the provincial semi-final. Anyone still labouring under the belief that their win
in the 1957 Leinster final had been a fluke was undeceived when Kilkenny and
Wexford renewed hostilities in front of 47,729 spectators amid torrential rain.
The holders led by three goals at half-time and won by 5-12 to 4-9.

One of the losers' goals was scored by Fr Maher's old friend Tom Ryan in his
final championship outing. "I don't know what category of forward you would
cast him in," Martin Codd wrote of the ever-colourful Ryan in his autobiography,
"but whatever it is he was very effective." What category? The Tom Ryan
category. He was one of a kind.

Ryan, who had got himself sent off in Kilkenny's defeat to Clare in the 1949
All Ireland junior Home final, had had a brief spell in the gardaí before taking
up a job as a storeman in St Senan's psychiatric hospital in Enniscorthy. His
arrival on the Wexford team in the autumn of 1953 was the final, critical piece
in the jigsaw – critical in that it served to liberate Nicky Rackard from the
depredations of enemy full-backs. Nominally the number 13, Ryan spent most
of his time making a nuisance of himself on the edge of the square, freeing
Rackard to roam at will out the field.

It need scarcely be added that Ryan was more than capable of taking care
of himself. After scoring Wexford's goal in the 1954 All Ireland final he was taken
out of it by Cork, for which he extracted due revenge upon Tony O'Shaughnessy
in the rematch two years later. Ryan's clashes with Mark Marnell, John Maher's
predecessor as Kilkenny's left-corner back, were the stuff of folklore, suitable
for the eyes of consenting adults only. A presumably apocryphal story of the time
had it that Marnell, no shrinking violet himself, went to confession before
every encounter with Ryan. The latter's brother Liam watched the 1955 All
Ireland final from a seat in the old Corner Stand alongside Tom Ryall, the future

chronicler of Gaelic games in Kilkenny. Twenty-eight years later Liam's son Harry wore the number 15 jersey as Kilkenny defeated Cork in the final.

How do you solve a problem like Galway? This was the year the authorities tried by giving them a bye into the All Ireland final, thereby pitting the champions of Leinster against the champions of Munster in the semi-final. How do you solve a problem like Tipperary? If you were Kilkenny you didn't. Not then. Not yet.

It wasn't that the MacCarthy Cup holders lacked for spirit or effort in front of a crowd of 53,337, more than the 47,276 who would pay to watch Tipp and Galway go through the motions a month later. Kilkenny hurled well in the opening quarter, but the selectors erred in omitting Mick Kenny, the attacking hero against Waterford the previous September. Tipperary led by a point at half-time, and with the young Jimmy Doyle, in his first year out of minor, sparkling on Paddy Buggy they pulled away for a 1-13 to 1-8 victory. The losers may have performed better than the scoreline suggested; with his beloved Wexford fallen by the wayside, Nicky Furlong transferred his support to Kilkenny, travelled to Croke Park and felt them "most unlucky" to lose as they did.

Notwithstanding that, the bottom line was unaltered. Another meeting of Tipperary and Kilkenny in a big match and another victory for Tipperary. The same old scéal. Move along there now, nothing to see.

Of the 14 All Ireland finals Kilkenny contested with Fr Maher as coach, the best – the most entertaining, the most absorbing, the most outrageously exciting – was that of 1959. With one team scoring five points and the other 17 points the game was wildly uneven, but the unevenness added to the drama and the last-reel twist in the tail was by Alfred Hitchcock out of Agatha Christie. Whodunnit? The most improbable of suspects dunnit. The Link Walsh's hurley dunnit.

It was an afternoon of contradictions. Kilkenny accompanied their five points with five goals and still didn't win. Waterford sent the white flag flying 17 times, a record for a 20th century final up to then, and very nearly lost. One man scored three goals, but his name has been lost to history because he didn't finish on the winning side. And Ollie Walsh, magnificent even by his standards, produced a goalkeeping display for the ages. Only a freakish piece of bad luck could have beaten him on the day – and it did. All in all the match had to have been quite something for John D Hickey to rate it more highly than the 1957 equivalent – and he did.

"Thank heavens it was a draw," Hickey began in the *Irish Independent* next day. "That was my predominant thought at the end of an epic combat at Croke Park yesterday, when, in an All Ireland senior hurling final that simply beggars description, a game that seems to make all words inadequate, Waterford (1-17) and Kilkenny (5-5) ended on level terms in a context that must rank as a landmark in the history of the GAA." Whether left "groping for words" as he had been in 1957, or dubious about their efficacy in conveying such Olympian heights of drama as he had just witnessed, Hickey was not a man to be easily deterred. On he prosed for a further 26 paragraphs and he didn't spare the superlatives.

Amid it all, including his consecration of Ollie Walsh as the greatest goalkeeper ever ("the good goalkeeper saves, but Walsh, who can come through a forest of hurleys in bewildering fashion, not only saves but breaks the heart of the opposition with mammoth pucks"), one line stood out by virtue of its very simplicity. Waterford, Hickey wrote, "were the better team".

That was as it should have been. By this stage they were the finished article, hardy and experienced and well balanced. Years of competing against the Barrs and the Glen and Thurles Sarsfields in the Cork Churches Tournament had proved to the Mount Sion contingent that man for man they were as good as anyone out there. The 1957 All Ireland final had shown them that playing well wasn't enough. The 1958 Munster final, a 4-12 to 1-5 trimming by Tipperary, had taught them the consequences of overconfidence and the perils of going to Thurles to face the home team.

The Cork Athletic Grounds was the venue when the sides met in the following year's semi-final, a game whose half-time score was so preposterous – Waterford 8-2 Tipperary 0-0 – that Micheál O'Hehir, on duty at the Connacht football final, rang the gardaí in Cork seeking confirmation. "If it was the other way around would you have believed it?" Frankie Walsh asked him mischievously after the All Ireland. The Kilkenny players were in the dressing room at half-time in the Leinster final against Dublin when someone announced that Waterford were winning by eight goals. To a man the team burst out laughing at this obvious fabrication. Walsh was his side's only scorer in the second half, but the damage had been done and Waterford held out against the breeze to win by 9-3 to 3-4 before beating Cork by a goal in the provincial decider.

They settled quickly in the All Ireland final and, with Seamus Power and Phil Grimes on top at midfield, led by 0-9 to 1-1 at the interval. But finals have a habit of throwing up unlikely heroes, and amid its myriad of sterling performers the first instalment in 1959 had a particularly improbable one: 19-

year-old Tommy O'Connell, the Kilkenny left-corner forward, born in Essex to parents who returned home when the war broke out.

O'Connell scored all three of his goals at the Railway End in the second half. The first arrived when a high ball in from Paddy Kelly hit the upright and came down for O'Connell, reacting the fastest, to flick to the net. Had he been in the square? It was borderline. Mick Mackey, the umpire on the far side, shouted a square ball but Nicky Rackard, his counterpart on the near side, was already reaching for the green flag. In view of his Kilkenny connections, his friendship with Tommy Maher and the knowing nod he gave O'Connell, it can be taken as read that Rackard was not disposed to do down the neighbours if he could help it. (Rackard and Mackey. The greatest forward line ever to umpire an All Ireland final.)

O'Connell's second came from an overhead connection and might have been stopped by Ned Power on the line. For his third he let fly on a breaking ball. The sliotar fizzed through a ruck of players and into the net. O'Connell's contribution allied to a goal from Dick Carroll helped the Leinster champions lead by 5-5 to 0-17 with time running out. The following two paragraphs constitute one version, corroborated by a number of observers and participants, of what happened next.

As county champions, Tullaroan not only had the county captaincy in the person of Seán Clohosey but also had two selectors, Paddy Phelan and Tom Hogan. Lory Meagher had captained Kilkenny to win the 1935 All Ireland final from midfield. Wouldn't it be fitting if another Tullaroan man were to do the same now? So Mick Fleming was withdrawn in the closing stages, John Sutton sent in and Clohosey switched to midfield. Like with Bob Aylward and Bill Walsh two years earlier, it was stroke politics of the usual, common or garden GAA kind. Unlike with Aylward and Walsh, it turned out to make a difference.

Sutton, a career midfielder and unaccustomed to wing-forward, was still trying to find his bearings when the sliotar broke in the area Clohosey had been patrolling, an area that was now vacant. Tommy O'Connell, not a million miles away in the corner, half-thought about making a run, then decided against. The Waterford right-half back Mick Lacey, with all the time in the world, sent the loose ball upfield.

Larry Guinan recycled possession near the Canal End touchline and found Seamus Power steaming in from the right with Frankie Walsh unmarked inside him. Walsh shouted to his Mount Sion clubmate for the pass. Power ignored him and let fly. He didn't make the best of connections; Ollie Walsh had the shot covered. But Jim the Link Walsh, the Kilkenny full-back, apparently believing that his goalie was not on his line, stuck out his stick. The sliotar struck it, spun off it and ricocheted past the helpless Ollie and over the line. Waterford 1-17 Kilkenny 5-5.

Amid the pandemonium Power, under the impression that Waterford were a point up – Frankie Walsh, "too frazzled to do the maths", thought they were a point down – had an opportunity to win the game but put it wide. For the first time since 1934, an All Ireland final had ended in a draw.

"Fury was let loose," was how Joe Sherwood described the second half in his ever-popular In the Soup column in the *Evening Press*. "What heart-palpitating stuff it was. Never a moment's respite for either players or onlookers. It seemed unbelievable that humans could keep going at such a pace. The harder Kilkenny hit to win their way back into the game (which they succeeded in doing), the harder Waterford hit back."

Equally impressed was the BBC commentator Kenneth Wolstenholme, there with a camera crew to make a documentary. "If you took these teams on a world tour to play a game like that you would have hurling played everywhere," he swooned, adding that Waterford's centre-forward Tom Cheasty had been his man of the match.

There is no gainsaying Frankie Walsh's contention that "it was a marvellous game and we were the better team but our backs were bad". Waterford were the better team, "of course they were", Tommy O'Connell agrees. "We got the goals and that kept us in the game." The Link Walsh was disconsolate back in the Hollybrook afterwards, blaming himself for costing Kilkenny victory and predicting that they wouldn't win the replay. The only ray of sunshine for him and his colleagues was the three pounds the county board gave each of them the next day in lieu of the wages they'd lose through missing a second Monday at work.

For the replay John Keane changed Waterford's training regime to encompass regular games of backs and forwards, a new departure for them and one which Frankie Walsh maintains "sharpened and toughened" the backs. One night in Dunhill, with Walsh Park being renovated, Austin Flynn was playing so well that he was stunned to be taken aside by Keane. "Austin, you've done enough tonight. Go in and get a rub." Come the replay Flynn saw the method in Keane's apparent madness. "We were much fitter. That was the telling part. John had pulled us back because he could see we were just right and he didn't want to overdo it."

Kilkenny's late misfortune of September 6th spilled over into October 4th. Mick Brophy cried off in the dressing room beforehand, necessitating a late and panicked reshuffle. Tim Kelly went centre-back and Mickey Walsh to right-half back, then to midfield shortly afterwards. "I didn't know where I was," Walsh laments. Worse was to come when Johnny McGovern, who'd gone off with a shoulder injury in the drawn game, had to be replaced after 15 minutes. Frankie Walsh: "When Johnny McGovern played well, Kilkenny played well."

An aspiring young photographer from Kilkenny called Tom Brett was on the endline and saw Tommy O'Connell being smothered by a Waterford defence now forewarned and forearmed. "He simply wasn't allowed to hurl." This event, or non-event, would furnish Gus Carey, a notable Kilkenny raconteur and wit who once gained entry to a packed pub on All Ireland night by (truthfully) informing the doorman that he, Christy Ring and John Doyle had 16 All Ireland medals between them, with one of his better lines. "Tommy O'Connell," quoth Carey dramatically. "The first day against Waterford in '59 he scored three goals. The second day Eamon de Valera saw more of the ball than he did."

Being pedantic about it, this may have been unfair on the president. Limited eyesight or not, de Valera was able to opine to Frankie Walsh, the victorious captain, on the podium afterwards that he thought Waterford might have gone for more goals. "Take your points and the goals will come," Walsh laughed. De Valera beamed.

Waterford were more focused than they had been a month earlier and Ned Power received far better protection. ("The Noreside forwards were not allowed to crowd the Waterford goalkeeper to the same extent as the drawn game," Seán Óg Ó Ceallachain noted in the *Evening Press*.) It finished 3-12 to 1-10 in favour of richly deserving champions, the total that had not been quite enough for the Déise men in 1957 proving more than sufficient two years later.

"Beating Kilkenny is worth two All Irelands," the secretary of the winners' reception committee pronounced. In the circumstances, who could have argued with him? Waterford might have won in 1957. They should have lost, however undeservingly, first time around in '59. The swings and the roundabouts and the fall of fate.

Kilkenny folk in the crowd of 77,825, the largest attendance to watch the county play prior to the redevelopment of Croke Park, were entitled to find some consolation in the fact that at least the Black and Amber were contesting All Ireland finals again. After the best part of a decade spent watching from the wings they were relevant once more. And the more far-seeing of their supporters would have derived solace from studying the young man who replaced Johnny

McGovern. In doing so he made history, having featured on the Kilkenny team unfortunate to lose by a point to Tipperary in the All Ireland minor decider a month earlier. He then showed up well against Dublin in the Oireachtas and Wexford in the Walsh Cup. Now here he was, ten days short of his 18th birthday, scoring Kilkenny's only two points of the second half, the first and last man to appear in both minor and senior finals in the same year.

He was from the postcard-pretty village of Inistioge and his name was Eddie Keher.

CHAPTER 9

Stirrings

'Twas quite a thrill as with great skill young Eddie took the frees
He never missed a single one and scored each point with ease
Poem commemorating Kilkenny's 1963 All Ireland title win

Three consecutive Leinster titles for the first time since 1947. Three autumnal appearances in Croke Park. One All Ireland triumph that was very nearly two. Had he been marking this particular exam paper Fr Maher would have been justified in awarding it an A-minus, the more so given that the student had inarguably started off in the B class.

The effects of the Maher revolution? It was not too early to say.

In the event, though, this was to be Kilkenny's lot for the time being. The initial surge of improvement under their new tutor had come to an end. It would take time for him to fill all the seats on the bus; one of Paddy Buggy's less edifying memories of the era was of the players practising handpassing exercises in one corner of Nowlan Park while the selectors looked on, barely bothering to contain their giggles at such arrant nonsense. To paraphrase an English international rugby coach of the 1980s, you can't give a county a brain transplant overnight.

Bad shooting – they hit 12 wides in 25 minutes during the second half – cost the holders dear in the 1960 provincial decider, a fine game that ended 3-10 to 2-11 in favour of a resurgent Wexford team that went on to floor Tipperary in the All Ireland final. As if to prove this was no one-off last stand, Wexford beat Kilkenny again the following year, by four points in the semi-final, and they maintained their grip in 1962, winning the final by 3-9 to 2-10. But 1962 did offer some consolation in the shape of the county's first National League title since 1933.

Of all Kilkenny's Croke Park triumphs this remains one of the least storied, undeservedly so since the proceedings, which brought themselves and Cork together in a big match for the first time since the 1947 All Ireland final, had the national media men in raptures. "A contest in the classic mould," raved John D Hickey. "Give us a Kilkenny-Cork hurling final at any time; they will never fail to produce the fireworks," gushed Paddy Downey in *The Irish Times*, dubbing it "one of the greatest" league finals. Despite a bus strike in Dublin, the pairing was sufficiently attractive to draw a crowd of 40,157. There were traffic jams leaving the capital afterwards and on the Naas Road the stream of homeward-bound cars stretched for miles.

Many in the attendance got what they'd come for when the 42-year-old balding gentleman in the number 14 red jersey beat Ollie Walsh for the opening goal after 15 minutes. Amid heavy rain which started in the 12th minute and continued for the remainder of the hour, and on turf as slippery as a skating rink (Walsh had lost his footing in attempting to save Christy Ring's goal), Cork led by 1-5 to 0-4 at the interval. They were unable to sustain their momentum, however, and Kilkenny, with Seamus Cleere supreme in defence and Billy Dwyer, who hit 1-5, and Eddie Keher (0-8) unstoppable up front, rattled off seven unanswered points in the closing ten minutes to pull away for a 1-16 to 1-8 win. "It is good to see them back," Mick Dunne proclaimed of the winners in the *Irish Press*. "For it is no disparagement on Cork or any other county to state that the wearers of the noble black and amber bring a glamour all their own to the major hurling struggles."

Mickey Walsh, known to his friends as Browley, had been around the place since 1955 and might have been expected to know most of the tricks of the trade. But in Christy Ring he found himself marking a man who'd been around the place since the autumn of 1939 and was acquainted with far more of them. "As cute as they come. Knew exactly where the ball was going to drop. He'd stand on your foot and get away that way. That's all he wanted, a yard in front of you." Cork's problem was that up front it was, to quote John D Hickey next day, "a case of Ring and Ring alone". Kilkenny possessed more picture cards and consequently greater scope when it came to deploying them, as they did to telling effect when switching Billy Dwyer from full-forward, where he'd been well held, to wing-forward. It was the matchwinning move.

Dwyer deserves a paragraph to himself. He may have been the best Kilkenny full-forward ever. He was unquestionably the most explosive and volatile. Only 5'8, he was low to the ground and mobile, stocky and bustling, blessed with a lightning ground stroke off both sides, not overly quick, but brainy and imaginative and absolutely fearless. Nick O'Donnell confessed he had to watch Dwyer "more carefully than any other player I played on". John Doyle called him "tough [no greater compliment from that quarter] but also a great hurler".

Off the field Dwyer was equally unpredictable. When Kilkenny flew to Chicago in 1964 they stopped to refuel in New York. During the stopover some of the players indulged in their own refuelling process. Back on the plane again, Dwyer took it into his head to pay a courtesy visit to the cockpit to ask if he could pilot it to Chicago. Moments later the cops were on the plane and Dwyer, with a gun to his head, was off it. He managed to catch the next flight, encountered someone in O'Hare airport who'd been at the 1963 All Ireland final and got a lift from him to Kilkenny's hotel. The roar of laughter that went up when Dwyer barrelled in was audible two blocks away.

While all this was happening on the surface of the millpond, something strange was taking place in the depths. Prior to the beginning of the 1960s the All Ireland minor championship had been dominated by Tipperary, with 12 titles to their credit, and Cork, who had six. Kilkenny had only four to their name (1931, '35, '36 and '50) and between 1956 and '59 had lost three finals to Tipperary. On the face of it there was no obvious reason why the situation should take a sudden and marked turn for the better, the more so given that 1959 was Eddie Keher's last year in the grade. But it did. Kilkenny proceeded to win three All Ireland minor titles in a row, 1960-62, the county's first and to date last treble in the grade.

Not that this was the result of sound planning, inspired management or enlightened nurturing of players. It just happened. That, at any rate, was how it seemed to Tom Walsh, the blond starlet from Thomastown who featured on the team in 1961-62 and hit an aggregate of 3-6 in the two finals. In 1961 his entree had consisted of 15 or 20 minutes in a trial match in Grennan for players from the southern clubs. "The benchmark was largely the under-14 group from four years earlier. Then you played in the trial match, the selectors saw you in action and you either heard from them afterwards or were never heard of again."

Being a special talent and fortunate enough to have come to prominence on the all-conquering Thomastown school teams of the 1950s, Walsh was never going to fall through the cracks. The same could not be said for equally or only marginally less talented youngsters from less successful clubs. With little collective training, even coming up to an All Ireland final, success in the grade was overwhelmingly dependent on the inherent quality – inherent, not latent, because no framework existed to draw out the latency – of the players eligible in any given year. One man who was interested in such esoteric concepts as frameworks, a smallish man in clerical garb, made a habit of materialising in the Kilkenny minor dressing room in the buildup to the All Ireland finals of the early 1960s. It wasn't his place to be delivering inspirational addresses from on high, but he looked and he listened and occasionally he spoke. And Fr Tommy Maher, in the words of Tom Walsh, wasn't someone "who went to a match to watch the action – he went to a match to observe players".

Noel Skehan can picture the scene at the last training session before the 1962 final, an evening that featured a memorable digression by Fr Maher on the joys of Irish dancing and the good habits – balance, rhythm, speed of footwork – the pastime could inculcate in a hurler. "He went from number one to number 15 and in a nice way explained what you should be doing. How to cope. What to do between the last training session and the day of the match. He basically showed us how to get our heads right. And he had one piece of advice for me that night. When you puck the ball out down, say, the left and it comes back too quickly, then go down the right with your next puckout. And if their half-back line is on top, drop the puckout to midfield."

Rank outsiders against Tipperary, who had captured no fewer than six titles during the 1950s, Kilkenny won the 1960 All Ireland minor final by a staggering 7-12 to 1-11. Their victory was founded on the midfield dominance of Joe Ayres, whose father had featured on the county's breakthrough minor side of 1931 (as per the liberal mores that obtained in the grade in those days, Bill Ayres was one of *seven* members of the team who were over age), and a hat trick from Tom Murphy from the Rower. Tipp were again the victims 12 months later, when Tom Walsh and Pierce Freaney hit 1-4 apiece, and likewise in 1962, when Joe Dunphy became the first and only man to captain two All Ireland minor-winning sides. On the defeated side for the third year in succession was one Michael Keating. Centre-back for the winners in 1961 was Pat Henderson, one of the most important Kilkenny players of his generation and one of the most important Kilkenny hurling figures of all time.

There was more to these minor teams than the players. The prime mover behind them was Mick Loughman. "Mick Who?" even a knowledgeable Kilkenny supporter of today could be forgiven for responding. Mick Loughman. The forgotten man of Kilkenny hurling.

Born in St Patrick's parish in 1896, Loughman was involved in the War of Independence and was interned. He went on to be one of the founders of Éire Óg, the city club that initially drew its players from Kilkenny CBS, and was involved with county minor teams from the 1930s to the '60s as manager, selector, fundraiser and general factotum. A postman by profession, he also worked in Stallard's Theatre in Patrick Street, now Zuni restaurant, where he ruled with a rod of iron. Nobody messed when Mick Loughman was on duty. He was a man of his time rather than a man for all seasons: austere, deeply religious, a gaelgeoir and a staunch Cumann na nGaedheal/Fine Gael supporter at a time in Irish history when political allegiance was about so much more than marking a box on a piece of paper once every few years. One of his specialties was to call to the homes of his young charges the night before a match; if they weren't in bed by ten o'clock, they wouldn't be picked next day. In another life he would have been a hermit or a warrior saint. As far back as 1992, Paddy Buggy posed in print the question of whether any one man would ever contribute as much to Kilkenny hurling as Mick Loughman had.

New blood of the type hothoused by Loughman was what was needed to break the stasis at senior level and new blood was what would help make the difference at Croke Park on September 1st 1963. Some of the new blood had made its mark earlier in the campaign, Tom Murphy's goal four minutes from time paving the way for a 4-9 to 3-8 victory over Wexford in the provincial semi-final and snapping Kilkenny's recent losing sequence against their neighbours. Dublin were seen off by 2-10 to 0-9 in a Leinster final that was as dour as the scoreline suggested. Cue a fourth All Ireland final showdown in seven seasons with Waterford.

If by now Fr Maher was part of the furniture with Kilkenny, he was a part that stayed in its own corner of the room. He was the trainer – it would be a few years yet before the term 'coach' stuck – and he remained so. The trainer, nothing more. Not the manager, not a selector, certainly not the chairman of selectors. Most of his communication was done with Paddy Grace, who would convey Fr Maher's views to the selectors; Grace himself was a non-selector but, given his force of personality, his views carried weight with the management. The lead-up to the 1963 final was the one and only occasion a Kilkenny management consulted Fr Maher directly. He was in bed when they rang and told him they couldn't agree on who should partner Paddy Moran in the centre of the field. Without hesitation he nominated Seán Clohosey.

The question would occasionally be asked in later years why Fr Maher, a man who had forgotten more about the game than most of the selectors he worked with had ever learned, didn't demand more of a say when it came to picking teams. Such reticence was probably a mistake; in later life Donie Nealon, his confederate on the Gormanston course, found that not being a selector when training a team was "an awful disadvantage". The obvious explanation is that Tommy Maher didn't feel it to be his place to press for a bigger role. As a young man he'd said goodbye to his hurling career without a second thought; he was going to be a priest and that was that. As a middle-aged man he was a trainer/coach – and that was that.

A constant bugbear of his was the selectors' preference for naming the team a few days before a game. Fr Maher wanted it picked as early as possible in order to have the time to coach the players in their positions. For him this wasn't a luxury, it was a necessity, and the passing of time would not diminish its importance. Shortly before the publication of his autobiography, Brian Cody was handed a newspaper cutting from ten days before the 1973 All Ireland final. "Kilkenny senior selectors were in conclave last night," it began, "but their discussion was for the purpose of giving team trainer, Fr Tommy Maher, a broad outline of the lines on which they were thinking about as to who they would call in to replace Eddie Keher, Kieran Purcell, Jim Treacy and Eamon Morrissey."

One man who would have seconded Fr Maher's preference for Seán Clohosey in 1963 had he been consulted was Eddie Keher. Clohosey was Keher's teenage idol, the most stylish player he'd ever seen. "Seán was playing in a difficult era for stylists, where the rules favoured a more robust style of play. He was a beautiful striker of a ball left and right. His ball control was class and he could latch onto a ball in the tightest of situations and use his speed over a short distance to break free to strike. He was a prolific scorer from any of the six forward positions, but his favourite position was centrefield where he had more room to display all his skills." Clohosey had had knee problems in both 1957 and '59. Now, in the final game of his intercounty career, he would give the performance of his life.

The man from the *Waterford News & Star*, whose pre-match observations so struck Fr Maher that he kept the article, was of a similar mind where Clohosey was concerned. The preview, a full broadsheet page, was written by Eugene Rellis, a Kilmacow man who was the *News & Star*'s greyhound correspondent and who as a footsoldier in their ceaseless battle with the *Munster Express* to appeal to a south Kilkenny readership wrote about hurling affairs Noreside.

On form, Rellis agreed, Waterford – a "high-powered unit of craft and mobility which showered such destruction on the opposition in League and Oireachtas" – were entitled to be favourites, seeing that Kilkenny were "comparatively young and inexperienced" and instead of improving since the Leinster final had gone backwards, as poor performances against an understrength Dublin in the Walsh Cup and Wexford in a recent challenge match had demonstrated. But Rellis had attended training in Nowlan Park, had liked what he'd seen and was convinced that the decision to start Clohosey at midfield was an enlightened move that could have "vital and far-reaching effects on the entire course of the game".

It was as well for all concerned that Eugene Rellis had not attended the training session that season where Oliver Gough, who had hurled for Wexford against Kilkenny in the 1957 Leinster final, bridled at a ground-striking drill and insisted on rising the sliotar and – oh dear – sending it high in the direction of the forwards. Fr Maher warned him. Gough persisted. Fr Maher sent him home. When Gough returned the next night not a word was said and the episode was consigned to history. That was Tommy Maher's way. Training was too important and scientific an exercise for emotions to be allowed intrude.

Less optimistic than Eugene Rellis about the prospects of the underdogs was Mick Dunne of the *Irish Press*. Of Waterford he wrote: "No hurling side that I have seen have displayed such a devastatingly effective cohesion. The fact that so many of these players have been together for so long accounts for this. Through nearly seven years in top-class senior hurling they have consolidated their splendid teamwork until now they move with a rhythm that is almost instinctive. They deploy the ball bewilderingly at times and they use the open spaces and create the extra man with telling effect." Seconding Dunne's prediction of a Waterford victory, John D Hickey declared in the *Irish Independent* that "All Ireland-winning sides do not grow up overnight, as it were, and I feel that Kilkenny are still in the process of development."

The latter point was undeniable. Who was the Leinster champions' centre-forward, after all? Johnny McGovern. Yes, Johnny McGovern. Yes, *that* Johnny McGovern. Bennettsbridge, liberally endowed with competent backs, had been trying him up front, as club teams are wont to do with defenders. Kilkenny didn't have a career centre-forward and would not have one for some time yet, so McGovern was burdened with reprising his club role. He wasn't thrilled about it, but he did have one man in his corner.

In training for the All Ireland final Fr Maher coached him in the specifics. As he wasn't built to go through or around Martin Óg Morrissey, McGovern was to break the ball down in front of himself and spread it out to the wings. That was all. Nothing more, nothing individual, nothing flashy. Keep it moving. A flick towards Denis Heaslip on his right, to Eddie Keher on his left or to Tom Walsh and Tom Murphy in the corners. They'd be floating into position to receive possession and from there on it was their problem. For the first half McGovern did his job well, getting out in front of his marker and moving the sliotar on, but on the restart Morrissey played him from the front, caught three or four balls in succession and the Bennettsbridge bulldog was called ashore, to be replaced by Oliver Gough.

If Kilkenny had learned a lesson from 1959 it was that points were the staff of life and goals an optional extra. Four years on they aimed to keep the scoreboard ticking over, a task rendered easier by the presence of the greatest individual points factory in the history of the sport. This would be the day Eddie Keher made his bones.

They also had Tom Murphy and Tom Walsh – almost absurdly callow, both of them, compared to Waterford's Napoleonic veterans, but every so often there comes an afternoon when experience curdles into age and youth translates as freshness rather than immaturity. Above all they had Ollie Walsh. As if to underline Sherlock Holmes's maxim about the imprecise nature of genius, Ollie would have his bad days on the big stage, notably the 1964 and '71 All Ireland finals. But 1963, despite the six goals conceded, was not one of them.

To Seán Clohosey he was more than a goalkeeper; he was a demi-god blessed with a combination of gifts from the gods. "A superb confidence in himself, a high degree of skill and a puckout that would invariably boom the ball down on top of the half-forward line. You knew you'd get that long puckout, which was fantastic. And when he was facing the other team's forwards, well... The other guy would swing. And swing with a bullet. Oh God! What happens next?! And then Ollie had the ball in his hand and was dancing out with it and hitting it a flake down the field. You'd be so delighted to see it. And you felt you couldn't let him down after what he had done for us." In the drawn game four years earlier, Ollie had been supernal. In 1963 he would merely be excellent.

Watched from the VIP seats by an Oscar-winning former Hollywood actress and her husband, Prince Rainier of Monaco, the 1963 All Ireland showdown produced 35 scores, a new record for a 60-minute final. In the process it demonstrated that, *pace* the cliché, goals, while helpful, do not always win games. If it had been exceedingly strange for Kilkenny to score five goals in 1959 and not win, how many kinds of extraordinary was it for Waterford to score six goals now and lose? Almost as oddly, Kilkenny hit 21 scores but had only four scorers: Eddie Keher (0-14), Tom Murphy (2-1), Tom Walsh (2-0) and Seamus Cleere (0-2).

It was not lack of grit that undid the Munster champions. After trailing by 11 points two minutes into the second half they had the gap down to two points with 90 seconds remaining. With glorious piquancy the closing point was scored by Keher with the second-last puck of the afternoon, his tenth free. Kilkenny 4-17 Waterford 6-8. A passing coroner might have attributed the losers' demise to being pinpricked to death by the 21-year-old from Inistioge.

To Seamus Cleere, the victorious captain, it was the balance and consistency of Kilkenny's display that won the day. "The points kept us on an even keel. At no stage did I feel we were going to lose." To Denis Heaslip the key was the simplicity of the gameplan. "Fr Maher told us to give the ball to Eddie Keher and he would do the rest. How right he was."

The two Toms had been dismissed beforehand as a pair of young and unknown corner-forwards. Tom Murphy wasn't fazed. Youth never is.

"Waterford's big names didn't know about us or care about us. So what? I hadn't any fears. I'd have had a lot more of them years later when I knew the consequences of All Ireland finals. But I thought, sure if I'm first to the ball, however good yer man is, I must have a chance..."

For the first of his brace Murphy got a flick on a dropping ball outside the square ("I don't know where the corner-back disappeared to"). For the second he pulled on a ground ball that lost momentum after one of the Waterford defenders got a half-block on it. It trickled in at the butt of the upright anyway. "I had gone up with Ned Power for a ball earlier and he'd landed on his shoulder and broken a rib. That's why he wasn't able to get down to it for my second goal." Power was replaced by Percy Flynn at half-time.

Interviewed in the dressing room afterwards, Fr Maher lauded his team's great spirit. "Whenever Waterford scored and seemed dangerous our forwards always replied, often with two scores for every Waterford score. It was indeed a great feat for Waterford to score six goals against Ollie Walsh, but our forwards were undaunted. They showed we were not a one-man team. It was a terrifically fast game, with very few stoppages. To me it seemed we got nearly 55 minutes of hurling out of the 60, which was a credit to both teams." That mathematical mind again.

The players were united in their praise for the trainer's decision to send them out early to puck around, a move deemed to have helped banish the nerves; Paddy Grace went as far as to declare that Kilkenny had never started an All Ireland final as well and that this was the reason why. Tom Walsh attributed much of the credit to Ted Carroll for holding the formidable Tom Cheasty. Ted in turn praised Ollie Walsh for his early saves. Tom Murphy declared he was very proud of his clubmate Eddie Keher. Fan Larkin agreed that he was the smallest player on the field but it hadn't worried him.

The indestructible John Grogan of Ballyhendricken, Ballycallan, now 87 and fresh from witnessing his 15th Kilkenny All Ireland triumph, popped up to proclaim his delight and hail a "great young team". And Princess Grace's thoughts on the game? "Fast, almost too exciting. It's marvellous," she told the *Irish Independent,* or at any rate was quoted as telling them. Yes, darling, absolutely fabulous.

Among the Waterford substitutes was Mickey Walsh, a National League winner with Kilkenny the previous year. He'd thrown in his lot with Mount Sion in the meantime, a move that meant he couldn't hurl with his native county. "Waterford asked me if I wanted to join the panel. I wanted to play hurling so I said yes." Walsh was to finish his career as a county medallist in three counties:

with his native Slieverue, with Moindearg in Dublin when he was working for Urney Chocolates in Tallaght and with Mount Sion.

Were Waterford overconfident? Frankie Walsh accepts they may have been. They were the worldlier team; they'd won the National League; they'd beaten Tipperary – the All Ireland champions of the previous two years – in Munster; and Kilkenny were crewed by a bunch of youngsters. This was surely Waterford's chance to win the second All Ireland to which the wealth of hurling they'd done over the past few seasons entitled them. Problem is, no team is 'entitled' to an All Ireland title.

Many of their supporters believed otherwise. One Jack Power, writing in *Gaelic Weekly* the following weekend, revealed that the Déise folk he'd encountered in Dublin on the eve of the final were concerned not with the result but with their margin of victory. "When I mentioned to some of them that pride comes before a fall they laughed at me and even went so far as to ask: 'What have Kilkenny apart from Ollie Walsh?' Well, I am sure my friends are now sadder and wiser men."

In the same edition of *Gaelic Weekly*, Tony Wall brought his powers of cold, reasoned analysis to bear on the game. He had, he revealed, paid particular attention to Keher on the frees and had spotted one where the sliotar did not come up properly (Fr Maher presumably empanelled a tribunal of enquiry in the Hollybrook the following morning) – "but still he shot it straight between the posts." Wall praised Seán Clohosey, who he said he had always found a hard man to mark, and pointed to the gaiscí of the two corner-forwards, about whose worth he had been dubious beforehand. "Tom Walsh likes to roam and Tom Murphy likes to be in around the square and a more effective pair would be hard to find."

The key line on the field, he maintained, was the winners' half-back line. Had Seamus Power and Phil Grimes, who between them scored 4-4 from the scraps that came their way in the full-forward line, been given a better supply they might well have won the match for Waterford, who Wall nevertheless reckoned lucky to have been within three points of their opponents at the final whistle. "When Kilkenny failed to Tipperary in the League earlier this year I rated their team as strong in defence and attack but poor at centrefield. Since then they have improved their centrefield 100%, improved their forward line considerably and just about retained the effectiveness of their defence."

Thus, after four championship collisions in the space of seven years, the Kilkenny/Waterford saga, at once a local rivalry and a Broadway extravaganza, ended. That Waterford should, in light of the consistent quality of their hurling, have won more than the one match they did is indisputable.

To Frankie Walsh, the 1957 defeat was the one that stung. "If we'd won that we might have gone on and won three in a row." Ever afterwards he did at least derive some warmth from the fact that all four encounters were proper games of hurling. "I never got a scratch playing against Kilkenny. I can't say the same about playing against Cork and Tipp." It would be 39 years before Waterford won another Munster championship, 44 years before they won another national title and 45 years before they contested another All Ireland final. Hurling was to be an infinitely drabber canvas without them.

The 1963 final marked the end of the line for Seán Clohosey also. By that stage he'd been playing intercounty hurling for ten years. He'd recently had colon trouble, he was married and all told he was getting too old and care-burdened for Sundays that began with a league match somewhere down the country and finished with him being press-ganged into going on the beer with Billy Dwyer till all hours and having to get up for work next morning. Early in 1963 he promised his wife that if Kilkenny won the All Ireland he'd retire. He was true to his word, albeit with one regret. One immense regret.

"I'd have liked a few more years with Eddie Keher. I think we could have built up quite a relationship." Against Waterford they'd combined splendidly together on the left-hand side of the field, Clohosey at nine and Keher at 12. "I wasn't great at sideline cuts. I mustn't have worked hard enough at them. But with Eddie in front of me it didn't matter. I'd look over at him, trotting along ten yards ahead of me. Flick the lineball to him. He'd turn. Whoosh, over the bar. I was as sure he'd score as I could be of anything."

The Tullaroan man's regret was shared by his Inistioge colleague. If Clohosey had never quite lived up to his "new Meagher" tag, ultimately proving to be the stylist whose career linked those of Langton and Keher, no matter. "Seán Clohosey's beautifully fluent style epitomised all the traditional grace of Kilkenny hurling," one scribe wrote. "One cannot think of a higher compliment to pay him as he now leaves the game to which he gave so much."

And so one of the great Noreside classicists departed the stage with two All Ireland medals to his name. Had it not been for the arrival of Tommy Maher, he might have departed without any.

CHAPTER 10

Pills

Bill approached football as an intellectual game, a game of strategy and execution. He saw it as an art form, a thing of beauty, something to be choreographed with everything working in harmony. He thought many other coaches were narrow-minded in their views. The prevailing philosophy when he started was how to make your team 'tougher' – being able to pound your opponent into the ground. Walsh believed that everyone who made it to the NFL level was already tough. He wanted to magnify the mental aspects of football

Al Saunders on Bill "the Genius" Walsh, mould-breaking coach of the San Francisco 49ers

A Nowlan Park evening from the mid-1960s. A Kilkenny training session with Tommy Maher supervising. And because it is a Kilkenny training session with Tommy Maher supervising, it is a training session that contains a couple of little lessons. Like every Kilkenny training session with Tommy Maher supervising.

This evening the object of the proceedings is to streamline the quality of ball into the forward line. Fr Maher points to Paddy Moran. "Now there's a man who can hit the perfect ball to the forwards."

A stopwatch is produced and the length of time taken between Moran's bas making contact with the sliotar and his delivery reaching its destination recorded. It is a signature Moran ball, crisply struck, skeeting (Pat Henderson's word, which translates from Johnstownese as 'skimming') above the heads of the half-backs, manicured perfectly for receipt by a member of the full-forward line.

For the second part of the lesson one of the lesser mortals is prevailed upon to hit a ball into the full-forward line. It goes high and, several hours later, comes steepling down coated in snow, an ideal defender's ball. This process is also timed. The moral of the story does not have to be rammed home to the players. The punchline has already been supplied.

"And this was back in the 1960s," Henderson reflects. "It never occurred to me at the time that Fr Maher was a teacher and was instructing people in the right way to do things. He'd studied the game and the conclusion he'd come to was that it was a simple game. Any aspect of it he saw as complicated he broke down into small, simple parts. Like taking a free.

"'What are the constants?' he'd say. The constants were the ball, the hurl and the posts. 'What will not change? The posts won't move.' So don't look too much at the posts. Worry instead about lifting the ball correctly. He had a teacher's ability to communicate and to get you to listen. If you were prepared to listen. And all the time he was developing your game further."

The 1964 All Ireland final and its lessons for Kilkenny, among them the inadvisability of trying to make a forward out of Seamus Cleere, will be touched upon in the next chapter. The 1965 provincial decider ended in a one-point defeat to Wexford, a result ascribable in part to the absence from the half-back line of the injured Cleere and Ted Carroll. Such reverses underscore the reality that the county's success under Fr Maher and afterwards was not an unbroken straight line.

He did not usher in some eternal sunshine of the Noreside mind. There were bad days and good days. There were days of rain as well as days of heaven. There were dead ends and cul de sacs and blind alleys. For all that Tommy Maher was a visionary, he was still only as effective as the competence of the selectors and the talent of the players allowed him to be. Bringing a county with him to a better place, and – crucially – bringing them there the right way, would take time. Every new season was a blank page, a great unwritten script. Many of them would not have a happy ending.

Yet there were evenings in Nowlan Park where none of that mattered. Tom Walsh puts it as succinctly as he can. Tommy Maher, he says, "never lost the thrill of hurling.

"Tommy on the training field – that was where his magic flowed. You had someone to inspire you, inspire you to play hurling with speed and accuracy. He saw the game as a team effort on every line, even down to the weakest link. And everything had to be done accurately. You didn't just handpass the ball, you handpassed it with accuracy." Make it short, make it simple, make it quick.

Walsh had encountered someone like Tommy Maher before, growing up at home in Thomastown: Peadar Laffan, the principal of the local boys' school and the uncaused cause behind the serial championship-winning Thomastown under-age teams. Any rare day that Laffan happened to be missing from the centre of the field was a day the world no longer spun. It was the same any evening in Nowlan Park that Fr Maher was absent.

If Kilkenny had been stuck for a centre-forward in 1963, they were stuck for a full-forward for years after it. Billy Dwyer's retirement left a void that would not adequately be filled until the advent of Pat Delaney and Kieran Purcell. In the meantime they would make do by attempting to convert defenders – Pa Dillon, Jim Lynch – into full-forwards, with a predictable lack of sustained success. Delaney and Purcell would change everything. But that was years away.

So they rubbed along as best they could. For 1966 the square peg they settled on was Pa Dillon. At full-forward his only job was to hold the ball up and create scoring chances for his corner-forwards. When the occasion arose he might try for a score himself, but Pa would never have won awards for his sleight of wrist and blue moons didn't come around too often. At full-back he'd at least been coached in what to do and how to do it. "That's how Fr Maher improved me as a hurler. Play the ball. Out first to the ball. Get it away. Get it out to the half-back line. Do that and your job is done. Up to then being a full-back was totally a man-marking job." At full-forward he was making it up as he went along.

Not that Pa was to blame for the 1966 All Ireland final. Kilkenny, fresh from their league triumph over Tipperary, were roaring favourites. Cork, who'd surprised everyone by coming out of Munster for the first time in ten years, were young and unconsidered. And none of them had ever played in an All Ireland final. And Kilkenny had beaten them comfortably in the league semi-final, although Jim 'Tough' Barry had taken heart from how well his youngsters had hurled in the first half, a moiety in which they'd driven no fewer than 16 wides. Next time the sides met, he promised, it would be different. And it was.

What happened when they did meet next time would give rise to one of hurling's more enduring clichés. You know, the one about Cork's ability to come like mushrooms. On Leeside it was the year of liberation. In Kilkenny it was the Year of the Pill.

Cork got the breaks, no arguments there. Seánie Barry's mishit free that came back off the Kilkenny defenders on the goalline and was finished off by Colm Sheehan. Tom Walsh having the ball in the net in the first half but being called back because Jimmy Hatton had already blown for a free. John O'Halloran's freakish goal 11 minutes from time when his attempt for a point from the right wing came down off the upright, flatfooted Ollie Walsh and bounced over the line.

But Cork, bubbling with the fearlessness and enthusiasm of youth, got the breaks because they were hungry enough to force them and sharp enough to avail of them. The final score read 3-9 to 1-10. Tough Barry was carried shoulder-high across the field in tears and the winners arrived home to a rapturous welcome from an estimated 60,000 supporters, many of them singing "We all live in a red submarine". The Beatles were long past their first LP by then.

The losers scrabbled around for excuses, or at least for explanations, and they found plenty. To Fr Maher, who began to worry when the team went for a few pucks on the beach in Clontarf on the morning of the game and a number of the players missed their ground strokes, they were overtrained physically. To John Teehan, Paddy Moran's midfield partner, they were overconfident. To Tom Walsh it was one of those days when nothing went right. "We played badly and Cork got the hop of the ball. These things happen."

That might have been that but for John D Hickey and his nose for a story. On the Tuesday, word emerged of strange goings-on in the Hollybrook Hotel on the Saturday night. No, not the player who'd had a couple of pints in the hotel bar; that had made no difference to either his performance or the outcome of the match, although had Kilkenny's collective eye been on the ball he wouldn't have been allowed near the counter in the first place. The story Hickey broke in the *Irish Independent* was altogether more colourful. Kilkenny, it transpired, had played badly because a number of the players had been given sleeping tablets the night before.

"Ah yes, the Year of the Pill," sighs Tom Walsh. "An absolute myth. Nothing came through my door on the Saturday night. At worst it was a couple of Aspros."

Hickey's story, which he'd got from one of the Kilkenny players at the post-All Ireland lunch on the Monday, was correct up to a point. One or two members of the panel had requested sleeping tablets in the Hollybrook the night before the game alright. But it was only one or two. Fr Maher was annoyed, Paddy Grace was furious and Dr Kieran Cuddihy, who felt his professional competence had been impugned, was incandescent. They called to Independent House late on the Tuesday, took Hickey to task and managed to force a half-hearted apology out of the paper. The story died a natural death, even if the phrase "the Year of the Pill" soon found its way into the Noreside hurling vernacular and was employed to frighten the children for years afterwards.

The 1966 All Ireland final was as chastening a defeat as any that Kilkenny ever suffered. Twelve months later, nobody was worrying about it any more.

CHAPTER 11

Tipp

Kilkenny for the hurlers, Tipp for the men
Traditional hurling saying

The rivalry dates back to the 1895 All Ireland final (Tipperary won it, of course), the parameters of the relationship to the 1916 renewal played in January 1917 (Tipperary won that too). After the final whistle the respective captains, Johnny Leahy of Boherlahan and Sim Walton of Tullaroan, shook hands. "We were better hurlers, Leahy," said Walton. "But we were better men, Sim," came the reply.

There and then the steps of the dance were formulated and codified. Kilkenny for the hurlers, Tipp for the men. It became one of the stone tablets of received hurling wisdom and it endured for nearly a century.

The longer it endured the more it calcified, received wisdom hardening into a self-fulfilling prophecy. Consider Babs Keating in his autobiography. "When I was growing up there was a feeling in Tipperary that you only had to show a Kilkenny man the blue and gold jersey and he would tremble. Very often that proved to be the case. The time was bound to come when a Kilkenny team would want to prove that they were different. It happened during the '60s."

Consider Michael Cleary, as stylish a wing-forward as ever came out of Tipperary and a keen student of the game, on his state of mind ahead of the 1991 All Ireland final. "Whether it was tradition or whatever name you want to put on it, I remember being very conscious that Tipp had this great record against Kilkenny in finals and being very confident – not in the sense that this was going to be handy or anything, but just that we would normally beat them in finals."

Consider Nicky English's autobiographical reflections on the same game. "It was as if the team *knew* that they had the measure of Kilkenny. As if the tradition of past meetings between the counties just gave Tipp an edge in confidence. When I was younger, I was totally dismissive when people talked of how 'tradition' could influence games. But the older I got, the more substance I could see in the argument."

Kilkenny's Via Dolorosa would have its full complement of stations of the cross. There was 1937 in Killarney where an ageing team, with Lory Meagher making his final appearance in the black and amber, were routed by 3-11 to 0-3 and the *Sunday Express*'s Londoner's Log columnist, on holidays by the lakes and fells, was moved to opine: "Tipperary were too strong and swamped Kilkenny, and the reason was obvious – they were faster, and this is an age of speed."

There was 1945 back in Croke Park and the disastrous first half in which Kilkenny leaked four goals, while at the other end what the *Irish Independent* described as "the robust, bustling, hard-hitting methods" of the Tipperary defence – Tipp readers would have parsed that quotation in a certain way, Kilkenny readers in quite a different way – were too much for the opposition forwards.

Above all there was the 1950 All Ireland final, a game in which the Leinster champions committed hara-kiri. "Kilkenny beat themselves," the *Indo* reported. There was no other way of putting it.

At half-time they led by 0-7 to 0-5 after playing against glaring sunshine and a near-gale. Dick Rockett, who was 19 and had driven from Slieverue in the boneshaker of a black ("there was no such thing as any other colour") 1939 Ford Prefect he'd bought from the Kilkenny Motor Company in John Street, hitting speeds of up to 30 miles an hour en route to Dublin, sat down on the Canal End with his friends and discussed how much the Leinster champions would win by. But it took Kilkenny 22 minutes to register a score in the second half. Jim Langton, who'd had a sparkling first half on a teenage Jimmy Finn, three times went for goal from 21-yard frees and failed on each occasion. Tom Walton missed another close-range free. Billy Costigan missed yet another. It was no day to be squandering such gimmes. A Tipperary team regarded as one of the most limited to ever leave the county won by 1-9 to 1-8. Via Dolorosa? This was Calvary.

If ever there was an All Ireland defeat that had lasting negative implications for Kilkenny, this was the one. The defeats of 1966 and '99, both when roaring hot favourites against young Cork teams, hurt in and of themselves, but outside the transient pain they left no legacy and in any case each was atoned for 12 months later. The 1950 defeat, however, crept into the bone and remained there, festering all the more painfully because it was a game that Kilkenny should have won with something to spare.

As if Jim Langton's agony was not enough after the three wasted frees, some truly malicious individuals put around the outlandish rumour that both his new green Anglia, registration number IP 7340, and Paddy Grace's new car, IP 7236, were the proceeds of the pair conspiring to throw the All Ireland final. Nonsense, of course, and all the more so in an age when people barely had two pennies to rub together. Langton had looked like winning the match on his own in the first half and a few days later, still distraught, was seen in tears on the Hebron Road near Nowlan Park. But gossip rarely contents itself with the facts.

"Any match you should have won but lose is a setback," Paddy Buggy muses. "That was the way with Tipp. They seemed to get the breaks. They were the better team most of the time. But there were days when they were lucky. The 1950 final was one of them."

The road continued on and continued ever upwards. Kilkenny tried again and they failed again and sometimes they failed better and sometimes they failed worse. The National League finals of 1950, '54 and '57: the usual story. The 1958 All Ireland semi-final; a good performance but not good enough. The Oireachtas finals of 1964 and '65: more of the same.

Peter Holohan was moved to pen a jeremiad in the *Kilkenny People* in March 1962. "Every time the counties meet the 'Tipperary hoodoo' raises its ugly head and while we have been able to lower the colours of the Premier County in challenge contests we have not succeeded in beating them in a league or championship match for more years than any Kilkenny supporter will want to remember... It is forty years ago this year since we last beat Tipperary in an All Ireland final. While we have been able to overcome great Cork teams we seem to find the Tipperary hurdle insurmountable. There is no good reason why we should not be able to hold our own against Tipp when we can do it against Cork. If we could match Tipperary in determination, perhaps, we could go a long way of the road towards breaking the 'hoodoo'. We can match any county in hurling skill but while Tipperary never lack for earnestness Kilkenny on the other hand occasionally show a tendency to lack that grim determination that is so characteristic of the Premier County and which has so often helped them to victory in face of the odds."

Holohan had more ochóning to do two years later following the 1964 All Ireland final. Here there was no question of the robust, bustling, hard-hitting methods of the Tipperary backs being the decisive factor. Instead Kilkenny were mown down by a blue and gold machine that in the words of John O'Grady – Cúlbaire of the *Tipperary Star* – possessed "a balance of talents, with more science than we'd ever shown".

As the years went by it would become an article of faith that Kilkenny, the reigning champions, had entered the game as strong favourites. The formbook suggested nothing of the sort; Tipp, their predecessors of 1961 and '62, had won the 1964 league Home final by 20 points against Wexford and the Munster final by 14 points against Waterford. Five down at half-time, the holders had cut the gap to two points a couple of minutes into the second half when the roof fell in on them. Tipperary, with a young Babs Keating resembling a reincarnated Mick Mackey on the 40, hit an unanswered 2-3 in the next eight minutes and there was no way back from that. Fourteen points was the difference between the sides at the end. Donie Nealon scored three goals.

Raymond Smith, as keen on racing as he was on hurling, came up with a neat equine parallel in one of his books. Kilkenny, he contended, could have been a two in a row team, possibly even a three in a row team – but, like Mill House, they had their hearts broken by Tipperary's Arkle of 1964-65. And yes, Nealon agrees, Tipp in 1964 *did* bear comparison with Arkle.

"We reached our pinnacle that year. A better team than in 1961-62. Mick Roche, Larry Kiely and Babs had come in since '62. We got lucky with the replacements." No less significantly, they also had Paddy Leahy in charge. "Paddy never took a coaching session but he was a great judge of a hurler. He'd seen a lot of hurlers over the years and Boherlahan, where he came from, was at the heart of it at the time. He had a lovely grandfatherly way about him, a lovely way of getting the best out of you. I don't think I ever heard him admonishing anyone. It was always a quiet word in your ear. And when we lost, he never ranted or raved."

Did Tipp bully Kilkenny out of it the same day? Certainly, according to Babs Keating in his autobiography, the defending champions' Thomasene full-forward line – Walsh, Forristal and Murphy – "had not had a pleasant time" against Doyle, Maher and Carey. But Tom Murphy disagrees. Tipperary "were much better" than Kilkenny in 1964 and that was that. Nothing more complicated. Nothing more sinister.

"Jimmy Doyle, Donie Nealon, Liam Devaney – real class hurlers. The other forwards were the playmakers. Nealon was the architect." As for the Kilkenny forwards being intimidated, not so. "We were youngsters. We had no fear of any of those lads. I'd have been more afraid playing Freshford when Pa was there."

Times had changed since Fr Maher's playing days. The winds of Vatican II were blowing through the seminaries of Ireland and nobody had to try and pretend that Tom Murphy was anything other than a clerical student in St Kieran's. Discretion was occasionally still the better part of valour, mind. Whereas the 1963 All Ireland final took place on September 1st, with the new seminary year starting the following day, the 1964 showpiece took place on September 6th, meaning the new seminary year had started the previous week – and once back, students were there until Christmas. Should he tell the college authorities he was playing in the All Ireland final and ask for permission to go to Dublin, a worried Murphy enquired of Fr Maher?

"Don't ask anyone," was the pragmatic reply. "That way no one will have to say no." To this day, Tom Murphy adds drily, nobody has ever questioned him over being awol from St Kieran's the weekend of the 1964 Al Ireland final.

The ill judged decision to move Seamus Cleere to wing-forward apart, maybe Kilkenny's only real fault in 1964 was to get in Tipperary's way. Cleere, the Hurler of the Year at wing-back the previous season, had impressed the selectors with his ability to storm up the field for Bennettsbridge and pick off points from long range. He was to regret being switched for more than one reason. Having scored the opening point against Tipp and feeling he had the measure of Mick Murphy, he set off on a solo run which was terminated with extreme prejudice by Michael Maher. "I soloed in and the next thing I was seeing stars. Maher wasn't a dirty player, but it was like running into a fireplace."

Shortly afterwards came the Oireachtas showdown where Tipp, back from New York and slow to settle, trailed by nine points in the second quarter before recovering to win by two. "Jaysus, Walsh," said John Doyle to Tom Walsh, baffled rather than sneering, "ye'll never bate us." It was a perfectly legitimate observation. Would the line of defeats stretch out to the crack of doom? In late 1964 it appeared that way.

Nor is there any gainsaying Babs Keating's assertion that at times the rivalry went beyond the boundaries of acceptability. Witness the incident in a Manhattan hotel in 1964 when a group of players from each county went down in the elevator in such tense, glowering silence that the American couple present couldn't wait for the doors to open and let them out.

All very childish, Eddie Keher agrees, but life was different then. "Nowadays players know players from other counties. They go to college together. Back then we didn't know these guys except as the enemy. They'd hit you a belt, you'd hit them back."

In time the jagged edges softened, then disappeared altogether. Martin Coogan and Jimmy Doyle grew close. Keher became friendly with John Doyle in later life and was one of the last visitors outside his family the man from Holycross had prior to his death in December 2010. Keher: "A terrific hurler. There was the whole Hell's Kitchen thing, but Doyle had skill and speed, which was often overlooked. He totally deserved all the accolades and the eight All Ireland medals."

Cards on the table please, gentlemen. Hell's Kitchen: reality or myth?

Tom Walsh: "Another myth. Totally. I don't know how it's reached the level of folklore it has. Every team had hard defenders. Dublin had Lar Foley. We had Pa Dillon, and none of them – not even Doyle, Maher or Carey – could touch Pa if you wanted real toughness."

Tom Murphy: "John Doyle had this animal magnetism about him. I wouldn't quite call it charisma, but he certainly had something. The other two, maybe not so..!"

Paddy Moran: "I was out at centrefield, so I didn't see that much of them. Doyle was more of a hurler. He used to run out the field. The other two never moved out. They were hard men. I couldn't say they were dirty. But they were tough. Fierce strong."

Birnam Wood came at last to high Dunsinane on May 22nd 1966 in the National League Home final at Croke Park. Tony Wall ("he wasn't huge for a centre-back, he wasn't a huge hitter, but he had a knowledge of the game and he always placed his clearances," says Eddie Keher) was flown back from UN peacekeeping duty in Cyprus to do his bit for Tipperary. In the dressing room beforehand, Paddy Moran and John Teehan decided between them that the latter would take Mick Roche and the former mark Theo English. The arrangement paid an instant dividend when Teehan hit the opening score from 40 yards inside the first minute.

Kilkenny needed that point. They needed every laboriously wrought point because this was an afternoon of apocalyptic weather conditions, they were playing with the aid of a tempest and their interval lead of 0-8 to 0-3 was not merely woefully tenuous, it was in the circumstances no lead at all.

So fierce was the gale that Pat Henderson, on winning possession in the corner at one stage in the second half, chose to solo up the field rather than hit it, on the basis that if he ran with the sliotar at least it couldn't be blown backwards. With the storm at its height Maurice Ryan from Clara, a brother of Fr Maher's old friend Tom Ryan, turned to the woman next to him and said, "You're good at praying. Say a prayer now!"

Somehow, in a second half that to their supporters lasted half an eternity, Kilkenny screwed their courage to the sticking place and gutted it out to win by 0-9 to 0-7. It was the county's first victory over their neighbours in a national final since 1922 and it was a milestone success.

Not that the banishing of the hoodoo led to sudden sunbursts and exchanges of hearts and flowers between the sides. This was Kilkenny and Tipperary, not San Francisco. March 1967 brought a rambunctious league fixture at Nowlan Park. A crowd of 20,000; 36 frees in the course of the hour (there would have been twice as many had Seamus Power, the former Waterford star, chosen to whistle for every infraction); the sliotar moving so quickly that the RTE cameraman couldn't keep up with the play; and Kilkenny winning by 5-7 to 2-7 after running up a 4-4 to 0-1 half-time lead. It was the day Mackey McKenna refused to go anywhere near the Kilkenny square on the grounds that Pa Dillon was "sharpening his hurley in there" and the day Babs Keating, as he told the world in his autobiography, flattened Dillon with a box near the end. That wasn't quite the whole story, according to the Freshford man.

"It was a great game, a huge crowd. The two of us were on the ground, getting up, and Babs hit me with a haymaker. What he didn't say in his book was that he'd broken my finger with a belt beforehand." The incident occurred four minutes from the end and Seamus Power, who by now had had quite enough, sent the pair of them off. "It would have been infinitely better for the image of the game of hurling if it had never been played," one newspaper sniffed afterwards. The next time Keating and Dillon, both Esso employees, met was by chance on the street in Callan. Babs later told a friend he "looked around for a manhole cover to dive into" before a hand was gingerly proffered and another extended to shake it.

Much more so than the other Kilkenny players of his generation or the previous one, Dillon possessed both the build and the bouldness to meet Tipperary on their terms. "Cork probably had more skilful players but with Tipp you knew what you were going to get. You were always going to be hit hard, you knew it and you had to be ready. I had the height of respect for John Doyle, for instance. Eighteen years there, eight All Ireland medals, 11 National League medals, never taken off. Played against the hardest of men. Played half-back, then came back and played corner-back. Gave everything he had for Tipp. An outstanding hurler."

As Dillon says, each county knew what to expect from the other. Johnny Leahy once ordered a Tipperary minor team facing Kilkenny to refrain from rising the ball on the basis that if they did so they'd "only be rising it for the Kilkenny boys to hit it". On the other side of the coin, Fr Maher told Martin Maher from Ballingarry, no relation but a student in St Kieran's in the mid-1960s, that he always liked to have a Tipp lad or two down the spine of a Kieran's team.

But Kilkenny were Kilkenny and Tipp were Tipp and scant was the meeting room for the twain, even if what the two counties had in common was far more important and substantial than what separated them. The Kilkenny view was stark. The rules were different, Tipperary were allowed to be physical and they were: end of. The Tipperary view was equally straightforward. The rules were different and Kilkenny weren't able for it: end of. One man's hatchetman is another man's teak-tough defender.

Raymond Smith tried his best to find a middle way when writing in the mid-1970s that Kilkenny "with better teams than Tipperary had continually failed to beat them in crucial tests. The reason for this had been the absence of a certain edge of steel in their play. The skill, polish and finesse were certainly there in abundance but championships are not won on pure skill alone. Thus Tipperary could often tie down better Kilkenny attacks."

An article in the programme for the 1972 All Ireland final contained an arresting extended metaphor to explain how the three leading counties went about their business. The chosen means of offence for Tipperary, the anonymous writer postulated, was artillery fire, that of Cork the machine gun, that of Kilkenny rifle shots. Even the respective jerseys, he (it couldn't have been a she) went on, were apposite, as Tipperary could only be blue with a gold band: solid, stolid, reliable. All very extravagant without being utterly absurd.

Yet by 1967 the first draft of a new screenplay had been written, quietly but in plain sight. From now on if Kilkenny were to lose to the old enemy it would be because they were hurled out of it, not because they were horsed out of it. For the Black and Amber had Eddie Keher, no longer a boy wonder and well able to mind himself. They had John Teehan, chosen for his size rather than his hurling – he hadn't been good enough to make the county minor team – but with his rough edges planed by years of Fr Maher's coaching. They had in the subs Frank Cummins, only young but a monster. They had Ted Carroll and, in the words of Liam Hinphey, his contemporary in St Kieran's, Fr Maher had "fierce faith" in Ted, both the boy and the man. Hinphey recalls playing football with Carroll on a St Kieran's team outclassed by St Peter's in Nowlan Park and the lad from Lisdowney soldiering on till the bitter end. He remembers him and his twin Mick playing for UCD in a Dublin championship match against a St Vincent's team intent on intimidating their younger opponents, Ted making a stand and a few of the chaps around him taking heart and picking it up from there. "Ted never said anything. He never had to. It was his performance on the field that mattered. That was all he needed to say and was why Tommy had him there as captain for Kieran's in 1957."

Above all they had Pat Henderson, and if Pat Henderson was from Johnstown and nowhere else he was partly of Tipperary – of Thurles CBS at any rate. Thurles CBS was a hurling hotbed when Henderson attended it, just after Jimmy Doyle and Ray Reidy, one of the greatest Tipperary minors ever but subsequently lost to the call of the cloth, had been through the school. There were concessions for hurlers and arrangements were made for Henderson, who travelled by bus from Johnstown, to train and play in the evenings. There he was raised on a diet of what the artist Tony O'Malley, who went to school in Callan CBS, termed "typical Christian Brothers hurling": hip to hip, man to man, honest to goodness fare. In a long-term context it helped him enormously.

Did it bring a facet to Henderson's game that would presently benefit Kilkenny? "I wouldn't have been conscious of this at the time, but yes. Going to Thurles CBS gave me an edge that stood to me in time. Putting a bit of physical stuff into it would be encouraged, let's put it that way."

Even if the county of Hell's Kitchen is also the county of Jimmy Doyle and Mick Roche and Nicky English and Eoin Kelly, it is scarcely overdoing it to suggest that most Tipperary fans of a certain vintage deep down prefer a doughty corner-back to a knacky corner-forward, a mindset the website Premierview encapsulated when branding John Doyle "the ultimate hurling icon in a county that likes its heroes uncomplicated, courageous and consistent... he probably best represents how Tipperary hurling sees itself." Whether the legacy of Hell's Kitchen served the county well or otherwise in the years following Doyle's retirement is a question that only Tipp folk can answer. The 1994 edition of the *Tipperary GAA Yearbook* contained an article entitled "Oh! For Men of Steel" in which the writer deplored "the stylish, faster players who are easily seen, scoring points and frees from all angles, lifting and soloing and playing 'namby-pamby', and fail, when called to the Bearna Baoil or when asked to 'take on a man' or fight for a fifty-fifty ball". Unrepresentative of forward-looking Tipperary hurling thinking as it undoubtedly was, it was still a screed that could never have appeared in the *Kilkenny GAA Yearbook*. A priest from Gowran was one of the reasons why.

Tony Wall – player, analyst, author and thinking man – confessed that he feared for the future of Tipperary hurling when he saw what Kilkenny were at under Fr Maher. If the first phase of the long war between the counties had belonged to Tipp, the next phase would be Kilkenny's. The same priest from Gowran was one of the reasons for that too.

And then 1971 came and went and for years stood as a landmark. In Cork they were distraught, or at any rate Christy Ring was; hurling was "only half dressed" without Tipp. In Kilkenny they were far from distraught, not so much overcome as overcome with schadenfreude. It was as if Little Nell had died all over again; they could scarcely read of the death of Tipperary hurling without laughing. Tipp "went out of hurling when class came in", as the gleeful explanation on Noreside had it? "Rubbish," replies Tommy O'Connell. "There's no way Tipperary could have won as much as they did in the 1960s if they were all hitmen." Quite.

If there was a criticism to be made of the county in the era of Tommy Dunne and Eoin Kelly, come to that, and it frequently was, it was that they were too classy, too nice, too neat, too stylish. Among the finger-pointers was John Doyle, who declared, almost plaintively, in 2005 that Tipperary had become like Kilkenny used to be and Kilkenny had become like Tipperary used to be, a role reversal that must have caused the old warrior no end of angst.

Some ancient prejudices died hard. Others never will. After complaining in the *Sunday Independent* about the size of Noel Skehan's bas following the 1983 All Ireland final, Raymond Smith – a native of Thurles, as Kilkenny people took good care never to forget – received a letter from an indignant reader that contained the unbeatable line, "May you and John D Hickey rot in hell and may the gods decree that Tipperary never win another All Ireland." The 1988 All Ireland junior final between the counties, with some highly predictable inherited spleen audible among the O'Moore Park attendance, moved the incisive and fairminded Westside of the *Clonmel Nationalist* to remark: "Kilkenny have among their supporters an element that would do better to cheer rather than sneer. Give me Cork any day, in victory or defeat!" Kilkenny's 2006-09 exploits so scalded the heart of one oldtimer in Ballingarry, meanwhile, that he told his nephew in Chicago that he'd "much prefer if the Black and Tans were around Ballingarry again".

Kilkenny, possibly without realising it, learned from Tipperary. Each one of the county's All Ireland-winning teams from 1967 onwards, the 1992-93 instalment excepted, was built on foundations of rock. The most perceptive observation made in the buildup to the 2011 All Ireland final came from Mick Roche: "We have wonderful ball players but Kilkenny have wonderful ball winners." When push came to shove on the afternoon of September 4th, Roche was proved correct. Tipp for the hurlers, Kilkenny for the men? So it seemed. Styles change. Wheels turn.

And some prejudices do wither. When the counties met in the 2002 All Ireland semi-final the world was a bigger place than it had been 35 years earlier and one with far more creatures in it. Henry Shefflin and Eamon Corcoran, the Kilkenny centre-forward and Tipperary centre-back, were friends and former Waterford IT housemates first, enemies a long way second. Nothing, not even the three goals he put past the Johnstown man 12 months later, became Lar Corbett like the pat on the back he gave PJ Ryan following one of the latter's improbable saves in the 2009 All Ireland final; goals are ephemeral, sportsmanship eternal. Few victorious captains have spoken as generously as Eoin Kelly, who'd won All Ireland colleges honours with Tommy Walsh, Jackie Tyrrell and Brian Hogan, did when lifting the MacCarthy Cup in 2010 and paying tribute to the fallen champions, "humble on the field and humble off it".

When Kevin Leahy from Clonmel, a grand-nephew of Paddy Leahy's, entered first year in St Kieran's in September 1978 the college president, one T Maher, was heard to announce in the staffroom: "Where hurling is concerned he's a thoroughbred." And Tipp's performance in the 2010 final, all imagination and verve and handpasses deployed at the optimum moment for maximum effect, was one the same reverend father would have been proud to have authored. How could it have been otherwise?

But on the first weekend of 1967 all of this was in the future, and the future would be a very different country to the present.

CHAPTER 12

Reckoning

SEPTEMBER 2ND 1967

Your name is Tommy Maher. You are 45 years old. You have lived half of your life.

In another 45 years' time, another lifetime away, someone will undertake your biography. (Call him Ishmael.) He will not hear a bad word about you from a single interviewee, most of whom will fall over themselves to hail you as "a man before his time". Granted, a friend of the biographer will speculate as to whether you, with your modest lifestyle and frugal tastes, may have secretly envied your old classmate Nicky Rackard, that buccaneer on the hurling field and roisterer off it. Guess that's one we'll never know. Pity.

On to more pressing matters. Tomorrow you face Them in the All Ireland final. Yes, Them. Again. Tomorrow and tomorrow and tomorrow.

You want to beat these fellas. You've always wanted to beat these fellas. You played against them 22 years ago, you've never quite got over that free Vin Baston gave against you and you still maintain it was a match Kilkenny could have won. You can't put that right now, you'll never be able to put it right, but you can help your county make up for it tomorrow.

You've been chasing the White Whale ever since. You've been planning for this day for weeks. You've been waiting for it since 1964, when Tipperary taught you the most painful lesson you've experienced in your time as trainer. In a sense you've been waiting for it since 1945. And in another sense you've been waiting for it all your life – literally all your life, because the year of your birth was the last time Kilkenny beat Tipp in the championship. True, you were 17 months old when the 1922 All Ireland final eventually went ahead, but let's not split hairs.

You've long been heard to fulminate about the selectors not picking the team early enough to allow you to do what a coach is supposed to do: to coach the players to play their various positions. Not this time around. You've had a good run at this one. You've had the players for weeks and they know exactly what you want them to do.

Don't use their bodies, as Tipperary do so well and have been doing since before John Doyle began eating babies for breakfast. Use their hurleys instead. Outrun Tipp. Outhurl Tipp.

You won't make the mistake of trying to fight fire with fire, as was the case that fractious Nowlan Park afternoon back in March. But your boys won't be standing back either.

You've long had your eye on John Teehan, a big lump of a lad you've worked on to do a job at midfield. It didn't happen for him at centre-forward in '64, but he did well against Tipp in the league final last year and you're optimistic he'll do so again today. Teehan won't hurl Mick Roche – who could? – but that's not what he's there to do. He's there to do to Roche what Tipperary have been doing to Kilkenny stylists all these years. And he won't win the physical battle by himself, but all going well he'll make damn sure Kilkenny don't lose it. Hopefully, anyway; you noticed in training a couple of weeks back that Teehan wasn't his usual self – all that work on the farm – so you've gone easy on him in the meantime to have him fresh for the big day.

Martin Coogan will be cherry-ripe too. You made him do a lap of Nowlan Park with Tom Walsh, the neighbourhood speed merchant, a few nights ago. There was only going to be one winner there. "Coogan," you told him when they were finished, "you won't be doing any more running. You've enough done. You can puck the ball around till the day of the All Ireland."

Apropos of Tom Walsh himself, you were listening to the wireless on Friday night and you heard Tom Ryall, one of the selectors, tell Radio Eireann's Liam Campbell that the decision to put Walsh at centre-forward could work out because Walsh's speed and ground hurling would trouble Tony Wall, great and all a man as Wall is, and help prise open the Tipperary defence. And you've noted that both Paddy Downey (aha!) and John D Hickey (hmm...) have gone for Kilkenny in their previews.

Logic says they should be proved correct. You don't have a single outfield player over 30; Tipperary have eight of them. And your forwards are aged 23, 23, 26, 24, 23 and 22. But three years ago Kilkenny also had a young forward line that was supposed to run the legs off an ageing Tipp defence. That wasn't how it turned out. This is Tipp, remember.

You've marked out the two teams in match-programme fashion on a lined A4 sheet, Kilkenny in blue ballpoint and Tipperary in red marker. S Cleere and Devaney, P Henderson and Flanagan, M Coogan and Nealon, and so on. Beside Paddy Moran's name you've written "quick delivery & low" and underlined it. You've drawn one arrow from Eddie Keher's name and another from Claus Dunne's name and angled them in behind Wall. "Get ball behind back," you've written and circled.

At the bottom of the page, in two columns, you've listed the subs and some final pointers. "Substitution. Broken hurley. Injuries. Frees. Cuts. Puck-out. Fear. Handpass from Tipp. Fouls."

You've underlined both 'fear' and 'fouls'. 'Fear' because while you don't want your team to be afraid of Tipp, at the same time you don't want them to be afraid of winning – and fear of winning could be an even greater danger than fear of Tipp. 'Fouls' because you don't want them giving away frees in front of goal and you don't want Mick Hayes *penalising them for hand on the back. And you'll say this to them in the Hollybrook beforehand.*

Will it be your finest moment if Kilkenny win? Well, winning in 1957 was a more important achievement in the scheme of things. And 1972 against Cork will never be matched for drama and dazzle. And 1974 against Limerick will be personal in a way unimaginable at this moment. And 1975 against Galway – yes, Galway – will see Kilkenny winning successive All Irelands for the first time since you were a boy. But all of that is ahead you. All that matters in the here and now is Tipperary.

What else? Oh yes, the walkie-talkies. You've long said that the dugout in Croke Park is no place to be analysing a match from and that the upper deck of the Cusack Stand is a much better vantage point. So that's where you'll be, with Tom Ryall beside you in the front row. You've been into Gray's in John Street and they've given you the loan of a couple of walkie-talkies. One for yourself, the other for Nicky Purcell in the dugout. Panasonic, 27 megahertz. Big but sleek looking. Fingers crossed nothing goes wrong with them.

After that unfortunate episode last year with the sleeping tablets – such a fuss about nothing and so unfair on poor Kieran Cuddihy! – you're heading up on the train in the morning. And Mick Lanigan, the new trainer, has the players as fit as they can be. But not too fit. This won't be like last year on that count either.

But when the train arrives in Dublin you'll head to that familiar old stomping ground, the Hollybrook Hotel. There you'll deliver your usual All Ireland speech to the team. A special word for every man. And an even more special word, for the day that's in it, for your full-back.

"Pa Dillon," you'll say. "You're regarded as being a kind of over-robust player. Well, today you won't be half robust enough."

That's about it. No more to be done.

Now as long as nothing daft happens that might ruin everything. Like your goalkeeper putting his hand through a window on the train on the way up, for instance... No, don't be silly.

The White Whale is in sight. The harpoon has been readied. Good luck, Ahab.

CHAPTER 13

Tom

You have a most wonderful career ahead of you
Tom Waldron, Kilkenny selector, to Tom Walsh on the train home after the 1963 All Ireland final

In the autumn of 1961, shortly after he won the first of his two All Ireland minor medals, Tom Walsh left home in Thomastown to work as a storeman for Dunnes Stores in their Georges Street outlet in Dublin. Among the floor managers there were the boss's daughter, the future Margaret Heffernan, and Arthur Ryan, later of Primark fame. To keep himself in shape Walsh trained with the capital-based Kilkenny senior players, including Seán Clohosey and Eddie Keher, in the grounds of Terenure College. Living in Walkinstown, his chauffeur to Terenure was Billy Dwyer. Stopping off in the Submarine bar for post-training refreshments with Dwyer was a regular if unofficial component of the proceedings. That was Dwyer, who was much the same man off the field as he was on it. Life was for living,

All went swimmingly for Walsh in his new job until the week after the 1962 All Ireland minor final. He didn't return for work till the Wednesday and was promptly lacerated by one of superiors for his presumption. Being by his own admission "an obstinate young man", he handed in his notice and finished up the following Saturday night. Before he left the building he went upstairs to say goodbye to Ben Dunne senior (always "Mr Dunne"), thanking him for the job and adding that he'd learned a lot there.

"I hear you're fairly handy with the hurley, Tom," Dunne responded. "Well, whatever you achieve on a Sunday, don't ever forget that Monday is the first working day of the week."

How handy with the hurley was Walsh? Plenty handy. Handy enough to win four successive county under-14 medals with Thomastown, to score 1-4 in the 1961 All Ireland minor final, to score 2-2 in the 1962 renewal and to hit two goals in the 1963 All Ireland senior decider at the age of 19.

To Micheál O'Hehir he was the "blond bombshell from Thomastown". To Fr Tommy Maher he was the prototype of a new breed of corner-forward, someone who rather than stand on the endline and play his position preferred to go roaming in pursuit of the sliotar instead. To the Kilkenny supporters he was a complement to Eddie Keher and in terms of raw electric excitement was arguably Keher's superior. "I was extremely fast, had good ball control and decent anticipation. I got into great positions principally by being able to read the game and getting into the right place at the right time."

Through it all Walsh remembered Mr Ben Dunne senior's words of wisdom about the necessity of maintaining a sense of proportion and the inexorability of Mondays and a new working week. Through the seemingly unending big-match disappointments against Tipperary until the road turned in the 1966 National League decider. Through the fortnight he spent in hospital following a wicked early pull by a Wexford defender in the Leinster final the same summer ("it was a dropping ball, he wasn't going for it, he pulled down on my face – I couldn't see for a week afterwards, the face was so swollen"). Through the shock defeat by Cork in the All Ireland final a few weeks later. Through his engagement to Angela Grace, daughter of the Kilkenny county GAA secretary.

Through it all he remembered old Mr Dunne and his words of wisdom. And then came a Sunday that had no Monday morning.

He doesn't find it difficult to talk about September 3rd 1967. He never has, he says.

The real oddity about the day was that if any Kilkenny player who just happened to hail from Thomastown and just happened to possess the surname Walsh were to be injured, it should have been Ollie Walsh. It *was* Ollie Walsh. The players and management attended nine o'clock Mass in St John's, opposite the railway station, before boarding the special to Dublin. Playing pitch and toss with Tom Walsh and a couple of the Bennettsbridge lads in the corridor, Ollie turned in his excitement at a prodigious pitch he'd made and put his arm through the glass of the compartment.

Tom Walsh can picture it still. "The blood flying out of Ollie's arm. Dr Cuddihy patched him up and they whisked him off to hospital when we got to Heuston and inserted stitches. I don't actually remember him arriving in the dressing room, but there was no question of him not playing."

Much to his surprise, Kilkenny played Walsh at centre-forward, on Tony Wall, rather than in the corner. In retrospect he can see the reasoning. In his fifth intercounty season he was "beginning to catch the game better, beginning to control the game, feeling more comfortable, starting to contemplate when to run and when to reserve my energy rather than running the whole time". He was stronger than he'd ever been. He was wiser than he'd ever been. He was as fast as he'd ever been. And against an ageing Tipperary defence that blustery autumn afternoon, speed killed.

It was no classic All Ireland. Kilkenny faced sun and wind in the first half but had money in the bank straight away. Keher went for broke from a close-range free at the Canal End in the fourth minute. The ball was blocked and cleared, but cleared only as far as Paddy Moran, whose bouncing centre deceived everyone and wound up in the net. From the puckout Kilkenny were awarded a free that Keher tapped over the bar. Four points up before the game had drawn its first breath. Sitting alongside Tom Ryall in the front row of the Cusack Stand's upper deck, walkie-talkie in his hand, Fr Maher allowed himself the ghost of a smile.

Tipperary gradually found their stride and Donie Nealon hit two rapidfire goals, bang bang, midway through the half. But Pat Henderson was a bulwark in defence and Ollie Walsh, none the worse for his mishap on the train, was supremely alert and light on his feet. To Fr Maher, the accident was a blessing in disguise. "Ollie was always a bag of nerves. The cut wrist was a help in that it gave him an excuse if he played badly."

The coach gave only one instruction via walkie-talkie during the hour. Early on he decided that Tom Walsh was being beaten by Tony Wall because he was dallying on the ball instead of moving it. Nicky Purcell, the county chairman, was in the dugout with Paddy Buggy, Johnny McGovern and Tom Nolan from Mooncoin, the other selectors. Fr Maher asked Purcell to go in and tell Walsh to pull on every ground ball.

So Kilkenny remained afloat. Even though Keher was unhappy with his freetaking and handed the responsibility over to Walsh, they trailed by only six points, 2-6 to 1-3, at the break. Manageable. More than manageable. The pattern for the second half was set when Ollie cut out Tipperary's first attack, cleared the ball 30 yards out and deposited it 35 yards from the enemy uprights.

It was now that Tom Walsh began to sense that Kilkenny had their opponents' measure and that the great day was finally at hand. Age had withered Tipp. The awesome power that had destroyed Kilkenny in 1964 had evaporated. "The beginning of the second half, these guys were dying on the ground in front of us. John Teehan was massive at centrefield. Ollie was outstandingly good in goal. Our backs were flailing into everything. The only regrettable thing was that we should have scored an awful lot more." It was Killarney 1937 in reverse. "Kilkenny proved beyond all doubt that hurling is a young man's game," Dermot Gilleece wrote in the *Daily Mail* next day.

They did score a goal almost immediately. Walsh made a mess of rising a 21-

yard free – how Fr Maher must have groaned – but pulled first time and sent it high towards the Tipperary net. The defenders on the line could only parry it skywards and Martin 'Goggy' Brennan from Castlecomer charged in to deflect the sliotar over the line.

Another five minutes and the sides were level following points by Walsh from a free, Keher with a classy effort from the left and Claus Dunne on the run, and Kilkenny hit the front in the 41st minute with a goal from Walsh, who teed up the ball on the ground for himself before directing a slashing left-handed stroke to the roof of the net. The buildup had involved another touch of class from Keher, this time with a flick of the sliotar backwards between his legs.

Shortly afterwards Walsh, who according to Tom Ryall in *Kilkenny: The GAA Story 1884-1984* "outpaced Tony Wall to a baffling degree", had a hurley broken off his knee by Len Gaynor. He could afford to laugh it off. "It didn't bother me, it didn't funk me. I was on fire with adrenalin."

From there Kilkenny ought to have won in a canter. To Pa Dillon it "should have been ten points" rather than the four it was (3-8 to 2-7). To Raymond Smith it might have been as much as 12. But Keher went off with a broken wrist, removing much of the team's firepower with him. Worse – far worse – followed six minutes from the end.

Paddy Moran was taking a lineball just inside the 50-yard line under the Cusack Stand when, in Walsh's phrase, "the hit came". He knew immediately he'd been hurt. "I put my hand up to my eye and saw blood and said, 'Jaysus, I'm in trouble.' Kieran Cuddihy came on to have a look. I asked him could he put a patch on it. He started waving his arms and I knew it was serious. The first-aid people came on. I walked off to the Cusack Stand side and into the dressing room."

There he was joined by his brother Martin. They knew Kilkenny had won before the ambulance arrived to take them to the Eye and Ear Hospital in Adelaide Road. The next 48 hours was a montage of fleeting, half-remembered sights and sounds.

A public ward with six or seven beds. Walsh slipping in and out of consciousness as the evening wore on. A couple of priests coming in to say hello. Prayers being recited. Fr Maher and Nicky Purcell telling Walsh that he'd had precisely the kind of match on Wall they'd known he would. A little boy from Sheriff Street who'd been hit in the eye with a bottle crying bitterly. Being wheeled to the theatre next day and seeing his mother Kathy, which disconcerted him: what was she doing there? Walking up after the operation in a private room. Francis McAuley, the surgeon, telling him gently that his left eye had been hurt very seriously, that eyes were peculiar items that worked in tandem and that, due to the danger of sympathetic opthalmia, the injured eye had had to be removed in order to protect the other eye.

More images, this time at greater length and better remembered. A further week in the Eye and Ear. His eldest brother Larry appearing home from the US: another shock. Being discharged. The taxi journey to Heuston Station, as Kingsbridge had been renamed the previous year, and the discovery that his depth perception was shot to pieces. "The buses seemed to be coming in on top of me. I felt very encroached on."

A disconcerting sort of homecoming followed with his father Patrick back in Thomastown. "Walking down the hall to meet him was tough for me. I felt his pain far more than he felt mine because he was surely thinking that my life was over. He wasn't a touchy-feely man – in fact, one night after I'd got a belt on the head in a club match in Knocktopher he gave out to me for getting cut – but he threw his arms around me, which he'd probably never done before." The next day Walsh went out in the car for a drive. "I had to test this thing." These days he wouldn't be allowed behind the wheel for six months.

Stoicism took over after a while. What was done could not be undone. His hurling career was over. Now he had to get on with life.

"These things happen. You play the game, you take the knocks. There was no malicious intent to knock my eye out – I'm fairly comfortable about that."

There were 64,241 paying spectators in Croke Park on the first Sunday of September 1967. Shades of Munster and the All Blacks at Thomond Park, Walsh reckons he's met every one of them in the meantime. The original eye implant he was given "wasn't great, but people were very kind". The current model gets weepy if he has a cold. Otherwise a stranger wouldn't be able to tell the difference.

Normality came dropping slower in some ways than in others. Attending matches was a trial for a few years afterwards, mainly because he felt that, when Kilkenny were beaten, other spectators were always about to say, "Ah, if only you'd been playing there today..." Fortunately he found by the end of the 1970s, to his considerable relief, that people had consigned him to the ranks of yesteryear.

Tony Wall gave his side of the story in John Harrington's rollicking 2011 biography of John Doyle. He and Walsh were trying to get ahead of one another as Paddy Moran shaped to take the lineball; Walsh turned back into him when he realised the sliotar was going to go beyond them; and as he did, Wall felt the handle of his hurley make contact with his opponent. He didn't realise Walsh had been hurt. He didn't even realise he'd had to leave the field until later.

Wall's account was corroborated by Fr Maher, who had seen what happened. "Tony Wall had no intention of knocking him out. The two of them were jostling as the sideline cut was being taken. As the ball was being struck, Tom went to go ahead of Wall, who put his hurl and arms out to stop him." Wall turned up next day at the post-match reception, which couldn't have been easy for him. Pa Dillon for one made a point of turning his back on him.

Fr Maher, who usually treated Kipling's two impostors just the same, was untypically animated in the dressing room after the game. Tipperary had been beaten at last, the hoodoo banished and his own ghosts from 1945 exorcised. His individual coaching had worked; his team had triumphed because they'd used their hurleys, and used them in the right way, instead of using their bodies. Then the news from the Eye and Ear began to filter through, getting worse with each update.

Given the venom with which the two counties had been going at one another for the past number of years, the rivalry degenerating in ever more unseemly declensions of pettiness, the differences between the pair magnified by their very insignificance, it was little surprise that someone would get seriously hurt. But what a rare and bitter irony it was, after all the belts dispensed early or late, brazenly or maliciously, that the blow that did such damage was an unintended one.

What should have been one of Kilkenny's greatest days was a day tarnished forever. The peach would always have a worm at its heart.

CHAPTER 14

Ollie

"No, no!" said the Queen. "Sentence first – verdict afterwards"
Lewis Carroll, *Alice's Adventures in Wonderland*, Chapter 12

The 1967 All Ireland final should have been the end of it between Kilkenny and Tipp. Old scores settled, the slate wiped clean, "the hurlers" finally and visibly "the men". As it happened, the rivalry had one more poisonous twist to it. When the counties met the following spring in the National League Home final, the settling of new scores from September was the first item on the agenda, the game a long way second.

The record shows that Tipperary won by 3-9 to 1-13 after leading by seven points at half-time. The record counted for little amid the fuss. One of the items that did matter was a photograph taken during the first half that captured Ollie Walsh slumped on one knee. It was the flashpoint moment of an eight-minute period during the second quarter that vibrated with nastiness. "Toxic," according to Pat Henderson. "Sickening," agrees Donie Nealon. "It was the only day in my career I felt a little bit afraid on the field."

Eddie Keher, playing at top of the right, was struck twice by his marker John Gleeson. Len Gaynor was struck by Keher. Ollie Walsh was struck by John Flanagan. Gleeson was struck by, of all people, Dr Kieran Cuddihy who, losing the rag after Keher had been felled the second time, ran in, hit Gleeson and was ordered out the gate by the referee, Gerry Fitzgerald of Limerick. To add a measure of farce to the episode, the man on the gate told Cuddihy to get a cap or hat, come back and he'd let him in. And he did.

The camera can lie, but in the case of Ollie Walsh and John Flanagan it didn't. On the extreme right of the shot was the Tipperary man, departing the scene of the crime. Jim Treacy and Pa Dillon were looking in Flanagan's direction, with Pa about to make a beeline for him. Seán McLoughlin was in the centre of the photo. Quoted in Dermot Kavanagh's biography of Ollie Walsh four decades later, McLoughlin said that he himself played the role of peacemaker on the day, "a role that I was not accustomed to". Jimmy Doyle, who was close by, declared that the incident was over and done with almost immediately.

Prior to the restart Gerry Fitzgerald – he may have been acting independently or he may have received orders from on high; a rumour to the latter effect subsequently did the rounds – lectured both teams in the centre of the field.

Whether it was that the players were listening or whether a sufficiency of boils had been lanced by then, the second half passed off peacefully.

That might have been that; it wasn't. The media might have been expected to be dutiful little boys and break out the whitewash for the sake of the good name of the Assoceeeashun; they weren't. John D Hickey didn't leave a tooth in it in the *Irish Independent* the next day.

"Hurling took a beating...eight scandalous minutes...acts of violence that must have sickened every spectator of the 27,892 attendance with a shred of respect for the precepts of law and order, never mind the canons of good sportsmanship...would be punished with a punitive sentence if perpetrated in civilian life instead of on a sportsfield...We have, I am convinced beyond all doubt, only Providence to thank that the frightening actions we saw did not have consequences that would startle us out of our complacency."

Hickey didn't let the affair lie, returning to it on the Tuesday under the headline "Juveniles did not deserve Croke Park 'scenes' – CENTRAL COUNCIL MUST ACT – Punitive measures now imperative". Think of the children, he implored – specifically the "hundreds of juvenile boy guests in the Nally Stand" who witnessed "Sunday's shameful affair", a match that "could do irreparable damage to the game if the Central Council does not take punitive measures to express its indignation about the whole sorry business".

He was sick and tired, he complained, of being told by certain authorities, "not without a distinct tone of chastisement in their voices, that it wasn't all that bad. Such misguided 'friends' of the game are its real enemies. In this enlightened age, a time when 'sacred cows' are being assailed on all fronts, it is time for those responsible to face up to the duties of their offices. If they again turn the blind eye to what happened on Sunday the Association could well find itself compelled to forfeit its hurling revival plan with a scheme to save the game from extinction."

Although Tommy Maher grumbled about Hickey's match report to his Inter Cert maths class on the Monday morning, the real umbrage was taken by the Tipperary county board, who launched a silly, unnecessary little war with the media that dragged on throughout the summer – silly because it was unwinnable, unnecessary because Hickey at any rate had not pointed the finger at Tipp any more accusingly than he had at Kilkenny. Banned from Semple Stadium, the *Irish Independent* retaliated by at one stage referring to Tipperary as "You Know Who". But that outbreak of bilateral childishness was only a sideshow. The mills of officialdom were beginning to grind in Croke Park. They did not cease grinding until a trophy head had rolled.

Among the witnesses called to the Central Council investigation was Ollie

Walsh, who it was assumed was there to give evidence against John Flanagan. Such assumptions were grievously misplaced. The bombshell detonated and both Walsh and Flanagan received a six-month suspension, with Eddie Keher and Len Gaynor cleared and John Gleeson warned about his future conduct. Where Walsh, who according to Seán McLoughlin shouldn't even have been summoned to the meeting, was concerned it was as patent a stitch-up as could have been imagined. One conspiracy theory had it that the GAA were out to get Walsh after he'd expressed his opposition to the Ban during the course of an appearance on *The Late Late Show*. "Apparently I was supposed to be next in line if Ollie wasn't suspended," Pa Dillon reports. "There might have been some cause with me. With Ollie, none."

Noreside was beyond convulsed. What especially outraged the inhabitants was not so much the blatancy of the miscarriage of justice, infuriating as that was, as its studied nature. This was not a case where someone was victimised due to honest incompetence on the part of the relevant authorities. It was a case where someone – a nationally famous sports figure to boot – was victimised with malice aforethought. Who breaks a butterfly on a wheel, as the London *Times* had mused in relation to a rather different public personality in rather different circumstances the previous summer? Walsh hadn't seen it coming and was as stunned as he was appalled. His son Michael was not old enough to take in the details but not too young to be unaware of how upset and shocked his daddy was. "Ollie was so clean and upright, a national hero," reflects Eddie Keher. "That was the part that really rankled."

The great man being in hospital with a stomach problem, Noel Skehan took over for the Leinster semi-final against Offaly in Portlaoise, a pedestrian affair that resulted in a 3-13 to 4-6 win for the All Ireland champions. What to do for the provincial final? An emotive special meeting of the county board heard Joe Walsh of Ollie's own Thomastown propose that Kilkenny not fulfil the fixture. Support came from Toby Kavanagh of the Rower-Inistioge and Bennettsbridge's Henry Drea. The atmosphere in Nowlan Park was so charged that Nicky Purcell adjourned the meeting for three days to allow tempers to cool. When it reconvened, a letter from Ollie was read out. In it he restated his innocence and requested that Kilkenny play the Leinster final. This they did, but their hearts weren't in it and Wexford saw them off by 3-13 to 4-9.

In the circumstances it was better for all concerned that it was Wexford rather than Kilkenny who fetched up against Tipperary on the first Sunday of September, where despite Mick Roche's blinding first-half performance the Slaneysiders won what was to be their last All Ireland for 28 years. Donie Nealon nursed his own what-if from the affair. "If only we'd had John Flanagan, who was young and strong and energetic, when Wexford came back at us in the second half..."

In a demonstration of solidarity with the victimised goalkeeper the 1968 Kilkenny championship was held up while he served his suspension. The final did not take place until April 27th 1969. It resulted in a 3-9 to 3-7 success for the Rower-Inistioge against Bennettsbridge. Eddie Keher would captain the county for the year.

Paddy Grace could not have failed to mention the league final and its aftermath in his report to county convention, which was held in the CYMS Hall in Kilkenny in January, and he didn't. "We find it difficult to know the reason for Ollie Walsh's suspension," he stated, adding that the episode had had "an overwhelming effect on the Kilkenny team generally, and the morale of the players was adversely affected." It was "through no fault of the county board", he protested, that the county final was not completed. The new season could not come quickly enough.

Offaly were a better team than they might have looked against Kilkenny in that 1968 provincial semi-final. What the four-point losing margin didn't show was that they'd played with 14 men for 50 minutes. They proved their worth for all to see at the same stage of the competition the following year when shocking Wexford, the MacCarthy Cup holders, by 5-10 to 3-11, all five of their goals coming in the first half.

It was no one-off. Offaly brought Kilkenny all the way to the wire on Leinster final day and could well have beaten them. They led early on, were level at half-time and were two points ahead seven minutes from the end when Pat Delaney struck for his second goal. The scoreboard showed the favourites 3-9 to 0-16 to the good at the finish. Unhappily for Offaly it was an ageing team, give or take Damien Martin, a young Johnny Flaherty and one or two others. The Faithful's breakthrough would have to wait 11 more years.

(In passing, modern researchers would do well to avoid taking old match reports as gospel. The papers the next day had Pat Delaney scoring three goals. In fact Joe Millea clearly scored Kilkenny's second goal shortly before half-time, doubling on a sideline cut from Mick Lawlor. *Caveat lector.*)

London, competing in the championship for the first time since 1903, provided the opposition in a novel All Ireland semi-final at Croke Park. Fr Tom Murphy, who as a newly ordained priest had been barred from hurling in 1967, marked his return to the fold for the first time since the 1966 All Ireland final by hitting three goals. Cork having easily disposed of Tipperary down south, the stage was set for a rematch of three years earlier. This time without the pills.

But not without some medical input all the same. The Bennettsbridge field day took place on the Sunday before the big game. As the afternoon wore on, Paddy Moran began to feel unwell and had to sit down. When he woke up next morning he had raging tonsillitis and couldn't get out of bed.

Kieran Cuddihy paid regular visits to Morans' as the week went by, on one occasion administering an injection at 4am. By Thursday afternoon Moran was able to rise and go for a walk. The selectors named him on the team for Sunday. His participation, though, was no fait accompli. On the train to Dublin on the morning of the match, Dr Cuddihy told Moran he'd be better saving his limited energy and going in as a sub if required as opposed to starting and inevitably having to be withdrawn. It was the 1967 final all over again. Crisis.

What happened next prompted one of Paddy Grace's finest hours. After the team arrived in Dublin the five selectors went into conclave in the Hollybrook Hotel. They'd decided after the final training session that Pat Kavanagh of the Rower-Inistioge would fill in should Moran be unable to start. Now, hypotheticals replaced by reality and a gun to their heads, they weren't so sure. Kavanagh or the less stylish, more robust Mick Lawlor from Coon?

They tossed the matter around for half an hour before voting three to two in Kavanagh's favour. Grace, taking some quality time out with his usual bottle of stout and half-one in a little alcove in the hotel, was so appalled when he heard of their decision that he called the selectors together and ordered them to try again. One of them was offended and told Grace that as county secretary his job was to write out the team, not pick it. Grace didn't bat an eyelid.

One selector who was far from offended was Tom Ryall, who had pressed Mick Lawlor's case during the initial debate but was outvoted. Not that Ryall was over the moon when, after a 20-minute discussion, the reconvened gathering settled on Lawlor over Kavanagh; the pressure of the situation was intolerable. Ryall was standing at the entrance to the Hollybrook as the Kilkenny minor team departed for Croke Park. "Are you sick?" Georgie Leahy, one of the minor selectors, asked him. "You look like a ghost."

Much to Ryall's relief, Lawlor proceeded to have a blinder. Had Kilkenny lost, he maintained later, he and the other selector who'd voted for Lawlor from the beginning "would have been run out of the county". For the record, the selector who had argued with Grace subsequently recanted, apologised and admitted that he'd been out of order.

Kilkenny were as well served in the fitness department as they were in the medical area. This was the third year of Mick Lanigan's physical training regime. Lanigan, from Patrick Street in the city, had won seven successive Irish 110m hurdles titles before injury deprived him of an eighth in 1965. He did his morning training, the long runs, in James's Park or Kilkenny Golf Club. He did his evening training, pure hurdling, in Nowlan Park, setting up three or four hurdles on the field under the bank and attacking them. Fr Maher, who had seen Lanigan train and in any case was a man to whom the words "why not?" came easier than "why?", suggested to the county board via Paddy Grace that he be brought on board in 1967 as physical trainer.

There was one slight problem. Lanigan was playing rugby with Kilkenny RFC at the time. "It was unusual, to say the least," he admits. "A lot of people thought it was a mortaller, not so much inside Kilkenny as outside the county."

His brief was straightforward. Try and get the players fit, Fr Maher told him, for the sport they were playing. (The term "game-specific approach" had not yet been coined.) With this in mind Lanigan, who had hurled at school and with James Stephens, spent a few months attending as many matches as he could in Nowlan Park, paying particular attention to the length of time players had on the ball and the distances they ran. If he hadn't already known it, his research brought it home to him that sprinting was an essential. What he categorically hadn't realised was that running backwards would form another element of the package.

"When the ball went over the head of a defender he had to turn and run back, in the same direction as the forward and the ball. So, and it sounds trite, we had to work out a regimen of how to run efficiently backwards – and as the players had to turn, how to turn as economically as possible. Some people didn't realise that this was necessary. Not in the beginning anyway. It was all, 'What's this about?' But once they started to use it in games they could see it was relevant. Training running around fields is training for running around fields. We needed the players fit, but fit for sharp short sprints."

The players were learning from Mick Lanigan. He in turn was learning from Fr Maher. "The biggest lesson I learned from him was to do the simple things well. Learn how to hit the ball on the ground properly. Learn how to take a sideline cut properly. Don't overdo your own perceived skills. Don't go on a solo run unless you were winning well. A ball will always travel faster than a player. He was very calm and level-headed, but he had steel when needed. He would have made a tremendous human resources manager."

Lanigan's first season ended with the 1967 All Ireland triumph. "Nobody from the county board ever complained or got in the way after that. It's very easy for people to consider you're a good trainer if you beat the old enemy in your first year."

Despite the absence of Justin McCarthy, injured in a motorbike accident ten days beforehand, Cork started the 1969 final as favourites and demonstrated why during the first half. Kilkenny, thanks mainly to Ted Carroll's impression of Lear defying the storm, just about kept their heads above water. The game swung off in a new direction shortly before the break when a point from Mick Lawlor and a Martin Brennan goal brought the Leinster champions back to within a goal of their opponents. It took its second twist ten minutes after the restart when Pat Delaney was stretchered off following a dreadful belt from Tom O'Donoghue, the Cork full-back. Quaintly, Mitchel Cogley wrote in the *Irish Independent* next day that "a Cork player whom I could name but, of course, mustn't, hit Delaney on the head" – and this under a photo that showed O'Donoghue staring balefully down at the poleaxed Delaney. Different times, different mores.

Filleann an feall ar an bhfeallaire. Mindful of Kieran Cuddihy's injunction, Kilkenny brought Paddy Moran on at left-half forward, switched Eddie Keher to the 40' and caught fire. Anger is an energy. Of the last 11 scores of the game, nine were waved by the umpire with the white flag at the Cork end. One was hit by Pat Kavanagh, in as a sub for Claus Dunne and paying his way with the point that gave the winners the lead 12 minutes from time. Another came from Moran. "I'd have loved to be there to see you score it after the week you had," he was told afterwards by Dr Cuddihy, who was otherwise occupied in the dressing room attending to Pat Delaney.

Delaney's injury meant that no fewer than three Kilkenny forwards had gone off badly injured in the last two All Ireland finals the county had contested: different times indeed. The tension between the teams at the official lunch the following day could have been cut with several knives. To give them their due, the Cork county board officials were mortified. Tom O'Donoghue did not wear red again.

The second Kilkenny goal was scored by Joe Millea, whose daughters Tracy and Sinead would continue to carry the family flag on camogie fields a generation later. Chuffed with his goal, Millea pére was almost as pleased with a lesser feat he accomplished later in the game, this one at the behest of Fr Maher. "No matter how badly injured you were, he used tell us, once you had the ball you should be able to hit it or pass it. Unless you were dead you should be able to do something with it. Well, I won a ball in the last ten minutes, was tackled, got a hurley into the face and won a free that Eddie Keher pointed. But I had managed to pass the ball before I went down, just like Fr Maher had preached."

Denis Coughlan, the Cork midfielder, was left gobsmacked by the turnaround. "I was shocked when I heard the final whistle. I just could not believe we'd been beaten."

Ted Carroll, whose immediate opponent Eddie O'Brien was taken off at half-time, as Seán McLoughlin had been two years earlier, went on to be named Texaco Hurler of the Year. Pat Henderson: "Fr Maher told us to hit the Cork forwards hard. We did, and though they were on top in the first half it took its toll on them. We wiped them out and they didn't have the energy left in the second half. And Ted was superb. Hitting man, ball, everything. His timing was perfection, meeting the man and the ball in the tackle at the same time."

Tom Murphy, the new curate in St John's in Kilkenny city, finished his intercounty career with a second medal in four All Ireland final appearances. He harboured no doubts as to the man to whom most of the credit was due. Tommy Maher made Tom Murphy a better player because he made him a more thoughtful player.

"He made me think about it. That was the real thing. I was a reasonably good player and I could read the game better than some. How I'd position myself, how to be opportunistic. Don't stand looking when the ball is cleared, he'd tell me. Move. So I'd have at least a step on the corner-back. What Tommy had, as well as this great hurling brain, was the ability to verbalise, which a lot of fellas don't."

Victory in 1969 marked Kilkenny's 17th All Ireland title and third in seven years. It was the first time since the 1930s they'd won more than one title in a decade. The sixties had been good. The seventies would be even better.

CHAPTER 15

Gormanston

My heart in hiding stirred for a bird – the achieve of, the mastery of the thing!
Gerard Manley Hopkins, *The Windhover*

It began casually enough, the way many great ideas begin. Alf Ó Muirí, the most fondly remembered GAA president of them all, wanted to help "bring hurling back". He knew Des Ferguson, the Dublin dual player. Seán Ó Síochain, right-hand man to the GAA's general-secretary Pádraig Ó Caoimh, knew Donie Nealon. Everyone knew, or at any rate knew of, Fr Tommy Maher. And Joe Lennon had recently pioneered a football instructional course in Gormanston College in Meath. It seemed only right and fitting that a complementary instructional course in the skills of hurling be undertaken. The ball was thrown to Ferguson, Nealon and Fr Maher and off they went.

Every weekend through the winter of 1964 and into the following spring they met in Barry's Hotel in Dublin. Three men, each a right-hander. A ball and a hurley, the tools of the trade. The wall of the room to belt the sliotar against, which was as close as they got to fieldwork. That was all they needed.

By and large they were thinking out loud. The hurling skills they possessed they'd acquired intuitively, even on occasion by chance. One day a young Donie Nealon had been blocking a ball in front of him when a man who was watching told him to hold his hurley at an angle rather than dead straight horizontally. This way, the stranger advised him, the sliotar would pop right up into Nealon's hand instead of falling to the ground and requiring him to rise it. Nealon did as bidden – and lo, he saw that it was good. Drawing up the Gormanston syllabus, a primer for instructing the instructors, would entail leaving nothing to chance.

Dick Fitzgerald had written *How to Play Gaelic Football* as far back as 1914. Because nobody had tried a similar exercise in hurling, Des Ferguson, Tommy Maher and Donie Nealon were travelling without a compass, naturalists handling species of flora and fauna that had long been visible but never examined under a microscope. They were identifying, categorising, naming, cataloguing. So they started, as they had to, at the very beginning, and in the beginning was the grip.

In the beginning was the grip, and the grip had to be the correct grip. That was non-negotiable. Right hand on top for right-handers, the left hand sliding up the handle of the hurley to lock with the right hand when striking. Left hand on top for left-handers. From this, everything flowed.

Nealon: "I don't think you'll ever reach your maximum or fully master the skills if you don't have the proper grip. It's very hard to develop the other side. If you haven't a full, proper swing, how are you going to get distance into your pucks?"

Grip. Swing. Striking left and right. Ground striking, with the stipulation that the player "must be able to strike left and right, and it must be a wrist-swing: short – not a cartwheel swing – ie stopped after the ball has been struck, to avoid accidents". Meeting a running ball. Rising the ball, jab-lift and roll-lift. Handpassing, seven different ways thereof. And so on.

Sometimes, they found, less was more in bringing about the mastery of the thing. Killing a ball in the air, for instance. Go back a couple of inches with your hurley angled, Nealon directs, and deaden it. "Watch the way Henry Shefflin does it. The ball doesn't go forward off his stick. It falls at his feet."

They weren't, says Nealon, "thinking of the Tipperarys and the Kilkennys. It was more the people after that, and after that again. The Bs and the Cs." They were preaching to the unconverted. For that reason, everything had to be made as simple and user-friendly as possible.

Each of the game's skills – they identified over 80 of them – was analysed and broken down into its constituent parts. Take striking the ball from the hand. An easy enough operation? The Gormanston trio didn't think so. They felt it to be one of the most complicated skills for a beginner to learn, demanding full coordination of body movement, good hand-eye coordination and proper use of the wrists. Here's how they demystified the process:

1. Hold the ball in the cupped left hand with the elbow slightly bent. The hurley is held upright in front of the right shoulder with the bas above head height. Eyes on the ball. Feet comfortably apart for good balance. Shoulders and feet in line with the intended flight of the ball.

2. Throw the ball to just above the height of the left shoulder and raise the hurley to the right in lock position (ie left hand locked under the right). Eyes on the ball.

3. Hips and shoulders rotate to swing the hurley. Eyes on the ball.

4. Hit the ball at a point in front of the left knee.

5. Body weight is transferred from right foot to left foot.

6. Good follow-through is necessary for accuracy and distance.

Each of them learned as they went along. Until he met Fr Maher, Donie Nealon had never realised how effective the handpass could be in clearing one's lines and moving the ball up the field – and this half a century before Jose Mourinho popularised the term "the transition from defence to attack".

Des Ferguson's eureka moment arrived on observing the premium that Fr Maher, a better hurler than he, and Nealon, who was more gifted than both of them, placed on practising the skills. So this was what it was about at the highest level, he decided. As a dual player with St Vincent's, Ferguson spent most of his time playing games. "You never had the time to practise, and you don't improve playing matches. I'm sorry I didn't practise more or have the time to do so. You have to practise the skills if you're going to acquire the skill."

The course was a learning curve for Fr Maher as well. To him, hurling was a game that was continually evolving. "In his eyes there was always a better way, or at least there might be a better way," says Brendan O'Sullivan, subsequently an All Ireland-winning minor and under-21 coach with Kilkenny. "And you could learn it from other people. That's why you should listen to other people, no matter where they were from. And he did."

Along with the technical specifics were general notes to which each of the trio contributed, detailing the varying requirements of the different positions on the field of play. The notes naturally reflected the habits and humours of the era. The full-back, "often a heavy man and not very mobile", had two functions. Beating the full-forward to the ball and clearing it was only the second function; preventing the full-forward from going in on the goalie was the first. The goalkeeper was advised, possibly unnecessarily, to be aware of incoming forwards, "whose ignominious business it is to 'bury' him". Look: it was the early 1960s.

Full-backs were encouraged to stick in the hurley, thus preventing the full-forward from connecting, rather than to pull first time and so risk being beaten to the pull. Corner-backs were advised to clear to the wings with ground striking unless they were Blackrock's Jimmy Brohan, who liked to get the sliotar into his hand before clearing it; wing-backs to play from the front; midfielders to avoid driving in random balls to the forwards; and wing-forwards to have the courage to shoot and to remember to follow up balls they'd delivered into the goalmouth.

Good habits were codified and exalted. At its root, the triumvirate maintained, hurling was a simple game of complex skills, a game based not on physical power but on command of the basics and on letting the ball do the work. The importance of hooking and blocking was emphasised, the shoulder charge condemned as a waste of energy.

In places it was a document of its time. In other places it was a document before its time, a paean to the primacy of skill, a road map to the future with its vision of a faster, more fluid game. While much of what the triumvirate wrote seems commonplace or obvious now, one can only hazard a guess at the trumpet note with which it fell on open ears.

Snitchy Ferguson (he disliked the nickname), a defender, authored the notes on defending. The other two wrote about forward play. Here is a taste of what they prescribed.

"The full-forward position gives great scope to the man who is a trickster, and this he must be if he is to overcome the great advantage every full-back has over his opponent. He must be able to twist and turn and sidestep and throw a ball out to one of his corner men. He is the man who, above all, must not play 'straight'. [This paragraph could only have been written by Tommy Maher and it could only have been written with his old friend Tom Ryan in mind.]

"It is the business of forwards to score. The first requirement of a forward, then, is to be able to shoot, to shoot hard and accurately. Any man of the six of them should be able to pick up a ball quickly in any part of the forward area and drive over a point or shoot straight and hard to the goals. How many forwards do we see even on county senior teams who cannot pick up a loose ball and drive it over the bar from a distance – all for want of practising it, which they could do on their own, by putting up some kind of target. Kilkenny owe many All Irelands to the ability of their forwards to do this, and when it is said that they were 'lucky' to win by a point, as they have often done, it should rather be said that they had forwards who were able to take their chances and pick off points.

"A forward, especially a half-forward, without a feint, a swerve, a sidestep is no forward. These are the tricks of the forward's trade – some of them anyway. A man who plays straight, runs straight, who is a bit heavy on his feet and cumbersome of body, might make a back man; he will not make a forward. A forward must be sprightly, agile, on the alert, a bag of tricks, always doing the unexpected. Therefore forwards, good ones, are always in short supply. In hurling – or in football, where traditionally the standard is low – you may get good backs and centre-fields, but after the team has played and lost the newspapermen will say that they could do everything except score while the opposition team, often with far fewer chances, was able to win. The credit must go to the forwards. But even in first-class counties it is easy to count the number of good forwards that appeared over a period of, say, ten years.

"The moral of all this is: the county that wants to raise the standard of hurling and win matches – and to win every now and then is essential for morale – must concentrate on drilling and training and schooling forwards in the things we have mentioned above. [A timeless exhortation. Tim Crowe from Sixmilebridge, a former Clare selector, has long bemoaned the county's habit of taking a promising youngster and trying to make a centre-back instead of a forward out of him.]

"A forward must behave and hurl in a cheeky, impudent and self-confident way. If he is shy and diffident and apologetic he will make no impression. For every player, but especially for the forward, it is necessary to feel at home on the field, confident in his own ability to measure up to any opponent. This comes with match practice – but character has a lot to do with it too. For want of feeling at home on the field the young player is very rarely able to do in a match a quarter of what he is capable of. This explains why old-timers – Ring, Purcell – are able to beat young fellows. With young players, especially young forwards, a trainer must try to do what is partly impossible: to put an old head on young shoulders.

"But hurling is such a fast game there is so much you cannot calculate or foresee, there is so much depending on individual ability and brilliance that only very general rules can be given. There are forward movements, there is combination, but little of it is worked out beforehand or even done consciously; it is done by instinct or intuition or a sixth sense – and more things happen by chance on a hurling field than newspapermen dream of. In practice there is no such thing as copybook hurling; those who look for a consciously worked out pattern in hurling will be disappointed.

"Because of the nature of the game of hurling, which is at its best in forward play, we have insisted above on the individual qualities of the forward: ball play, accuracy, self-confidence, trickiness. A forward is a man who can see without looking, who knows without thinking. Therefore he does not try to score when he is badly positioned; he does not pass to a comrade who is not free; he shoots for a goal rather than a point when the opportunity is there. You can hardly say that he decides to do or not to do these things; he just does them by instinct, by a feeling he has for his surroundings. If you say that it is not possible to teach such things you are partly right. And therefore Rings are few and far between. But such qualities are latent in many players and can be brought out and perfected by practice and coaching, especially in the early years. Since these qualities are more vital for forwards than for other players the importance of careful selection of forwards who have this natural ability is obvious."

Weekend followed weekend in Barry's Hotel. More skills, more components, more deconstruction. Des Ferguson kept meticulous notes. Phone calls from his home in Kells to Kilkenny and Nenagh. A bill for 22 shillings for lunch for the three of them. ("Wholesome food. Like food was then.") He kept meticulous notes because he had to. "It was for Croke Park and they had no money. They genuinely hadn't. Their attitude was, 'Get it done, but don't be costing money because we can't afford it.'"

Every so often Ferguson would call in to Croke Park. At the time three terraced houses stood together on Jones's Road, one of which was the GAA's headquarters. "A creaky oul' stairs and Miss Moriarty at the top of it. 'Who do you want to see?' If your business was deemed important, Pádraig Ó Caoimh would come out and see you and discuss things. Then off you went. That was it. Ó Caoimh and Seán Ó Síochain and Miss Moriarty. The three of them running the GAA."

After each meeting Ferguson brought the fruits of their labours back with him to Kells, where they were typed up on a Gestetner machine by a colleague in his school. Presently the format for a week-long course, with lectures and discussions and practicals, took shape. Not a *coaching* course: an *instructional* course. 'Instructional' courses were fine where the upper echelons of the GAA were concerned. 'Coaching' courses smacked of professionalism, reeked of the dreaded other codes and carried implications of the suppression of individuality.

From all corners of the island the believers descended on Gormanston College during the second week of August 1965 to hear the new gospel. There were priests and Christian Brothers and clerical students. There were also lorry helpers and bakery storemen and sewing-machine mechanics. Everyone was given a form to fill out. *Ainm. Seoladh. Slí Bheatha.* Are you attending the course as a representative of your county's coiste iomána? Are you attending so as to become a hurling instructor or for the purpose of improving your own hurling standards? How competent a hurler are you (intercounty/club/ beginner)? As well as lectures and practical demonstrations there was golf, handball and a céilí mór with a demonstration of dancing. Musically minded participants were encouraged to bring their instruments.

Tommy Maher was no turbulent priest. But Gormanston gave him a pulpit he hadn't had access to before. The homily he preached was one of simplicity and imaginativeness, of the relevance of skill and the importance of proper practice. As always, demonstration accompanied theory. *Don't tell: show.*

He even coached a sceptical Des Ferguson in the correct way of taking a sideline cut. Fr Maher's solution was to take a divot. He produced a matchstick and placed it half an inch in front of the sliotar. Aim at the matchstick, he commanded, not at the ball. Ferguson took a swing. "And she flew!"

The course, which fittingly was launched by Alf Ó Muirí, lasted for a week.

It was meant to be a one-off. The crowd shouted out for more. A more advanced syllabus was drawn up and recognition granted by the Department of Education.

Among the attendees that first year was the most popular and respected individual ever to attend the course, a man not just liked and admired but revered and adored. Ned Power, universally described as "a gentleman of the highest order", had won an All Ireland medal in goal with Waterford in 1959. He was now 35. His days playing hurling were behind him. His days thinking about hurling were only beginning.

He'd come to the right place. Fr Maher, whose coaching Power maintained was the factor that had made the difference for Kilkenny against Waterford in 1957, "was the first man who made me really think about hurling", he would frequently declare afterwards.

Gormanston did not solve the age-old conundrum about who guards the guards. But it did provide the answer to the question of who coaches the coaches and how, and it lit a candle in the hearts of men of goodwill. Maybe, Donie Nealon ruminates, "we went into too much detail". Or maybe not; John Hanley from Clarecastle and Ned Power found further skills to identify and catalogue. They didn't stop until they'd reached 120.

The faithful and the converts continued to flock to the Meath countryside and in ever greater numbers. Justin McCarthy came from Cork, Liam Hinphey – now back in his native Derry after his time in Kilkenny – from Dungiven. The 1970 course catered for first-year and second-year attendees and, complementing the usual classes on psychology, responsibilities of a coach, principles of attack and defence and the rest, had Pat Fanning speaking on 'The Club of the '70s', Seán Ó Síochain discoursing on 'Communication and Co-operation' and a functionary from the Department of Education droning about 'Sport in Education, Sport in Society'.

Gormanston was endlessly enlightening and thought-provoking. Even better, it was enjoyable. Late nights were not infrequent. Liam Hinphey was the unofficial Minister for Fun. Justin McCarthy took part in matches in 1970 despite the small inconvenience of the plaster on his leg from his motorbike accident (he cooled the injured limb at half-time by pouring water through the plaster). One morning John Moloney, the finest referee of his generation, came to Des Ferguson complaining about some joker doing woodpecker impressions in the dormitory and keeping everyone awake. Some investigation by Ferguson revealed the culprit to be Moloney himself.

Entertaining a contingent in his house one night, Ferguson went up to the attic and brought down a coaching booklet written by a Christian Brother in the

1940s. "Find out who your referee is," it advised. "Discover his failings. Coach your team accordingly."

Gormanston's was an altogether less cynical gospel. The New Testament, not the Old.

"All Irelands were won out of Gormanston." Thus goes the claim. True? False? Misty-eyed mythology?

True in the case of Offaly in 1981 and '85. Dermot Healy had been a Gormanston regular in his early 20s. Anything he hadn't already learned from Tommy Maher he picked up there.

Similarly true in the case of Galway in the same decade. Cyril Farrell was another Gormanston alumnus. Like Donie Nealon, he too had his mind expanded by the store Fr Maher placed in the handpass and the hallucinogenic vistas this opened up for the progressive coach. "His methodology with people was very good, very down to earth," says Farrell. "He was coaching before coaching was even heard of. He showed me what the handpass was all about. Up to that you'd be banging away. I'd never seen it developed the way he had developed it." *Ma-aaaaan.*

True in the case of St Mary's of Athenry, thrice All Ireland club champions between 1997 and 2001. A formative influence on the team was Tom Cloonan, father of Eugene, who'd attended Gormanston in 1972. The main lesson Cloonan brought back with him to Athenry BNS and employed in his coaching was that tough physical training had no place when it came to improving the skills. Hurling was about speed of reaction, not powers of endurance.

And true also in the case of Ger Loughnane's Clare, for Ger Loughnane's Clare included a healthy contingent from Clarecastle, not to mention a Clarecastle captain, and many of the Clarecastle contingent had encountered John Hanley, a graduate summa cum laude of Gormanston, long before they encountered Loughnane.

Before he took himself to Gormanston, Hanley had been a hurling enthusiast. Upon immersing himself in its waters he became a hurling apostle. Gormanston didn't just fire his ardour, it heightened his consciousness and armed him with the wherewithal to pass on his new knowledge.

Other than Tull Considine paying the occasional visit to St Flannan's to demonstrate overhead striking and sundry other bits and pieces during his school days, Hanley had never seen the skills of the game showcased on a formal, officially sanctioned basis. As a result, Gormanston was "a tremendous learning process" for him. What specifically piqued his interest was the emphasis placed on positional play. "Not only did they show us how to hold the hurley correctly and how to perform and develop the skills, they showed us how to use the skills in various positions." One size did not fit all. A forward needed a different approach to a centrefielder. A centrefielder's job was not the same as that of a defender. Some of the skills were common to all positions. Others were more important or useful in discrete areas.

Even as basic an exercise as striking a ground ball came with a bundle of lessons attached. Hanley: "With ground hurling a player learns how to hit the ball on both sides. He learns how to address the ball properly. He learns footwork. He learns how to sidestep. And look at how few players can sidestep any more. They charge through rather than sidestep."

Energised, Hanley went back to Clarecastle with his notes in a folder and fire in his veins. That winter he prevailed on his brother, a hotelier in Liscannor, to open up his place for a gathering of the clans. For years afterwards a small club could not win a juvenile title in Clare without Hanley being told by grateful club elders that it was all due to Gormanston.

What John Hanley learned in Gormanston, he also passed on back home in the boys' national school in Clarecastle. Correct grip was one of the building blocks, for Gormanston had alerted Hanley to the joys of purity and a right-hander with his left hand on top chilled him to the marrow. Among the pupils in the school at the turn of the 1980s was a youngster from nearby Madden's Terrace called Anthony Daly. John Hanley would be the biggest influence on Daly's career. Not Father Willie Walsh or Father Seamus Gardiner in St Flannan's. Not Ger Loughnane. John Hanley.

"Every day that there was a dry ten minutes he'd have us out hurling. He was top class on the technical side. He gave you a massive foundation. He showed you how to position yourself, how to protect yourself, how to block and hook, where to be under a high ball." And something interesting that Daly, one of that breed who aren't speedy but who never look in a hurry because their basic technique is bombproof, noticed when he graduated to the Clarecastle senior team: colleagues who hadn't gone to Clarecastle BNS and been coached by John Hanley were way more liable to receive knocks and stitches. Among the multitude of lessons he imparted, Hanley had shown his charges how to protect themselves, a skill in its own right.

Daly may have spent his early years with Clare as a soldier in a losing army, but he had learned his hurling in cadet school. That was John Hanley. That was Gormanston.

It wasn't all about future champions. Liam Hinphey knew a teacher in the depths of Tyrone. The man had only the vaguest idea about hurling, he'd never played in his life and his school had to travel 40 or 50 miles to play a match. Yet inspired by the flame lit in Gormanston, this teacher produced "the nicest little team you ever saw. That's what Gormanston did." And when Hinphey returned to his own school in Dungiven and showed his notes from Gormanston, his Gaelic football and soccer colleagues gaped. The material was far ahead of anything they were using.

Hinphey spent some time on the dark side as trainer of the Derry footballers. Everyone else seemed to think it was about laps and weights and endurance. He knew better. He knew, because he'd learned it from Tommy Maher, that intercounty training was about performing the skills at optimum pace. Get that right, Hinphey realised, and fitness wouldn't be an issue.

"The secret of Gormanston was that it gave enthusiasm to the enthusiasts. It was a counting house for inspiration that established a network for people from the weaker counties. If there may have been an overemphasis on the social side at times, it was amply repaid in terms of the effort put in when they went back to their counties and got stuck in at the coalface."

Gormanston's tentacles stretched all the way into the under-age arena of the early 1990s. Ned Power, a man far too straight and upright to be a sophisticated political animal, had had an unhappy experience coaching Waterford in 1982-83 and thereafter lacked the stomach to be part of a management team. The county had a richly promising under-21 outfit in 1992, though, and Tony Mansfield and Peter Power, the manager and coach respectively, were neither too proud nor too stupid to spurn the sage on their doorstep.

Besides, they needed guidance. They were worried about Tony Browne and Johnny Brenner – specifically about the pair's striking, which was too coarse for comfort. So they arranged for the team's next challenge match to be taped and they sent the tape to Ned Power, a man who once spent the entirety of a car journey from Kilkenny to Dundalk debating with Noel Skehan the merits and demerits of the hurling grip vis a vis the golf grip, imploring him to identify ten faults. Power sent it back a few days later complete with a list of ten areas for specialist coaching. Among the faults he'd spotted were Brenner's habit of twisting his hurley prior to connecting, Browne's striking off his left and Paul Flynn's freetaking technique. Waterford went on to win the 1992 All Ireland under-21 title. It was the county's first All Ireland triumph since their 1959 MacCarthy Cup success. Gormanston again.

"Have you got a name for the book?" John Hanley enquires by way of a parting question.

"Something about a hurling godfather? Or a messiah? Good. No better title. Des and Donie were great men. But they'd admit that Fr Maher was the messiah."

CHAPTER 16

Grace

And yet in the papers on Monday morning you'd see a quote from Grace
"Our boys were bad, 'tis very sad, they couldn't last the pace
They'll never win the All Ireland, still we won't despair
We'll feed them up, we'll train them well and maybe they'll be fair"
From a poem entitled *Grace – Before and After* **by Tom Coyle**

"The train isn't going out until four o'clock on Saturday, but you can travel up the next morning," Tom Walsh, the county chairman, informed Shem Downey, a butcher in Ballyragget, a couple of nights before the 1947 All Ireland final.

"No," said Shem, "I've already arranged for someone to come in and cover for me on Saturday."

Walsh frowned at the thought of this additional expense for the county board. "A pity you didn't tell us that earlier," he replied acidly. "We wouldn't have picked you."

That's how it was then. But it wouldn't be that way for much longer. Three months after the All Ireland final, Paddy Grace, the right-corner back to Downey's right-corner forward, became secretary of the county board. Kilkenny hurling would never be quite the same again.

Grace had already done his county handsome service. An All Ireland minor winner in 1935, a senior medallist in 1939, the losers' best performer against Tipperary in 1945 and one of the heroes of the hour in 1947 after beating his marker Joe Kelly, Cork's champion sprinter, in the race to a loose ball to put Kilkenny on the attack for Terry Leahy's winning point. He was to spend the next 37 years doing them more service still.

He was politicised by an incident that happened him one day while wearing the stripey jersey. He broke his hurley in a clash. A replacement was thrown in from the sideline. After the game one of the Kilkenny officials took it back. Grace remonstrated, pointing out that it was his hurley that had been broken and he was entitled to a replacement. No, he was flatly told, much to his anger. It was not long afterwards that he stood for the post of county secretary. Kilkenny hurlers would want for little while he was around.

When Donal Óg Cusack, not merely the most interesting and courageous GAA person of his generation but one of the most interesting and courageous Irish people of his generation, spoke in his autobiography of Kilkenny being a "land of milk and honey", admiration as well as envy was detectable behind the apparent jibe. A land of milk and honey? That was due to Paddy Grace more – oh so much more – than to anyone else. He was, as scores of former heroes have attested, the ultimate players' man.

"He looked after us, he did what he could for us," says Seamus Cleere, the 1963 All Ireland-winning captain who unbidden recalls the ticket arrangements for that final: six tickets per player, with an option to buy four more. "He left a legacy of looking after players, and Ned Quinn as chairman drove that on further," says Pat Henderson. "We haven't had discontent in Kilkenny because the players come first always. That's down to Paddy Grace."

The sight, so beloved of Cyril Farrell, of children pucking around on the field in Nowlan Park following a match? Another byproduct of Grace's tenure as secretary. His greatest concern, an article in the 1972 *Kilkenny GAA Yearbook* affirmed, "is for the welfare of the players. Equally important with him is his great desire to enable young boys to play the national games and if he had his way every young boy in Kilkenny would have a hurley free of charge."

He and Tommy Maher were not chips off the same block, their membership of the 1945 All Ireland team apart. Maher was a forward, Grace a defender. Maher's career was cut short by the seminary's siren call; Grace hurled for as long as he could. Maher was a priest and teacher, Grace an insurance agent. Maher was intrigued by hurling as a scientific exercise and brought his powers of logic and analysis to bear on it; Grace's calling was to make Kilkenny great and keep them great. Maher liked other sports; Grace was in favour of the Ban and made no apologies for it. Grace died in office at 67; Maher lived on till a ripe old age. But it was Grace who identified Maher's talent and brought him in to train Kilkenny, and it was Maher who returned the favour by bringing the county to heights unattained for four decades.

Grace knew what players needed the occasional couple of bob and what players were trying it on with him, demanding refunds for the price of mythical taxis from Dublin and whatnot. He knew which supporters to give out All Ireland tickets to because he knew which of them were Nowlan Park regulars and which of them weren't. He had a healthy contempt for the suits in Croke Park and he made no secret of it.

And no, maybe he didn't keep the minutes of county board meetings as efficiently as another secretary might have. And every now and then he might come across a set of county minor or junior medals he'd put away in a drawer at home in Newpark, forgotten about for a year or two and now had to furnish belatedly to the winners. But so what? The genius of the man was in the fixity of his purpose and the warmth of his spirit, not in dotted i's and crossed t's. "I never saw him take a note about anything he had to do," Tommy Maher once said. "Yet he never forgot anything he had to do."

The stories about Paddy Grace are legion. Some are, in a nice way, unprintable. Here are a few that give a flavour of the man.

◆ The 1971 All Ireland final. Jim Rhatigan, a cub reporter with the *Kilkenny People*, is doing a sideline colour piece and somehow finds himself in the dressing room at half-time. To say that nobody takes a blind bit of notice of him is not quite accurate; Paddy Grace offers him a tot of whiskey. (Mr Rhatigan wishes to put it on record that, being a young man of impeccable virtue and professionalism, he declined.) Fr Maher does most of the talking during the interval, which concludes with much banging of hurleys off tables and floors. "Like a wardance," Rhatigan reminisces. It is not his first encounter with Paddy Grace. Bitten by the soccer bug after the 1966 World Cup finals in England and a prime mover behind Emfa FC, who subsequently joined the League of Ireland and became Kilkenny City, Rhatigan was on flag-day duty for the club one time, collecting money for new footballs, when Grace gave him ten bob. "If any Gaelic football team asks you for the loan of a ball," he added, "don't give it to 'em." The daddy of this remark was uttered by Grace to Donie Butler, a neighbour of his in Newpark and later the commercial manager of the FAI, who'd done scoreboard duty in Nowlan Park during the 1960s before he too fell in love with the garrison game. "I don't mind you getting involved with soccer, Donie," Grace declared with tongue only half in cheek. "But for the love of God stay away from that oul' Gaelic football!"

◆ The night of the 1959 All Ireland final, whether the draw or the replay. One Kilkenny player touches Grace for a fiver in the bar of the Hollybrook Hotel. He goes upstairs to join some of his colleagues. "I've fooled Grace," he announces, waving his bounty. "You haven't fooled Grace," says a voice behind him. Yes, Grace has followed the player up the stairs, just to let him know he's keeping an eye on him. But he allows him to keep the fiver and share it.

◆ A league match in Cork sometime in the 1960s or '70s, long before the advent of the motorway, when the journey home to Kilkenny entails a three-hour trip via Mitchelstown, Fermoy, Cahir and Clonmel. To the astonishment of a car containing a group of players and officials, a leg appears out of the driver's side of the county secretary's car in front of them. Grace is driving with one foot on the pedal and the other out the window.

◆ A Killkenny player who travels a distance for training submits a wildly excessive bill for mileage. Grace takes him aside, tells him he's overdoing it and orders him to resubmit the bill. When a second bill, this one more in keeping with reality, is submitted the player receives double his mileage. It wasn't that Grace objected to the player getting his expenses and a bit more on top. Not remotely so. It was that he objected to being taken for a ride.

◆ A Friday evening in Lenehan's pub near Nowlan Park. A couple of men down the far end of the counter are engaged in a loud argument about the best hurlers in the country. Not a single Kilkenny player is mentioned in the discussion. Grace, in for a drink to mark the end of the working week, grows more and more irked until he can no longer contain himself. Out he goes to his car, opens the boot, comes back with the MacCarthy Cup, dropkicks it down the bar and announces, "That'll stop yer effin' arguing." It does.

◆ All Ireland day one year in the 1970s. Grace, as is his custom, is with the minors. A suited flunkey, oozing pomposity, detains them at the players' gate behind the Cusack Stand. Where are their passes? Grace turns to the players. "C'mon, lads, we're going home!" The flunkey's face drops and he hurriedly ushers them through. The players are delighted. They already have the opening score of the afternoon on the board.

◆ Early 1979. Chunky O'Brien, dismayed after being substituted in the 1978 All Ireland final, has retired. He's at work in Smithwick's brewery one afternoon when Grace calls. They repair to one of the many Parliament Street hostelries opposite the gates of the brewery. By the time they're finished, Chunky has come out of retirement. He'll finish the season with an All Ireland medal, an All Star and the man of the match award in the All Ireland final.

◆ Late 1979. Kilkenny are off to the US to play the All Stars. Sponsorship of the scheme has recently been taken over by Bank of Ireland, with the result that there will be stopoffs in New York, Chicago, San Francisco and Los Angeles. The *Kilkenny People* are happy to send John Knox, their GAA correspondent, but they won't pay his full fare. Knox goes to Mick O'Neill, the county board chairman, for help. He finds a sympathetic ear. A week or two later, Knox is approached by Paddy Grace in the tunnel under the Old Stand in Nowlan Park. "Hey you," says Grace, "why didn't you ask me about going to America?" He has a reason for wondering, for Paddy Grace and John Knox go back a long way, back to when the latter was a young lad and Grace in his Royal Liver persona used to call to the Knox household in Fatima Place every Saturday around lunchtime to collect the weekly payment on a policy. The policy was for a penny more than the weekly payment figure, but Grace never collected the additional penny. Thus he became chez Knox "the man who didn't collect the penny". If Grace was affronted that Knox hadn't gone to him first he soon got over it, assured him he'd be on the plane and would be looked after when he got to the US. The county board helped cover Knox's fare and he had a great trip, spending a lot of time with Eamon Langton and the late Eamon Hennessy. "As the years passed, Paddy and I became great mates. We never drank together, we never socialised together, we simply got on and showed each other respect. That was what Paddy valued. Mutual respect and honesty."

◆ The early 1980s. Kilkenny GAA in grave financial trouble, like a number of other counties in Leinster at the time. Grace comes to Paul Kinsella and Brendan O'Sullivan of the Schools Board, to whom the county board gives subsidies for hurleys every year. "No matter what happens, lads, there will always be money for schools' hurling in Kilkenny."

◆ John O'Shea of the *Evening Press* and later of the charity Goal. Not Grace's favourite journalist. Maybe it was his splash before one All Ireland about how the Kilkenny players were getting fewer tickets than the Cork players were. Maybe it was just that John O'Shea was, well, John O'Shea. Whatever the reason, one night Grace tried to throw him out of Langton's. Wait... "He didn't *try* to throw me out," O'Shea reports. "He *did* throw me out." The pair of them kissed and made up in later years. What's more, the passing of three decades and the dawn of a new world of Wags and Baby Bentleys and fake blood capsules threw the existence of men like Paddy Grace into new relief for O'Shea. Because Grace, idiosyncratic as he was, stood for something. For a love of the game, for amateurism, for a certain standard of behaviour and values, for decency and honesty. "Isn't it fantastic that someone would fight like that for something he believed in? Something that he wasn't in for the money?"

By the way, John, now that we're at it, can we blame you for retiring Keher? "Tsk. Eddie had reached the age of reason. He must have known what his body was telling him. I merely ushered his decision along and made it easier for him by breaking the story. Anyway, retirement afforded him the opportunity to sample the golf courses of Ireland – and did he sample them. He should thank me for giving him the push."

♦ The buildup to the 1983 All Ireland final. Grace's health is failing. His mind is not. The Kilkenny players want to purchase extra tickets and are dropping hints about not doing this or that if they don't get their way. Grace kicks up a fuss and announces he won't be giving in. It's all a bluff. After some pushing he discovers who the ringleaders are. His curiosity satisfied, the problem vanishes. The players get what they wanted.

♦ He married Maureen. It was the beginning of a beautiful friendship and a unique double act. Together they understood the GAA in Kilkenny and beyond. How it worked, the players, the clubs, the people. When the throngs descended on Esker, their house in Newpark, the week before an All Ireland final they both – Maureen as much as Paddy – knew without any reference to book or ledger who deserved tickets, who got them, who had access to them through Croke Park anyway and who was chancing their arm. Maureen was the ambassador, no matter how intense the pressure became. Paddy was Paddy.

♦ Paddy and Maureen. There followed Richie, Angela, Nuala, Rena, Mary, Paddy junior, Ursula, Frances and Terry. Angela would marry Tom Walsh from Thomastown. Frances, better known as Frankie, would marry Michael Walsh from Tullaroan. Their first child was born in 1983. They called him Tommy. The good Paddy Grace did for Kilkenny hurling would live after him in more ways than one.

♦ His phone number was 21211. At a time when it was one of the few phones around, there wasn't a baby born in St Luke's Hospital to a family from the Newpark or Johnswell Road area that the call wasn't made from the hospital to Graces' and the good news passed on.

♦ He died much too young in the summer of 1984. "An extraordinary man in an extraordinary job," Monsignor Tommy Maher declared during his funeral homily. "He recognised everyone and was recognised by everyone."

How would Grace manage if he were around today? Truth be told, he wouldn't get on too well. There is no room in the GAA of the 21st century for a Paddy Grace. There never will be again. Then again, there will never be another Paddy Grace.

The poem quoted at the beginning of this chapter was written by a man living in Middlesex and paid tribute to Grace's habit of – even mania for – publicly writing off Kilkenny's chances prior to All Ireland finals. It finished with the following lines.

And in the papers on Monday morning you'd see a quote from Grace
"Our boys were fast, I knew they'd last, they were first in every race
I knew they'd win the All Ireland, ah our pick is very strong
Sure I was saying it in the papers that they'd win it all along"

CHAPTER 17

Epic

Kilkenny 3-20 Cork 5-11...And so help me God, I hope it's a draw!
Micheál O'Hehir, September 3rd 1972

It would be easy and convenient to say it was apparent from the outset that Kilkenny would dominate the first half of the 1970s, that a decade and a half of Fr Tommy Maher had honed their game and broadened their horizons and that they were consequently wristier, craftier, better. It would also be untrue. There was no obvious indication that the seventies would be, if not socialist, then striped.

Admittedly some straws in the wind were noticeable on close inspection, chief and critical among them the fact that the county weren't stuck for forwards any more. Pat Delaney had established himself. Kieran Purcell and Mick Crotty were on the way. No longer would the county be forced to try and convert a Pa Dillon, a Johnny McGovern or a Jim Lynch from defender to battering ram. Neither would the battles they lost in the 1970s be physical battles. The presence of John Teehan in 1967 had marked a new departure. From now on Kilkenny would never lack a midfield enforcer, from Frank Cummins, omnipresent during the 1970s to 1982-83, through Michael Phelan in 1992-93 and Andy Comerford and Derek Lyng in the noughties right up to Michael Fennelly, simultaneously Hurler of the Year in 2011 and Robocop.

And Keher and Henderson were still there as the 1970s dawned. And though there would never be another Ollie, he would soon be more than adequately replaced. And one man who wasn't going anywhere was Tommy Maher. With the team that won the 1957 All Ireland he'd been the janitor, the painter and decorator. With the team that won three All Irelands during the 1960s he'd been the foreman and site manager. With the team of the 1970s he would be the architect. Not since James Hoban from Dysart, Callan designed the White House had a Kilkenny man overseen such an impressive creation.

Where in the pantheon do the Kilkenny team of the 1970s rank? Not as high as the Tipperary team of the 1960s, Babs Keating has asserted on the basis that – his words – Kilkenny were winning All Irelands in the '70s with the same players Tipp had been beating in the '60s. Eschewing the temptation to cite Mandy Rice-Davies at this juncture, it remains a matter of record that both Frank Cummins and Pat Delaney were only finding their feet in the intercounty arena in the late 1960s and that Kieran Purcell's first All Ireland final was that of 1971. Here were three men who weren't wispy or willowy or stylists in the classical Noreside mould. Cummins, Delaney and Purcell were all capable of going through brick walls for a shortcut and invariably quite happy to do so. They and Pat Henderson supplied the steel; Eddie Keher and Chunky O'Brien were the silk merchants.

It might have been an even better team than it was. Two words: Tom Walsh.

To hold that Walsh's presence would have rendered the Kilkenny of the 1970s stupendous as opposed to merely brilliant is a reasonable proposition. A pointless and at this stage irrelevant proposition, to be sure, but what is hurling conversation but a tantalising tale of what-ifs and might-have-beens, frequently told by drunken idiots in a pub, signifying nothing? In his own words, Walsh "wasn't going to fall off the stool". All being well he would have continued till, at the earliest, 1975. Eddie Keher, three years older, was the benchmark he used. Keher kept at it till 1977; Walsh imagines he'd have managed the same himself.

"I can't say what way my life would have gone, obviously, but I took care of my body and was an avid keep-fit person. The rule change would have helped me, and helmets might also have helped. I certainly think I'd have enjoyed hurling much more in the 1970s. And Keher and myself had this symmetry. We thought about the game the same way. I think I'd have had a lot of fun. I think I was ready to take on the mantle. But I never got hung up over it. I was glad for what I'd had."

Like their predecessors of the 1930s, the third great Kilkenny side in the annals of the sport were required to learn to lose before they could win. The 1971 All Ireland final, the first of five successive September appearances, resulted in a three-point defeat to Tipperary. Any one-score defeat in a final prompts regrets; this one prompted more regrets than most. To Fr Maher and to just about everyone else in Kilkenny, it was a game that should have been won.

Tipp took the spoils less because they had "the men" than because Ollie Walsh, still feeling the effects of an appendix operation, had what was generally accepted to be his worst game ever and because Pat Henderson was also a mile off the pace. If any Kilkennyman was entitled to an off-day it was Ollie, while in Henderson's case there were comparable extenuating circumstances. He'd hurt himself burning rubbish at home not long beforehand, crammed too much training into too short a timescale in trying to get himself right, "was flying" with the Fenians a few weeks before the final but was overcooked by the time September came around.

As with Waterford in 1963 and later with Galway in 1990, it wasn't a lack of scores that did for Kilkenny. They hit 5-14, 2-11 of it from the stick of Eddie Keher, a new individual record for an All Ireland final. The problems were at the other end, so much so that the *Tipperary Star* was moved to acknowledge that the winners "had their share of luck, without which they might not have succeeded", chiefly in the form of Roger Ryan's goal early in the second half – Seamus Hogan hit a ground shot that appeared to be going wide but rebounded off the post for Ryan to tap home – and Dinny Ryan's clincher in the dying minutes. "While some may argue opportunism rather than good fortune, Kilkenny did not have the same going for them," the *Star* was sufficiently gracious to concede.

"We were bad up the centre that day," ochóns Kieran Purcell, whose thunderbolt of a late goal counted for naught. "One of those matches we should have won. Without a doubt. And against Tipp, to make it worse."

"Be careful what you do when selecting the goalkeeper," Fr Maher had warned the management before they sat down to pick the team. They weren't careful enough. "That was one day we didn't cover ourselves in glory," Johnny McGovern, a Kilkenny selector for most of the 1970s, sighs.

It was and they didn't. But they would be granted plenty of days on which to atone.

Kilkenny had a new goalkeeper in 1972. Noel Skehan had been knocking around the place since picking up the first of three All Ireland medals as a sub-goalkeeper in 1963, understudy to his cousin Ollie Walsh. Now his time had come at last. He went into the job thinking it was precisely that, a job. He wasn't long there when he discovered it was nothing less than an intellectual exercise. One man was responsible for his enlightenment. Guess...

The first piece of advice Tommy Maher imparted to Skehan went something like this. "Noel, I'll tell you one thing. If it's up in the Hogan Stand you follow that ball. You never take your eye off the ball. If you follow it your concentration will be perfect." That was the beginning of it. That was only the beginning of it.

Further instructions followed as the year went on and as the years went on. It gradually dawned on Skehan that Fr Maher had evolved his own philosophy of goalkeeping. Reading between the lines, it's apparent that some elements of it derived from years of watching Ollie Walsh and of seeing not so much what Ollie did so brilliantly as what he didn't do so brilliantly. Fr Maher didn't want another matador. He wanted an accountant.

"See the square?" the coach asked his new goalie. "I want you to control that area. I don't want you to be diving around making fantastic saves. Do not let play develop in front of you. Be on your toes. Concentrate. Out to the ball before it drops. Make the save simple. Don't make a simple save glamorous, make it as simple as it is."

There was more. Lots more. Have control of your full-back line. Let them know when you want them to let the ball through to you. Talk to them. If a ball is going a couple of inches over the bar, don't try to bring it down. A ground ball coming in? Never wait! Go towards it! Saving a shot? Kill it on the stick, don't let it rebound! (And here Tommy Maher would, being Tommy Maher, demonstrate the necessary wristwork to Skehan). And *don't* puck the ball down on top of a Wexford half-back line containing Mick Jacob and Colm Doran!

All this was not imparted the first night or the second night or the third night, but over time the sponge absorbed the moisture. "Every evening in training he'd mention something. 'You should work at this or that.' He taught me so much. By the time he retired my reflexes were no different but my goalkeeping was totally different. All the credit is due to him. I came in to replace Ollie, who was bigger and taller and more famous. I was succeeding the best goalie in Ireland. Just do what you've been doing, Fr Maher emphasised. 'Don't try to emulate someone who's 6'3.'"

As time went by and Skehan settled into the role, he was encouraged to dip his toes into the waters of tactical puckouts. One ploy had Frank Cummins and Chunky O'Brien staying wide while Skehan belted the sliotar straight down the middle and Kieran Purcell or Pat Delaney, whichever of them was on the 40 at the time, came out to meet it. Another had him aim for one of the wing-forwards and Cummins or Chunky running for the layoff. Win the puckout, start the attack. "Fr Maher was all the time analysing the team we'd play and how we'd combat them. Was he 20 years before his time? Thirty years?"

If Fr Maher would have been intrigued by the Cork team of the noughties, with their choreographed movement, their off the ball running and their handpassing, he'd have railed at one aspect of their game: the short puckouts. It may sound strange for a man who hymned the importance of retaining possession, but for Fr Maher there was a right place to be hitting a bespoke-tailored pass and there was a wrong place.

Skehan: "Oh, he'd hammer you for a short puckout. If I saved a ball the attack would start there. But even if you hit it out to the half-back line you were still in danger. For three reasons. You were putting pressure on yourself to hit a safe puckout; you were putting pressure on the half-back to win possession; and he still had to turn and hit it – and he might half-hit it or be hooked or blocked. Puck it out to midfield or beyond and he couldn't be. Fr Maher wanted you to find a man, yes, but a midfielder or forward. Not a back. Too dangerous."

Among the crowd in Nowlan Park for one of the last training sessions before Kilkenny took on Cork in 1972 was Liam Hinphey, down from Dungiven to get in the mood for the week that was in it. The atmosphere was so relaxed as to border on the narcoleptic; at one stage Hinphey went out onto the field and chatted to Ned Byrne. Fan Larkin had a knee problem and wasn't doing much. Hinphey drove him home to Larchfield from Langton's afterwards and Fan admitted he was worried about the knee.

Also among the attendance was what comprised the national GAA media corps at the time: the GAA writers from the three daily papers and Mick Dunne from RTE. Paddy Downey and John D Hickey descended on Paddy Grace, whose spake about how Kilkenny had no chance "against this great Cork team" was so transparently risible they could only grin. Afterwards they nabbed Fr Maher, who spoke at length about his team's prospects. When they'd stopped scribbling he asked them had they finished, upon which he stated off the record that he didn't see Kilkenny winning. "I don't think our forwards are up to it." This revelation made no difference to the two reporters' big-match verdicts; both already favoured Cork on foot of their destruction of Clare in the Munster final. But as to whether Fr Maher was for once spinning them a line or whether he really was genuinely apprehensive, Paddy Downey was never quite sure afterwards.

Downey was one reporter Fr Maher was fond of. "A nice guy and a good reporter, very fair." John D Hickey, who was generally regarded in the Kilkenny camp as being a Tipperary fan with a typewriter, he'd had some run-ins with over the years. One time after training he was talking to him in the doorway of Langton's when Pa Dillon happened along. Hickey saluted Pa and stood there with him for a while, taking it upon himself to impart some advice to the Freshford man ahead of the upcoming Kilkenny/Tipperary match. "Pa, if I were you playing on [Seán] McLoughlin next Sunday here's what I'd do." Pa stood back, affronted. "John D, if you were playing on McLoughlin next Sunday you'd do feck all!"

The GAA writers who attended training before an All Ireland final always had a pool as to what the team for Sunday would be. Fr Maher didn't realise this for some time. One year he gave the XV to Paddy Downey before anyone else and Downey won the bet. Flushed with victory, Downey told Fr Maher about it later. Amused, the latter informed Downey that if he was observant enough he'd see the team out there on the last night of training, even if only for a short while. A nod being as good as a wink to a blind journalist, Downey scooped the pool every year afterwards.

The day after that underwhelming night in Nowlan Park, having dropped Fan Larkin home and paid due homage in the shrine to hurling that is Delaney's of Patrick Street, Liam Hinphey, who was friendly with Justin McCarthy from Gormanston, drove south and watched Cork training. He was stunned. They looked like a team ready to take on the entire Russian army and put them to flight. Everything was precise and perfect and carried out at speed. "It was total regimentation." After waiting around for ten minutes to meet McCarthy afterwards – another contrast with Nowlan Park, where one could literally walk in among the players – he told the Cork midfielder that the session had been infinitely superior to the one he'd witnessed 90 miles north-east the previous evening. "No bullshit, ye're way sharper and fitter than them," Hinphey said. McCarthy, who was worried that Cork might have been overdoing it, went home to Passage reassured.

Hinphey and his friend Terence McMacken, a fine soccer player, retired for a post-training beverage or three to the Arcade, Paddy Crowley's pub in Oliver Plunkett Street. There they fell into conversation with Paddy O'Driscoll from the Cork county board and various other punters. Hinphey ventured the opinion that Cork's training session had been much more impressive than Kilkenny's.

At this Terence McMacken chimed in. "From what I've seen last night and tonight," he announced, "Kilkenny will murder ye on Sunday." Sound of faces hitting the floor all round.

"You can't train like that the week of a final," McMacken elaborated. "That was Cork's All Ireland tonight. Kilkenny are ready to play their All Ireland. They were just winding down last night."

Fr Maher had a concern of his own the same week. It had been ten years since his goalkeeper had played in an All Ireland final of any description, and to compound matters his goalkeeper was also his captain. So a few days before the match he asked Noel Skehan to call up to visit him in his office in St Kieran's where they spoke for over an hour. Correction: Fr Maher spoke for over an hour, enumerating the demands of the occasion and advising Skehan on how to deal with them. The sun was shining outside, a smashing day in late August. "Don't forget to bring a cap, Noel," was the trainer's closing line. As it happened, Skehan didn't possess a cap, but he went straight down to Tommy Duggan in the Monster House in High Street and bought one. The first Sunday of September was an equally glorious afternoon. Skehan wore his new headgear against the sun in the first half.

Fr Maher wasn't forgetting he had a new midfielder in Chunky O'Brien, who had grown up in 76 Assumption Place, an Ollie Walsh short puckout from Nowlan Park, and had spent his childhood pucking the ball back to Ollie during training sessions. Nor did he forget about the man O'Brien would be marking: Justin McCarthy. Justin knew nothing about Chunky; Fr Maher knew plenty about Justin from Gormanston, not least about how his hurling brain worked, and he was determined that Chunky fire an early shot across McCarthy's bows. For weeks before the final he drilled it into Chunky that the first ball he got, no matter where on the pitch he got it, he was to strike it off his left "so that he will know you're able to hit left and right". The first ball Chunky got came to him in the middle of the field in the eighth minute. He promptly sent it over the bar *off his right*. At half-time he felt compelled to apologise to Fr Maher for such a flagrant breach of orders. "That was what I thought of the man."

Rank Kilkenny's All Ireland triumphs since their first in 1904 and 1972's sits at the top table. At the head of the top table. The victories of 1939 and '47 were more poundingly tense. That of 1967 was more meaningful. That of 2006 would be more important for what it heralded, and those of 2009 and 2011 would be historic in differing ways. But nothing beats 1972 for sheer crazy exhilaration.

Pat Henderson cleaning up all around him in the closing quarter. Pat Delaney running at the Cork defence, bouncing the ball off the ground and back into his hand as he thundered onwards. Skehan, who "had more shots to save than in three or four other All Ireland finals", conceding five goals and preventing twice as many. Chunky O'Brien, instructed by Fr Maher at half-time to "hold onto the ball as long as you can", obeying orders this time and driving forward, sliotar glued to stick, his style of soloing in counterpoint to Delaney's. The blood-boltered Keher helping turn the tide when switched from the corner to the wing. High drama. High opera.

Seventeen minutes of the 40-minute second half had elapsed when Con Roche hoisted a monster point, struck from somewhere out on Clonliffe Road, between the Canal End uprights to put Cork 5-11 to 1-15 in front. It was to be their last score of the afternoon. By then Jack Lynch, the Taoiseach, had left Croke Park for Dublin airport, from where he flew to Munich for talks with Edward Heath, the British PM.

Kilkenny's response was swift, sustained and unrelenting. Keher a goal from a close-range free to ignite the comeback. Keher a point from a free. Delaney a point on the run, flogging the sliotar in front of him as he went, with Keher coming out of nowhere to third-man the pursuing Seamus Looney. Frank Cummins, despite looking like he was about to lose control of the ball at any moment, panzering through for a goal. The sides level now and the pace ferocious.

Keher the lead for Kilkenny with a snap point from the right after Pat

Henderson and Frank Cummins had made the ball do the work in moving it up the field: a score embossed with the Maher trademark. Mullinavat's Mossy Murphy, dropped for the final but on after half-time for Ned Byrne, a point after O'Brien put the ball on a plate for Keher and Keher served it up to Murphy: two ahead. Kieran Purcell a point created by a wristy ground flick from Keher: three ahead. Delaney, again on the run, a point: four ahead. Two more Keher frees to extend the gap and the closing score from the irrepressible Delaney. Kilkenny 3-24 Cork 5-11.

Our old friend John D Hickey, never shy of rounding up platoons of personal pronouns and sending them into battle, revealed he became so engrossed in proceedings that midway through the second half he found himself with a match in his mouth, frantically trying to light it with a cigarette. It was that kind of encounter, scintillating and absorbing and unrepeatable, a match to turn nerves to jelly and make strong men quiver. Like the 1967 final it was a game that took place on John Kinsella's birthday. Unlike the 1967 final it was a game that left Kinsella, the winners' left-half forward, gasping for air. "Even in five years the difference was huge. The 1972 final was so much faster."

The military metaphorist in the match programme had not been entirely correct. Kilkenny destroyed Cork not with rifle fire alone but by bringing war upon them across a number of fronts. They hit the enemy from all angles and they hit them with an assortment of ordnance. The creeping barrage of scores from start to finish; the high-explosive detonations that brought the three goals in the second half; and then the sniper fire, a sequence of kill shots by cold-eyed triggermen, precise and remorseless.

Supposedly the older team, Kilkenny were galloping on long after Cork, like a straggler in the last half-mile of the Grand National, had slowed to a walk – a tribute to Mick Lanigan, who was doing a round of the pitch in the closing moments when Con Roche turned around to him. "Ya fecker, Lanigan, you've beaten us again!" En route to Munich, Jack Lynch received the bad news from his pilot. At least it wasn't a one-point defeat this time.

Even the winners' injury problems worked to their advantage. Fan Larkin had arranged with his James Stephens clubmate Georgie Leahy, a first-year selector, that he'd raise a hand as a signal if he felt his knee giving way, the contingency plan being that Martin Coogan would come in at left-corner back with Jim Treacy switching over to the other corner. The best laid plans... When Coogan, a left-hander, replaced Fan he went straight in at right-corner back, entirely off his own bat. It shouldn't have worked, and if it hadn't the selectors would, as Leahy says, "have been crucified". But Coogan caught the first ball that came his way and drove it down the far end of the field. Sometimes a game takes on a life of its own.

The following conversation between a pair of stunned Cork supporters on their way out of Croke Park found its way into print. Apocryphal as it may be, it's still too good not to reproduce.

First Cork supporter: "Ooo know, boy, if it wasn't for Ray Cummins [who scored 2-3] we'da been murdered."

Second Cork supporter: "C'mere, ooo – we *were* murdered!"

A month or two later Fr Maher encountered Justin McCarthy at a coaching function back at the scene of the crime. McCarthy, likewise a man for whom a game never finished with the final whistle, took his friend aside and asked him to explain the turnaround.

"My philosophy is that you have to keep that bit in reserve for the day itself," Fr Maher responded. "Our priority was to keep the lads fresh. Ye left yer fitness in Cork. We kept ours for Croke Park." The answer, which McCarthy quoted in his autobiography, proved to the latter that, off the field at any rate, Cork "were still years behind Kilkenny".

Fr Maher had a hand in the county's victory in the curtainraiser too. Coached by Dermot Healy and captained by Brian Cody, the Kilkenny minors beat Cork by 8-7 to 3-9, with Billy Fitzpatrick contributing 3-4. It was Noreside's first September double since 1935, the day Paddy Grace captained the minors and a young Pádraig Puirséal helped chair Lory Meagher, the senior captain and the Prince of Hurlers, across the field in triumph in his sodden jersey, soaked and immortal.

CHAPTER 18

Limerick

When we went up to play that match, whether there was one Eddie Keher or ten Eddie Kehers playing, we were going to win. We were just primed

Eamon Grimes

In the 1972 *Kilkenny GAA Yearbook* the county chairman Mick O'Neill, looking back on the Black and Amber's first All Ireland senior-minor double since 1935, asserted that the next ambition must be the breaking of another barrier. Not since 1932-33 had Kilkenny won successive MacCarthy Cups. If the plum looked ripe for the plucking at the beginning of the year, on the night of the Leinster final it appeared all but harvested, washed and ready to be served as a garnish.

Against a team that had taken them to a replay the previous year and that would push them all the way once more in 1974, the champions made every post a winning post. Eight points up on Wexford at half-time, 14 ahead with 15 minutes to go and ten in front at the end. The final score was 4-22 to 3-15. "Everything just went perfectly on the day," Mick Crotty avers. "Everybody seemed to contribute right around the field." Raymond Smith wrote that he had "never seen a more brilliant display of hurling through a full game against worthy opponents". It was like St Kieran's against North Mon in 1961 or Kilkenny against Waterford in 2008, a performance to be preserved and set to Wagner's 'Ride of the Valkyries'. It was champagne hurling from start to finish, the county's most devastating performance of the decade and of the Maher epoch – and, as is often the way of these things, it would count for less than nothing come teatime on September 2nd. Crisp was incomparably the classiest horse at Aintree the same year, but that didn't count for much at the winning post either.

It was after the provincial final that, as Pat Henderson puts it, "the dominoes began to fall". Things began to go wrong for Kilkenny. They didn't stop going wrong until well into the second half of the All Ireland final. Events, dear boy, events.

Eamon Morrissey emigrated to Australia: one man gone from 1972. Jim Treacy injured an Achilles tendon, Brian Cody being summoned from the minor ranks of the previous year to step into the breach: two down. Kieran Purcell had his appendix out a fortnight before the All Ireland final: make that three. Eddie Keher injured his collarbone and was a non-starter: now it was four. Chunky O'Brien was going over John's Bridge a few days before the final when he ran into Pat Delaney, who told him he had a dose of the flu. A sea of troubles indeed. At one stage Paddy Grace was even moved to ask his son in law Tom Walsh, however jokingly or otherwise, if he couldn't "come back again". It says something about the team's aura that, the injuries notwithstanding, all but one of the national newspapers tipped them to win the final. The odd man out was the one from the banks of the Suir that flows down by Mooncoin, Pádraig Puirséal.

Against another team Kilkenny might have survived and the hacks been proved right. Against a team with destiny on their side they could not hope to. And in 1973 destiny was on Limerick's side in a way it hadn't been since 1940 and would not be again for the next three decades.

Various pieces, fitted in over the years, contributed to the mosaic. The winners' mentality that the four in a row Harty Cup feats of Limerick CBS in the mid-1960s seeded in a generation of youngsters. Joe McGrath's arrival as county trainer and the enthusiasm he brought with him. The National League success of 1971 followed by the near-miss in the Munster final against Tipperary, both of which convinced them they were on the right road. But why the pieces combined and cohered so joyfully in 1973 as opposed to any other season? "It just happened," according to Ned Rea. As simple, as profound and as good an explanation as any.

Rea, the husband of a Ballyragget woman and chairman of Faughs in Dublin for 17 years, comprised a part of the explanation himself. At a time when full-forward mammoths like Ray Cummins and Tony Doran roamed the land, Limerick needed their own wrecking ball to provide space for Eamonn Cregan, Frankie Nolan and the rest. In Rea, a career corner-back six feet tall and weighing 15'7, they found their man.

He'd been dispensed with at full-back following the defeat by Wexford in the National League decider in May and watched the narrow Munster semi-final win over Clare from the bank in Semple Stadium, standing a few feet away from Jimmy Doyle. A while afterwards he was visiting his grandmother in Limerick Regional Hospital when he ran into Jackie Power, the team coach, who was in to see Rory Kiely, the county chairman. Power enquired if Rea would like to play full-forward. Rea, who'd done so at underage level, reckoned it would be "no big ordeal".

Had Power asked him to try walking across the Shannon, it's probable that Rea wouldn't have viewed it as any big ordeal either. None of them would have. Commemorated by a statue in Annacotty, Power, the left-corner forward on the county's All Ireland-winning outfits of 1936 and '40, was strategist, man-manager, everyone's favourite uncle and a living link with Limerick's rainbow-coloured but gradually fading past. "Sometimes you had to wonder were we playing for Power rather than for Limerick," Rea muses. "We felt we had to give a little more because it was Jackie," Seán Foley, the young left-half back, agrees.

Rea subsequently wore the number 14 jersey in a challenge against Waterford at the Gaelic Grounds and scored 2-1. On returning to training he worked harder than he'd ever done in his life, so much so that Power, worried he might crock someone in his enthusiasm, took him aside two weeks before the provincial final and told him to relax, he'd be playing.

Lost in the provincial wilderness since 1955, the summer of Mackey's Greyhounds, the earth's axis spun at last for Limerick in Thurles on July 29th, one of those breathless, pressure-cooker Munster final afternoons of rose-hued mythology. "The day of the moving goalposts," Eamonn Cregan terms it. "The day that luck finally went in our favour."

It did so partly because Rea did what he'd been put there for. He barged. He bored. He broke loose balls all over the place for teammates to extemporise with. Modesty precludes him from admitting he had a hand in each of the six Limerick goals. Near enough to it, anyway.

The destination of the silverware fined down to the last puck of the game, a Limerick 70. Seán Foley, approaching the sliotar, found himself overtaken somewhere around midfield by Richie Bennis, the team's close-in deadball specialist. Ever afterwards it was claimed in many of the homes of Tipperary that the sliotar veered wide. Ever afterwards Foley kidded Bennis that if he'd taken it he'd have put it straight over the black spot and left no room for argument.

Hunkered down behind Bennis, Bernie Hartigan, the left-half forward, followed the sliotar's flightpath and saw it sail inside the right-hand upright – "not by much, but it went in a straight line all the way". Cregan, in position in the left corner, hadn't a clue whether the ball was in or out but roared for a point regardless. The umpire signalled it. Limerick 6-7 Tipperary 2-18. Bennis and Foley exploded like human firecrackers out the field. Among the thousands of Limerick supporters who flooded onto the pitch was a young Cashel-based Christian Brother, Michael O'Grady, who cut his hand getting in over the barbed wire.

London, who'd upset Galway by five points in the quarter-final, were disposed of the following Sunday in the All Ireland semi-final, a game vaguely notable for the fact that Rea had the "eerie experience" of being marked by his brother Gerry, the exiles' full-back. As eyes turned to Croke Park, the main preoccupation was with Pat Delaney, the man who had helped destroy Cork in the second half the previous September. What were Limerick to do about him?

Ten days before the final Dick Stokes, another hero of the past on the management team, went to Cregan, told him the selectors were thinking of switching him to centre-back and asked would he like it. Cregan's first thought was for Jim O'Donnell, who'd started there in the Munster final after turning the tide in the semi-final when coming on against Clare. His second thought, and his answer, was that it was "up to the selectors".

They knew what they were doing. So did Cregan, who played most of his club hurling with Claughaun in the number six shirt. Whether Kilkenny realised that or not, they surely weren't aware that his stronger side was his left. "So under a dropping ball I was going left to right, which would upset anybody sticking up his left hand. Switching me wasn't as big a gamble as people made it out to be." His own plan for Croke Park was no more complicated than was necessary: stop Delaney getting the ball into his hand.

In common with his teammates, Cregan was more worried about getting through the remaining training sessions in one piece, especially as he'd injured a knee against London. The sessions that year were, he says, "animal". Blame it on his brother Mick, Joe McGrath's replacement as trainer and "a typical army man". Cregan reels off his sibling's instruments of torture. To warm up, six laps of the field, which had to be completed within a certain time ("exceed the time and you had to make up for it on the next lap"). Ninety minutes of hurling training. Then the real killer, 45 minutes of physical work. Ten press-ups, eight tuck jumps, six squats and a sprint the width of the pitch, 90 yards. Repeat the sprint another nine times. A two-minute recovery period was followed by short sprints called doggies. "And we did that from the first week in January to the Thursday week before the final." Limerick reached Croke Park one of the fittest teams in history.

An enlightened county board put up the Dublin-based Rea and O'Donnell in a hotel for the fortnight leading up to the final and ensured they were covered for in work. Training attracted attendances unseen since the 1930s. Cregan realised that something special was afoot the night he spotted Pat Fanning, the former GAA president, up from Waterford and looking on. The panel travelled to Dublin on the Saturday afternoon amid much hullabaloo in a train driven by Mick Lipper, a CIE employee and the mayor of Limerick.

All Ireland weekends are rarely complete without a moment of mild farce. Eamon Grimes, the captain, fell asleep after breakfast on Sunday morning and was left behind in the hotel. They were halfway to Croke Park before someone noticed he was missing and the bus did a u-turn. Cregan went to the toilet moments before the team took the field and emerged to find the dressing room empty. In between – and accounts of this episode vary, but the following version is as plausible as any of the others – Grimes had climbed up to the window over the toilets and hauled in a young man who accompanied the team out onto the field. His name was JP McManus.

Limerick were ready and trained to the minute. Ready for the "almighty roar" Mick Cregan had warned would greet them as they hit the field. Ready and hardened by the years of heartbreak. Ready to hurl the game of their lives. They did. Kilkenny? They were ready only for the knacker's yard.

No Keher, no Treacy, no Morrissey. Delaney with flu. Purcell on the bench. Frank Cummins only half-right. It soon got worse. Liam O'Brien and Richie Bennis began pulling at the throw-in and Bennis connected with O'Brien's nose just under the eye. (The foundations of Limerick's victory, Pádraig Puirséal reported in the *Irish Press* next day, were "laid at midfield".) The left-half forward, Johnstown's Paddy Broderick, who wore glasses, couldn't see in the rain and had to be replaced at the interval by Purcell, still feeling the effects of his operation. "I thought I was fit until I went on. Then I knew I wasn't."

A sea of troubles? An ocean of them.

The action witnessed by a rain-soaked attendance of 58,009, among them a trainee teacher from up the road in St Patrick's, Drumcondra, called Ger Loughnane, who wore a green and white paper hat in honour of his neighbours, involved an early collision that jolted Eamonn Cregan's torn cartilage. The cartilage might have popped out; instead it popped back in. "Luck really was on our side," Cregan reflects. True, but they'd travelled a sufficiently arduous road since 1970 to have earned it.

The challengers led by 0-12 to 1-7 at the interval. The protagonists were level six minutes into the second half when what may or may not have been the turning point arrived. Mick Crotty palmed the ball from close range at the Railway End to the far side rather than the near side of the Limerick goalie Seamus Horgan, who thus had a split-second extra to react and to touch the sliotar over the bar. "From my point of view it was the wrong decision," Crotty concedes. "But I felt there was more room on that side of him."

To be fair to Crotty it was a brilliant save rather than a bad miss, and even if the ball had hit the net the fact is that Limerick still had 34 minutes to retrieve the situation – a Limerick team that were, Mick Lanigan told the papers afterwards, "stronger and fitter and faster". In the event, Mossy Dowling scored a goal shortly afterwards with the nearest thing to a pushover try witnessed at Croke Park prior to 2007 ("the boys came in behind me and pushed and the momentum carried me into the net"), and the Munster champions made the best of their way home from there to win by 1-21 to 1-14. "A well deserved win in 1973," read the entry from Frank Cummins in the visitors' book in Ned Rea's pub in Parkgate Street, across the road from Heuston Station in Dublin.

The rest was hysteria. Cheering crowds, marching bands, Mick Mackey greeting the new champions in Castleconnell on their way home. Bernie Hartigan, a non-drinker, reckons he visited every pub in the county between September and January, "places in west Limerick, places up the mountains I was never in before then in my life and never will be again". Another player, afloat on a sea of alcohol through September and well into October, made a tactical decision to go on the dry for the month of November. So well did the detoxification process work that he repeated it every subsequent November.

There is a parallel sporting universe, accessed only by way of the imagination, where contests of the past are replayed in an endless loop and result in outcomes that differ from history in accordance with one's taste. In this twilight zone, Crisp is not handicapped by the concession of 23 pounds to Red Rum and Kilkenny are not handicapped by the concession of injured players to Limerick, with the result that Crisp is the Aintree hero of the spring of 1973 and Kilkenny are the Croke Park heroes of the autumn of '73. But the race is not always to the most talented horse or team. Sometimes the race is to the bravest horse, the grittiest team, the performer with fortune on his side on a particular day or in a particular year. Thus it was in 1973. Anyway, knowing the tribulations Limerick would endure over the coming decades, would any Noresider with even the slightest aspiration to sportsmanship begrudge them their fleeting nectar?

It was Limerick's day and Limerick's year. Where Kilkenny were concerned it was a day for Murphy's Law and a year for Murphy's Law. They won seven All Stars that winter nonetheless. If it may not have been a coded signal on the part of the selectors as to their opinion of the best team in the land, there were plenty of people on Noreside happy to interpret it as such. And after all, to paraphrase Scarlett O'Hara, 1974 would be another day.

So: what would have happened had Kilkenny been at full strength in 1973?

Limerick folk have always pointed out, with some justification, that the replacements can't have been too bad, and – with more finality – that it was Limerick's year and that Kilkenny wouldn't have won even had they had Eamon

Grimes's "ten Eddie Kehers". To Fr Maher, the what-ifs of 1973, all the more acute in view of Kilkenny's copybook performance in the Leinster final, didn't cause any loss of sleep once the balance sheet had been righted the following year. Yes, with a full team Kilkenny might have beaten Limerick in 1973 – but would they have won in '74 if they had? "In retrospect it was great that Limerick won. Otherwise they'd have had no All Ireland since 1940."

Noel Skehan: "Good question. You could say we wouldn't have won in '74 had we won in '73. But when I think of the people on that team, and of Fr Maher, I'm not so sure."

Pat Henderson: "There has always been a doubt in my mind that we would have."

Crisp, the moral victor at Aintree in 1973, never received the opportunity to right the perceived wrong inflicted on him by Red Rum. For him there would be no 1974. For Kilkenny there would be. In hurling, unlike in steeplechasing, there is always another year.

Happily from their point of view, Limerick were back in Croke Park after getting a run on a young Clare outfit early in the provincial decider and sauntering home by 14 points. Kilkenny made harder work of getting there; Wexford played with 14 men for the second half – 40 minutes – of the Leinster final following the dismissal of Phil Wilson, yet stormed back from arrears of seven points at the break to be level at the death. Rather than have the spare man twiddling his thumbs at corner-back, Kilkenny took off Jim Treacy at half-time and sent on 20-year-old Nickey Brennan with instructions to make himself useful around the middle of the field. It was Brennan who won the injury-time free that Eddie Keher converted from a tight angle under the Hogan Stand for the narrowest and most scarcely merited of victories, 6-13 to 2-24.

Galway were swept aside by 15 points in the All Ireland semi-final in Birr, a game in which Brennan lined out at left-half back and had what in his opinion was a "solid but unspectacular" game on Gerry Coone. The selectors didn't see it quite the same way and called up Tom McCormack of James Stephens, another member of the under-21 team, for the All Ireland final.

McCormack was as surprised as anyone else on hearing of his summons. He was even more surprised to discover just how low-key the atmosphere was. After giving it some thought, he came to the conclusion that this was because Fr Maher and most of his troops had soldiered through several campaigns together. They trusted him and he trusted them. There was no shouting or thumping of tubs because there was no need for shouting or thumping of tubs.

McCormack assumed he was there to make up the numbers, a player for the future. The Thursday week before the final, he learned this wasn't quite the case.

Fr Maher sat him down after training, told him he'd watched him with the under-21s and had been impressed. Not only that, he liked what he'd seen of McCormack in training in Nowlan Park. This staggered McCormack: had he not been doing little more than pucking around at the town end while the real business was taking place down the other end of the field between the first-choice backs and forwards? Not quite, it transpired.

"Fr Maher wanted to observe, he said, how I mixed and interacted with the older players, both in training and afterwards in Langton's. Then he asked me two questions I'll never forget. First, did I believe I could fit into the team if he needed me during the match, which really made me sit up and think. And second, would I be nervous if I was called upon? My confidence had been built up a lot by training with the older players, so I said no. It was only afterwards I realised that he'd allowed me the anonymity of training with the also-rans at the town end so I could blend in. It was planned by him and was a masterstroke."

Project McCormack didn't end there. The night the team to play Limerick was announced, Fr Maher detained the youngster in Langton's beforehand and suggested he go home now to avoid the hubbub. And on the day of the final he solved two potential problems at a stroke, detailing Eddie Keher, who the older he got the more nervous before a big match he became, to take McCormack under his wing during the puckaround. McCormack, who like Tommy Maher himself 29 years earlier was making his championship debut on the most daunting stage of all, was so awestruck pucking around with hurling's superstar that he forgot he was supposed to be tense; Keher in his turn was so busy being avuncular that he didn't have time to be. There was one last-minute piece of advice from the trainer. "Hurl your own game. But listen to Henderson."

If Kilkenny were a different team to the one they'd been the previous September, so too were their opponents. They were weary, in mind as well as in body. The commando training that had energised them in 1973 enervated them in '74. Limerick made the mistake, common in new champions, of trying to retain the title by retracing the path they'd taken to gain it. Matt Ruth from Ballyragget was a member of the panel and was taken aback by the intensity of their preparations.

"Very hard physical stuff. Completely different to what I was doing with Kilkenny later on. The training with Limerick was as hard, nearly, as what teams do now, although it didn't start as early in the year. Sprints, press-ups, all of that. If you finished in the last three you'd have to do ten press-ups. So if you started off badly you could end up doing badly all night. It had worked for Limerick in 1973. But a lot of the players maybe didn't have the stomach for the same again in '74."

There was another difference from 12 months earlier. This time, for Kilkenny, it was personal. It wasn't that Limerick had beaten them the year before; it was that, for a number of Kilkenny players, some of their Limerick counterparts had not been gracious in victory. Not for all Kilkenny players. To Pat Lawlor there was "absolutely no issue" with Limerick. To Mick Crotty there was "nothing built up". To Pat Henderson, on the other hand, there was "a nastiness about our games with Limerick". RTE's Donncha Ó Dulaing fetched up in Kilkenny the week before the final and pounced on Henderson for a few words for his radio programme. Have you a message for Limerick next Sunday, Ó Dulaing enquired? "Watch out," Henderson responded.

It set the tone, one that Fr Maher picked up on in the Hollybrook Hotel on the Sunday morning when speaking about "the sneering that went on from Limerick" the previous year. You owe it to yourselves, he told his players, to win and win handsomely. Rarely has a Kilkenny team been as motivated as the one that took the field at Croke Park on September 1st 1974.

Nickey Brennan may have lost his place, but he was as much in tune with the mood as were any of men who started. "Without question there was a fierce determination given the result in 1973. You must remember that some of the great rivalries and on-pitch encounters in the early '70s took place between Kilkenny and Limerick players. To say no quarter was given or asked would be an understatement. To put it bluntly, there was no love lost between the players. For all the skill and technique Fr Maher brought to hurling, the game was ferociously raw on many occasions. Even Kilkenny's best hurler of the era, Eddie Keher, was more than able to defend himself in the most physical of encounters. Fr Tommy may have worn a white collar, but don't think for one minute that he did not realise the need for his players to show total commitment against every opposition. He taught you to respect your opponent but not to fear him. He had a great ability to get players to believe in their own ability to succeed."

Limerick led by 0-6 to 0-1 after 11 minutes. That was as good as it got for them. When the challengers opened the throttle there was no stopping them. Two goals in as many minutes from Mick Brennan and Keher, the latter's a penalty, propelled them into a 3-7 to 1-9 interval lead and by the final whistle the gap had stretched to 12 points, 3-19 to 1-13. The holders, for whom Matt Ruth hit the opening point of the second half, managed only one score in the closing 32 minutes. "Kilkenny were never going to be beaten by Limerick in consecutive

All Irelands really, were they?" asks Billy Fitzpatrick, whose first senior final it was.

Keher finished with 1-11 to his name, making it 5-35 for his four outings in the 1974 championship. Henderson, putting his hurling where his mouth had been, was positively brilliant – "Granite Henderson", John D Hickey called him in the *Irish Independent* the next day. Nicky Orr may have been the captain but Henderson was the leader, as Orr, his fellow Johnstown man, was happy to acknowledge. "I was inspired, and I think everyone else in the side was, by the tremendous play of Pat Henderson. To have a man like him in front of you, you just couldn't help but do well."

Tom McCormack had an uneventful afternoon, largely if not exclusively as a result of the identity of the man on his right. Hurling his own game did indeed, as per Fr Maher's instructions, mean listening to Henderson. "He had these calls. 'I'm going to catch.' 'I'm going to pull.' Pat Lawlor and I listened to him and acted accordingly."

Lawlor: "Playing alongside Pat Henderson had to be the best thing that could happen you as a wing-back. He was outstanding. He played with his brain as well as being a very skilful hurler. I'd come off after a Leinster final and people would be saying that I'd had a great game and Henderson hadn't. That was actually deliberate. Before the match he'd tell me to drop in behind him. He'd go up with Tony Doran or whoever, hold him off and the ball would come through to me, sweeping up behind them. A brilliant player and a brilliant motivator."

Two generations later, Kilkenny's victory over Limerick in the 2007 All Ireland final would constitute the least memorable of their triumphs in the Cody era. Of their triumphs in the Maher era, however, few were more satisfying than success against the same county in 1974.

It didn't answer the question of what might have been in '73. It merely raised it.

CHAPTER 19

Keher

Eddie Keher was the best hurler ever to come out of Kilkenny. Shefflin is a good man, DJ was good, but Eddie was best of all
Theo English, 2011

Stephen Keher from Ballydooley in Roscommon was 24 when he joined the Garda Síochana in March 1922, one of the earliest recruits to the new police force in the new state. After training at Garda headquarters in the Phoenix Park he was posted to Kilkenny city that September, thence to Tullaroan and subsequently, in August 1931, to Inistioge. It was in Inistioge that he met Noreen Browne, whose family ran the newsagents shop in the square. He and Noreen married in 1935. They had a daughter, Eileen, in 1938 and a son, Eddie, on October 14th 1941.

How different would the modern history of Kilkenny hurling be had Stephen Keher remained in the city or in Tullaroan? Not very. How different would the modern history of Kilkenny hurling, and of hurling itself, be had he not been sent to Noreside in the first place? The reader is invited to spend an idle hour speculating.

The Kehers' son learned to take frees at an early age. It wasn't a conscious decision on his part. Martin Walsh, the principal in the school in Inistioge, didn't want a seven-year-old mixing it in the goalmouth with the big boys and decided to put him out of harm's way, taking the frees and dropping them into the square. By then Keher had already changed from left hand on top to an orthodox grip at the behest of Michael Noonan, an older boy from around the corner and later the parish priest of Portarlington. By the age of 12 he was, unsurprisingly, a good freetaker, albeit one who relied largely on intuition. Before he was very much older he was a student in St Kieran's and encountering a man who would show him that freetaking was not about intuition but rather was – or could be – a science based on a system.

His introduction to the school was an awkward one. Stephen Keher had written to De La Salle College in Waterford as well as St Kieran's. The decision to send his son to the latter instead of the former was an 11th-hour one. By the time Eddie arrived in St Kieran's there was no room for him in the dorms, with the result that he was forced to spend the first term sleeping in an attic above the glasshall, sharing a room with four or five other refugees. Of rather more concern to him was the discovery that the teams for the junior leagues had been chosen by this stage. But his reputation had preceded him and a place was speedily found once a row over which team would get him had been settled.

Tommy Maher returned to St Kieran's at the beginning of Keher's second year. Under the junior dean's aegis the teenager would acquire a new freetaking technique; not a habit, which was how he'd taken his frees up to then, but a method. Taking frees, he learned, was a process entailing a number of distinct and separate components, among them the correct placing of the feet, the stance and the follow-through. The most important element of all? Rising the ball in the first place. "Fr Maher's whole philosophy was to practise the skills over and over again. If that's drummed into players often enough, then when the autopilot is on, as it will be in an important match, these habits will kick in and the practice will pay off. You don't have time to think in a big match. It's about doing things automatically."

The 1957 All Ireland colleges final in Thurles was his initial coming of age, the afternoon Keher stepped forward into a new version of himself. At 15 he had no right to be doing anything of the sort. To the day he dies, Liam Hinphey says, he'll see Keher making those runs up the left-hand side of the field that shredded the St Flannan's resistance. He won his second All Ireland colleges medal in 1959, this time as captain. "I can declare quite confidently that had I not gone to St Kieran's, hurling would not have played such an important part in my life. I would not have been prepared for the county team and probably would not have been considered."

If ever a lad did not deserve to finish on the losing side in an All Ireland minor final it was he. He played in two and shone in both. Kilkenny were a little unfortunate in 1957, losing by 4-7 to 3-7 to Tipperary after conceding two soft goals in the second half. Keher, still 15, hit four points in a manner the *Irish Independent* described as "reminiscent of Terry Leahy and Jim Langton".

Two years later they were more than unfortunate. Having led from the 20th minute, they were a goal ahead with three minutes left in spite of the loss of the injured Fan Larkin at half-time. Then a sideline ball was wrongly awarded to Tipperary, which led to them winning a 21-yard free which should also have gone the other way. The rigging danced and Tipp won by a point, 2-8 to 2-7. But there was little doubt that the man of the match was the chap in stripes who'd landed six points, even if – as in 1957 – his fellow forwards were not on the same wavelength and a number of passes he gave went astray. Such imprecision wouldn't have occurred had he been wearing black and white hoops and surrounded by colleagues who knew what he'd do next. "Eddie Keher was in a class of his own," the *Kilkenny People* reported. "Easily the outstanding individual performer of the 30 he delighted the vast crowd with his jinking solo runs, deceptive swerves and beautifully executed points. His display was representative of Kilkenny hurling at its best."

The call-up to senior ranks followed immediately. Keher featured against Dublin in the Oireachtas and Wexford in the Walsh Cup before being added to the panel for the All Ireland replay against Waterford. After a quarter of an hour he was in for Johnny McGovern. There he would remain for the next 18 years, his two points in the second half serving as a preview of forthcoming attractions.

Keher was more than just another handy minor. He was more, even, than an exceptionally gifted one. He was a boy wonder who unlike many another boy wonder developed into a man. Seán Clohosey by his own admission wasn't physically able for the vicissitudes of the lions' den against Tipperary. Keher, who was bigger than Christy Ring, was more than able. John Doyle named the three most dangerous opponents he faced in his career as Ring, Jimmy Smyth of Clare and Keher. That tells its own tale.

That Keher would not be an overnight sensation was due to the surroundings in which he found himself. The 1957 All Ireland-winning team was disassembling. The Kilkenny side of the 1960s would not be fully formed until well after the cream of the three in a row-winning minors had found their way upwards. A National League medal did come his way in 1962, but the feeling had taken root in some quarters that Keher, irrespective of his youth, was capable of more than he was showing and was rather too laidback for his own good.

The night of the last training session before the 1963 All Ireland final, he was going in the front door of Langton's when he encountered his old mentor. Fr Maher, who may or may not have agreed with the laidback theory but had unquestionably heard it, fixed him with gimlet eye. "Now Eddie, make up your mind to be dug out of these lads on Sunday."

At all costs, Keher decided, he had to convert his first free. But the first free Kilkenny were awarded against Waterford was a tricky one, at an angle out on the right, hard against the sideline. So he played the percentages and lobbed it into the square. Ninety seconds later an easier free presented itself and Keher was off and running. By afternoon's end he'd had 14 shots and scored 14 points. Having cleared his throat with those two points in 1959, he was now trumpeting his talent from the rooftops. Valhalla I am coming.

He joined the hosts of heaven long before the end of his career. Every season between 1959 and 1972, bar 1964, he accumulated over 100 points. In 1971 he surpassed Nicky Rackard's 1956 record of 30-35 from 19 games by hitting 8-141 in 17. For three decades his championship total of 35-334 in 50 appearances stood as a record until surpassed by Henry Shefflin. His scoring total from play, 19-135 or an average of 3.84 points a game, weathered the passing of the seasons also, although Shefflin had closed to within four points of it by the end of 2011.

In his ten All Ireland finals Keher scored 7-74; Henry Shefflin managed 4-60 in his 11 appearances up to 2011, his truncated contributions in 2007 and 2010 included. Keher's 2-11 against Tipperary in 1971 was the highest total by a player on a losing side, and his 2-9 against Cork the following year remained the highest total by a player on a winning side until Nicky English surpassed it in 1989. His All Ireland scoring figures read as follows:

Year	Placed balls	Play	Total
1959 replay:	0-0	0-2	0-2
1963:	0-10	0-4	0-14
1964:	0-2	0-0	0-2
1966:	0-6	0-1	0-7
1967:	0-1	0-2	0-3 *
1969:	0-6	0-2	0-8
1971:	1-7	1-4	2-11
1972:	1-7	1-2	2-9
1974:	1-6	0-5	1-11
1975:	1-5	1-2	2-7

* Went off injured after 43 minutes.

An annus mirabilis? Keher didn't have one. Every year was an annus mirabilis with him, to the extent that what initially was the astonishing eventually became the mundane. For "Dog bites man" read "Keher hits big total".

As the GAA statistician Leo McGough revealed, Keher scored from play in 94 per cent of his championship outings (Henry Shefflin did likewise in 84 per cent of his up to the end of 2011 and DJ Carey in 79 per cent of his); he scored at least one point from play in 92 per cent of them (Shefflin did so in 82 per cent and Carey in 66 per cent); and he scored a goal in 34 per cent of them (Shefflin and Carey 37 per cent each).

All through his career Keher did nothing but score. For seven successive seasons he was the game's leading marksman: 10-85 in 1966, 13-65 in '67, 9-76 in '68, 16-77 in '69, 8-70 in 1970, 8-141 in '71 and 20-134 in '72. He averaged 3.30 points from play in his All Ireland final appearances compared to Shefflin's 2.45 and Carey's 2.33.

It need hardly be added what a joy he was to play with. Ask Mick Crotty, provider of the monstrous handpass for his second goal against Galway in 1975. "If you passed the ball to Keher or he stood over a free, all you had to do was run back out to your position for the puckout." Besides, being built to take care of himself, tough opponents he could cope with. He preferred them, in fact. Tipperary's Mick Burns, on the other hand, was an uncomfortably sticky proposition because he wasn't a hard nut and he didn't try to be. "A great wing-back. I always found it harder to play on a skilful half-back than a half-back with what you might call 'a reputation'. The skilful guys concentrated on the ball. They dashed out ahead of you, whipped up the ball and away down the field with it."

The first All Star team was selected in 1971. Keher was left-half forward. "For his consummate artistry, the poise and grace he brings to his chosen sport," the citation read. It could not have been better phrased.

The greatest Keher goal? Impossible to say, but Kieran Purcell nominates one he scored at the Gaelic Grounds in a National League game at the height of the rivalry with Limerick. The sliotar was going wide near the corner flag on the left. Seamus Horgan, off his line, was watching it dribble out. Keher, almost on the endline, pulled left-handed from the most fantastically acute of angles. The ball hit the near post, ricocheted off the far post and in over the goalline. "Is it luck with you or have you a gift?" Purcell asked him at half-time.

The most important Keher goal? Probably the one that precipitated the avalanche against Cork in 1972. Twenty-two minutes left, Kilkenny eight points down and Keher standing over a 21-yard free a little to the right of centre. "What would you do, chum?" Micheál O'Hehir enquired of his viewers. "Would you be satisfied with a point? You have a long time to go. Or would you go for a goal? Here he comes! And he's got it!"

The precise moment when Keher began to transcend said chosen sport is not easy to gauge. Perhaps it was in 1975 when, as part of their buildup to the All Ireland final, *The Irish Times* despatched Paddy Downey to interview Fr Maher and, rather more imaginatively, a female staff writer to interview Keher. The latter duo met up over Cidonas in a Kilkenny hotel bar. The ensuing article might have been written by a starry-eyed teenage girl.

"Not only is he elegant in build, but he has an ascetic look that you can imagine melting into the bank atmosphere... Almost Plantagenet. Or else a senior brother in a closed order. Or a behind-the-scenes, policy bank man... The flaring egotism and pride of a Jane Austen heroine..." Phew.

Such was the tenor of the piece that the editor of the *St Kieran's College Record* was moved to observe, with his customary elegant astringency, that "when somebody called Elgy Gillespie writes of Eddie Keher that 'his long face is reserved, almost devotional, his nose is thin and arched, and his large beautiful eyes have the spirituality of a man who contemplates,' then press coverage of Kilkenny, and of St Kieran's, has reached a sublime level of objectivity that even Ms Gillespie's association, as pupil and colleague, with Paddy Downey cannot tarnish. For Ms Gillespie has no known connection with the college, the city or the county (other than that of being a sympathetic visitor to all of them). She is not subject to the authority of a past pupil of the college. She has no intimate knowledge or experience of hurling, and may very well have lived in the belief that Nowlan Park is a new housing estate in Kilkenny named after Liam Nolan. In short, the woman has nothing at all to gain by being nice to Kilkenny, to St Kieran's or to Eddie Keher, whose virtue is, in any case, beyond question."

To children in the Ireland of the 1970s, among them the Tuam band The Saw Doctors who decades later namechecked him in a song, Keher was the man. There was the photograph with Muhammad Ali. An *Irish Press* editorial and an appearance on *The Late Late Show* following his retirement. Chairing the Kilkenny jury for the National Song Contest one year with Gay Byrne desperately hoping that the phone link between Montrose and the Springhill Hotel would work. His three eldest children, Eamon, Clodagh and Deirdre, popping up sometime in the late 1970s on an RTE programme, unimaginable now, entitled *Whose Baby?* in which panellists attempted to identify the famous parents of the featured offspring. The doctorate from the University of Limerick. A place on the Team of the Century and another on the Team of the Millennium and no debate, still less an argument, about either.

The biography was an inevitability. Ultan Macken, a Galway man living in Dublin, was at the time the GAA correspondent of the *RTE Guide*. Every year he'd attend the Leinster final in Croke Park. Every year he'd see Keher doing what Keher did so well. Keher's role in the destruction of Galway in the 1975 All Ireland final concentrated Macken's mind further, painful and all an afternoon as it was for him. The next step was obvious.

Eddie Keher's Hurling Life took Macken, a son of the acclaimed novelist Walter Macken and a fan of Raymond Smith's GAA books, three years to research and write and involved regular trips to Kilkenny to interview the player, numerous teammates and Fr Maher. Macken spent the weekend of the 1977 county final chez Keher in Newpark Lawn in Kilkenny city and at one stage even took part in a training session in Nowlan Park. The original draft of the book, which went on sale in 1978, ran to 300 pages, but Mercier Press cut it back to 150 pages. The finished product garnered considerable publicity in view of its subject's profile and ended up selling about 3,000 copies, a respectable figure without being overwhelming.

The final chapter of the career was short and silly and messy. Rower-Inistioge lost that 1977 county final to the Fenians. Coming on top of the three games it had taken them to dispose of Muckalee-Ballyfoyle Rangers in the semi-final, Keher was left disappointed and drained. After the team ate in the Newpark Hotel that night Dick Bolger, the Rower-Inistioge representative on the county selection committee, asked him if he was okay for Kilkenny's league match the following Sunday. Keher replied that he was "wrecked" and couldn't see himself turning out.

When the team was announced without E Keher in it, John O'Shea of the *Evening Press* put two and two together, rang Newpark Lawn and made it add up to four. Before he knew it Keher, who in his innocence didn't consider his immediate playing plans or lack thereof to be newsworthy, was all over the headlines and being shoved into a retirement he hadn't actually contemplated and now couldn't disentangle himself from. When the Kilkenny seniors and minors took the field at Croke Park the following September, it was the first time since 1957 for the county to be involved in one final or the other, 1973 apart, without Eddie Keher being togged out.

It may have seemed like the end of everything when he retired. But Kilkenny survived, just as they would a generation later when DJ Carey's departure in 2005 was followed by MacCarthy Cup success in 2006. Call it the line of apostolic succession. Jim Langton gave way to Keher. Keher gave way to DJ. DJ, who scored goals that seemed never to have been scored before and who, to misquote Raymond Chandler on the oeuvre of Dashiell Hammett, scored them over and over again, gave way to Henry Shefflin. Unto every generation is born a great Kilkenny forward, as Paddy Buggy liked to observe.

It took Buggy, who idolised Langton, a long time to concede that DJ Carey may have been his superior. Eventually, and not without a considerable mental struggle, he did. In Buggy's eyes Langton was "the stylist supreme", Carey the greatest artist he saw on a hurling field – and Keher a better, more effective forward than either.

"Langton's striking was beautiful and crisp. He had such rhythm in his arms. He was much the same build as DJ. Good shoulders, a good pair of hips, not easy to upset. Neither of them was a big man but they were both strong men. Keher on the other hand was a big man and one who always rose to the big occasion. If I were asked to pick a man who'd win an All Ireland for you as a forward I'd go for Keher." And Shefflin? Well, that's one for another day. But this much can fairly be said. While Carey and Shefflin may have equalled or even bettered Keher in some aspects of the game, they never surpassed him. Because Keher was unsurpassable.

Why he roll-lifted the sliotar where Shefflin jab-lifted it is easily explained, by the by. "You couldn't jab-lift it in my time. No grass. You might take a 21-yard free and there'd be loughs of water everywhere. Your best chance of rising the ball then was to roll-lift it. That was what I stuck to. Even placing the ball for a free meant taking extra care because at the time the rims were much more severe than they are now. You took the smooth part of the ball for rising so that you weren't cutting across the rims. Fr Maher was always advocating a ball like a baseball. He couldn't see the need for rims."

Keher is not a member of the In My Day Club. Ask him if the hurling of the 21st century is better than that of his era and he replies instantly that "it has to be". The skill level is higher, the equipment and pitches better. "Every sport develops because people look at the players and try to emulate them and do things better. And you have the science now. Fantastic pitches, lovely sliotars, hurleys made to measure. Hurling has to have got better and it *is* better. The skill level is phenomenal."

Phenomenal. Like Keher himself.

CHAPTER 20

Galway

The hurlers of both counties [Kilkenny and Wexford] favour the lifting and handling game, although their striking differs, Kilkenny's being sharper, more fluent and economical, scientific almost to the point of mathematical calculation and technical precision

Paddy Downey, *The Irish Times*, October 7th 1975

Another luxuriant winter on Noreside, another celebratory *Kilkenny GAA Yearbook*. Peter Holohan, the editor, hailed 1974 as "without doubt the greatest year in Kilkenny hurling history". This was getting to be a habit. But Mick O'Neill's wish from the *Yearbook* of two years earlier – successive All Irelands for the first time since 1932-33 – had not yet been made flesh. The new season would see this oversight rectified.

Interviewed in the *Yearbook*, Mick Lanigan cast some light on the secrets, such as they were, of the Kilkenny training regime. Physical strength, he stressed, was not a prerequisite. The training sessions were "short and sharp" and entailed ten minutes warming up, a quantity of ground hurling and a practice match of 20 minutes per half, extending to 40 minutes per half coming up to an All Ireland final. The wind-down consisted of physical exercises and a few sprints.

"The skills of most players will increase as they grow older and all the trainer has to do is to ensure the players are fit enough to sustain this skill over the full period of the game," Lanigan elaborated. "A trainer has to become part of the team, to knit the players into a cohesive unit. He has to ensure that all the players are motivated 100 per cent towards the task in hand and if the trainer fails in this regard he is unsatisfactory. In Kilkenny we tend to spend more time during training on playing hurling than most other counties. If you ask a player to do, say, 20 sprints at short intervals he might say it is impossible but if he is asked to play in a seven-a-side match he will work harder and it will be of greater benefit."

One thing that made life easier for everyone, Lanigan avowed, was the presence of Fr Maher. "He knows more about hurling than anyone I know and it is impossible not to be impressed by his accurate analysis, whether it is of Kilkenny or our opponents. I think it would be impossible for any player, under Father Maher's influence, not to give the last ounce of his energy. We have had many books on hurling. I look forward to the day when we will have one by Father Maher."

(A quick sidebar. Lanigan, later a member of the Senate, secured sponsorship via a business contact for some gear for the team – a set of shorts or socks – prior to one of the All Irelands. The sponsors were an obscure Dublin bank with an office in Manchester. Anglo Irish Bank.)

Another encomium to the coach came from Kieran Cuddihy, the team doctor, at that stage two decades in town and by now *Kilkenniores sunt Kilkenniis*, who declared: "I don't know if he ever played chess. But if he did I'd be confident he would have been a grandmaster."

To Pat Lawlor, Fr Maher's eye for a player was "like an x-ray. He was a great reader of players and always emphasising the importance of peripheral vision. How to anticipate something happening and take action before it happened." Analysing the strengths and weaknesses of the opposition was second nature to him. Going through the individual match-ups prior to the 1973 All Ireland final he came to Lawlor, who'd be marking Bernie Hartigan. "You'll be too fast for him," was all Fr Maher said. And Lawlor was. I know my own and my own know me...

If all was right off the field, all was similarly ship-shape on it. The stalwarts of the 1960s – Ollie Walsh, Ted Carroll, Seamus Cleere, Martin Coogan, Paddy Moran et al – had vacated the stage and been replaced. Ned Byrne had departed to set about adding seven Irish rugby caps to his All Ireland medal, but the troupe now included Billy Fitzpatrick, the star of the 1972 minor team. The individual joins were invisible because the collective transition was seamless. And the team's defensive sheet anchor remained as fixed and unyielding as Kilkenny Castle. Pat Henderson, who'd spent his first couple of years on the team trying to protect Ollie from marauding forwards, had long ago learned from Fr Maher what to do at centre-back and what not to do.

"The most important thing for the half-back line was to be solid. Don't let the ball pass you and you end up facing your own goal. Be unrelenting under the puckout. Fr Maher wasn't too interested in dramatic catches. Block the ball, drop it at your feet, hit it. On to the next line and let them take it from there. Exhibition stuff wasn't his cup of tea. He mightn't say it, but he didn't like a guy turning around to hit a ball 80 yards. Much better to hit a quick 50-yard ball that the opposing team would hate. I'd know what type of ball to hit and to what position. That was the unseen part of coaching. And the forwards were encouraged all the time to anticipate, and the more you practise the better you anticipate. Tom Walsh was very good at that in the 1960s, always breaking fast for a ball. But in the 1970s we had real ball winners in Delaney and Purcell. Any kind of ball. You could put it down on top of their heads. Like with the Kilkenny forward line under Brian Cody."

It may not have been a team of all the talents but it was the next best thing, an outfit with perfect balance. A brilliant goalkeeper. Defenders who were physically strong, defenders who could hurl – Henderson fitted both categories, obviously – and, to Skehan's right, the one and only Fan Larkin. An iron fist/velvet glove midfield pairing. A forward line that combined self-sufficiency and a jagged edge with incisiveness and accuracy, topped off by the presence of the triggerman to end all triggermen.

It also had its share of unsung heroes, notably Pat Lawlor – Kieran Cuddihy's favourite player – in defence and Mick Crotty up front. For the 1971 All Ireland final Lawlor had featured at midfield, where he modelled himself on his fellow Bennettsbridge man Paddy Moran. "His positional sense, how he made room for himself – Paddy was an expert at that," Lawlor says. More comfortable in defence, he thereafter made the number five jersey his own. The number ten shirt belonged to Crotty, who didn't do much talking either. He didn't have to. "League or championship, Crotty was just Crotty," according to Kieran Purcell. "The bigger the occasion, the better he was. And with Keher, you didn't have to look for him. He was always in the right place."

Purcell himself was one half of the kind of attacking double act not seen in the black and amber before or since. Purcell and Pat Delaney. They hewed wood, they drew water, they made goals and they scored them. They weren't dissimilar in looks and physique, but in terms of style they were no twins. Purcell, who had played in goal for the county at under-age level, was the more gifted hurler, Delaney the stronger man ("way stronger", Purcell insists). Purcell preferred centre-forward to full-forward because of the extra space it afforded, excelled under the dropping ball – a byproduct of his Gaelic football background in Windgap – and was an expert when it came to guarding his catching hand. Delaney was set low to the ground and directed the attacks with a baton of steel. He wasn't subtle and he didn't try to be.

"Between them they gave Eddie Keher the freedom to exercise his skills as distinct from having to take a lot of abuse," Pat Henderson says. Over time, Keher agrees, it became second nature to him to read their game and feed off them. "They added years to my career." It was usually left up to the pair of them to decide when to switch with one another. In practice this involved Delaney doing the ordering. "Hey, Purcell, come out!" "Hey, Purcell, go back!"

Bliss it was in this dawn to be alive and a Kilkenny hurler. "It was just brilliant," Liam O'Brien recalls wistfully. "People would actually stop and let you cross the road." Groupies were few, Wags had yet to be invented, but there were guest appearances and awards ceremonies and trips to America, and though the booze flowed ceaselessly a certain air of innocent enjoyment suffused it all. Not every member of the team hailed from a traditional hurling powerhouse, which made life on the other side of the velvet railing a little miracle for the ones who didn't. Kieran Purcell, for instance, was from Windgap, where nobody had ever won an All Ireland medal. "To come from a small club and be put on a team like that…"

Johnny Campion drove the Hehirs bus that carried them to matches. Bill Sullivan, a butcher in John Street and sidekick of Paddy Grace, and PJ O'Neill from James Stephens, better known as Flukey Nale, were among the faces in the dressing room. One of the team's most fervent supporters was Felicity Lewis, a jovial Church of Ireland lady from opposite Langton's in John Street. Tom Brett took the photos for the *Kilkenny People*. In his own way he too was living the dream.

"It was such a buzz. They were my heroes. I admired them so much. There was no such thing as a telephoto lens at the time so you were literally almost in the goalmouth. Ollie was the goalie when I started off and when he'd go to clear a ball he'd always bring it out to the side. I'd have to physically get myself back out of the way because otherwise he'd have run into me. I never realised how big many of them were until I'd see them stripped in the dressing room. It was probably the stripes that made them look thinner.

"Semple Stadium wasn't a great place to take photos. When you stood up you were in people's way. Often you'd get a stone in the back of the head. An occupational hazard. But Croke Park on All Ireland day was alright. I'd stay in a B & B on Jones's Road, which meant you had a parking space, and go to the handball on the Saturday night. Then next morning it was straight across the road and in. There was no formal arrangement for taking a team photo, nothing to suit TV like there is now. I'd have my back to the Canal End. The lads liked having their photo taken, but they also liked to pretend they didn't. I'd try and get them together before the officials came along and took over. I'd shout, 'Lads, give us a picture, please!' 'Hurry up, Tom!'

"One year I felt subconsciously there was something wrong with the picture. It turned out someone was missing. I should have known who it was: Fan! He had a fixation about where he wanted to be photographed. It was always in the back row with the big guys, right at the end. But this year he was late out because he was getting an injection from Kieran Cuddihy. [True. The picture of the 1972 All Ireland-winning team contains 14 players.]

"You could move around the pitch during a match back then instead of having to stay in the same spot the whole time. And that Kilkenny team were so good, so consistent, that sometimes you could sense a goal coming and you could get yourself into position for it. Pat Henderson once told me I'd seen more action in Croke Park than any Kilkenny hurler of the previous 40 years. He probably had a point."

Langton's and Nowlan Park were the popular places of pilgrimage for the faithful, their Lourdes and their Fatima. A third was the Hollybrook Hotel in Clontarf, where Kilkenny had stayed on All Ireland weekend since 1957. In this metropolitan home from home the supporters did not forget where they came from. One year a barman announced on the Sunday night that they'd sold more Smithwick's in the past 24 hours than they'd sold all year.

Then there was Wexford. Always. Every summer without fail. How Wexford kept coming back year after year, their spirit unbroken, is one of the untold stories of 1970s hurling. Kilkenny had the better players, but not by much. They had the better team, but often only barely. And they had better guidance from the sideline, at least if Fr Maher was to be believed. At half-time in one Leinster final the Kilkenny selectors were fretting about what moves to make. Relax, he told them politely. "We'll let the Wexford lads make the changes because they generally make the wrong ones."

Was it possible to feel sorry for Wexford? "I do now," Pat Henderson offers. "Not then."

The 1975 showdown proved to be far from the thriller of the previous year. Aided by 11 Wexford wides in the first half, the holders led by four points at the interval and went on to win by six, 2-20 to 2-14. The *Irish Independent* named Brian Cody, here to stay as Jim Treacy's successor, as their sports star of the week. Cody finished the year an All Star. His citation read: "For the supreme self-assurance and the exciting spirit of adventure he has shown at such an early stage of his senior career."

The win against Wexford should have been the precursor to a rematch of 1972 with Cork. Mick Crotty married Evelyn on July 30th and honeymooned in Rome. The newlyweds had scarcely touched down in Dublin airport when they heard some sensational news. Galway had beaten Cork in the All Ireland semi-final.

Cork may have been, and probably were, overconfident – understandable but not forgivable, seeing that Galway had been coming for a while and in 1972 were All Ireland under-21 champions with a group that included Frank Burke, Joe McDonagh, PJ Molloy and Iggy Clarke. What's more, far from being dark horses in 1975 they were the season's form horse after winning the National League for the first time since 1951. Along the way they beat Cork in the quarter-final, Kilkenny in the semi-final – a game in which Fan Larkin was sent off for fighting with his marker Pádraig Fahy ("You did the manly thing by dropping your hurley, Fan," John Moloney told him, "but I'm still sending you off!") – and Tipperary in the final.

"We put a lot of time into building the team during the league," recalls Seán Silke, the Galway centre-back, "and winning it gave us a bit of momentum. And we had a number of players who'd been doing well in the Fitzgibbon Cup. Inky Flaherty, a great Galway hurler of the past, was an army guy and he knew how to train a team. He was very positive and encouraging. But the big thing was that the players had come up through under-age ranks, had gained experience and were now ready to deliver."

The All Ireland semi-final took place on one of the hottest days of one of the hottest summers of the century. Cork may have been "a bit rusty" after winning Munster, Silke surmises. In any event Galway hit them hard and hit them from the off. They scored a couple of goals early on, they continued to get scores at opportune times and come the end they had two points in hand, 4-15 to 2-19. Modern Galway hurling began that afternoon.

There was no shilly-shallying from Fr Maher when interviewed by Paddy Downey for *The Irish Times* prior to the All Ireland final. Galway, he predicted, wouldn't get early goals, they wouldn't score more than two goals in the course of the game and while they were the faster team and might get a couple of breakaway scores, this was unlikely to be enough. "Otherwise I can't see them beating us."

For the benefit of readers who might have missed it amid all the fuss about Galway, he pointed out that Kilkenny had a considerable incentive themselves. "This team has now got to show that they are as good as, if not better than, the teams of the thirties." They had been together for so long, he added, there was practically no coaching necessary any more. His next words could have been uttered in 1957. "In the past we have had great teams of individuals, but let's not overlook this fact: there was little or no effort at coordination in those days. Nowadays combination teamwork is almost perfected; there is no point going out without it."

Why did coaching matter, Downey enquired?

"In the past, I suppose, great players like Christy Ring got certain things wrong hundreds of times. Then they did it right once and they knew it was right. They had discovered the correct methods by trial and error. Few will do that nowadays. They must be taught and they must acquire the skills pretty quickly and effectively or they will not carry on at the game. That's why coaching is absolutely necessary. I remember when I was laughed at for practising the handpass. When I began coaching the Kilkenny team, nobody handpassed the ball, it just wasn't done. Nowadays you're lost if you don't use the handpass. It has speeded up the game and made it more attractive. Some people would like to abolish it and go back to hip-to-hip and shoulder-to-shoulder belting on the ball, but I don't agree with that at all."

His system of coaching? Explain, demonstrate, practise. "Take a player who is not good at lifting the ball. You don't say to him, 'Lift the ball the right way.' You get down to it yourself and you say, 'This is the right way.' You bend your back and place your hurl almost parallel to the ground and you hit the grass about two inches at your side of the ball. Then you slide your hurl in under the ball and in that way you will never fail to lift it."

Contemporary freetakers did not impress him, it appeared. "The one thing that matters, the ball, they will look at the ball for only a couple of seconds. And they will look at the post for 20 seconds, which counts for nil, provided they've taken up the right stance. To do it the correct way you stand over the ball and say, 'I'm going to get you off the ground, I'm going to get you up anyway.' And when the ball comes up you automatically hit it. You can't miss it."

Downey closed the interview with a gently hopped sliotar of his own. Did Fr Maher enjoy his job? The response may have surprised him.

Asked in 1957 to coach Kilkenny, he answered, he had "accepted reluctantly and, reluctantly, I have continued to the present day". Granted, he'd "had a modicum of success" and he couldn't say he hadn't enjoyed it. "But there are times when I say to myself, you're the biggest idiot that ever was; instead of training a team on a summer's evening you could be relaxing at the seaside.

"But I have enjoyed it, yes, and I suppose I've brought a certain amount of pleasure to the players. But if I were starting again and knew what was in front of me, I don't think I'd do it. But that's true of everything in life, isn't it?"

Seán Silke has carte blanche to blame Galway's failure in the final on the county losing the collective run of itself during the buildup. He doesn't because the county didn't. Training went well in Kenny Park in Athenry. There was an air of excitement that never reared out of control and became a frenzy. The local naysayers didn't give them a chance; the optimists took refuge in the indisputable fact that Kilkenny were getting old. Then the game started. All too soon, and not wholly because this was the first 70-minute final, it was over. "It passed us by. Most of the players didn't play as well as they could."

After a rasper of a goal from Frank Burke in the 19th minute, Galway went

22 minutes without a score. Kilkenny led by 0-9 to 1-3 at half-time and kicked on. Within a few minutes of the restart the gap had stretched to eight points. Play Micheál O'Hehir...

"Oh, lovely fielding by Brian Cody! What a wonderful young hurler he is! And here comes Michael Crotty...And this is Eddie Keher...And that's a goal!"

Crotty hit five points. Liam O'Brien, on the way to the Hurler of the Year award, was unstoppable. Fan Larkin had his revenge for the league semi-final by rendering Pádraig Fahy "almost as inconspicuous as if he were at home in Carnmore", to quote John D Hickey next day. Kilkenny 2-22 Galway 2-10.

A bloodless victory, yes, but it was never going to be otherwise. Galway had performed about as well or as badly as rank outsiders and big-day debutants were entitled to. Raymond Smith rounded up Eamonn Cregan and Mick Burns afterwards and quoted them in the *Irish Independent* to the effect that – naturally – the game would have been entirely different had Kilkenny faced Munster opposition. What everyone failed to recognise, understandably enough in view of the margin of defeat, was that this would be no one-off September appearance for Galway. The Tribesmen were back to stay. Hurling acutely needed an emerging new power. Now it had one.

The winning captain was Billy Fitzpatrick, who a month later in Dungarvan picked up his second successive All Ireland under-21 medal as Kilkenny defeated Cork in a coruscating affair, 5-13 to 2-19. At Fraher Field he was required to play his part. At Croke Park he'd been required simply to play his position. That and kiss the Archbishop of Cashel's ring beforehand.

"If you looked for a better team to come into, a better forward line, you couldn't have got one. Imagine having Pat Delaney alongside you, doing all the hard work and taking the knocks. I suppose I was meant to be doing most of the running. I was only learning the game. Learning it with a great group, but learning all the same."

One crutch that aided Fitzpatrick was Fr Maher's matchday *cúpla focal*. "A great motivational speaker. He'd talk to us around 12.30 on the day of the final. No roaring or shouting. Prior to that you'd be in bits. I would be anyway, the nerves taking over. But after listening to him you'd forget about how nervous you'd be and you could settle into it."

For the edification of readers of the *Kilkenny GAA Yearbook* that winter, Peter Holohan roped in Smith and Pádraig Puirséal to anoint and contextualise the MacCarthy Cup holders. To Smith they should have been, if not a three in a row team, then at any rate a four out of five team. Like Pat Henderson does, he identified 1971 rather than 1973 as the one that got away. "Had the selectors shown the courage to start Skehan in 1971 they must have beaten Tipperary... On his 1966 or '67 form Ollie would never have conceded a few of the goals he let in that day." They were not, Smith went on, a great side in every position, but they were ever dangerous in attack "because of the triangle of Keher-Delaney-Purcell".

Skehan, who he had never seen concede a soft goal in the championship, he now considered to be better than his predecessor: "Only Ollie could have kept Skehan out for so long." And he had kind words too for Henderson, "brilliant" in the 1972 and '74 All Ireland finals. "He may have some of the Tipperary steel in him but he is a stylist in the true Kilkenny sense."

Pádraig Puirséal, who'd been watching Kilkenny since 1926, had broken bread with men who had seen them even earlier than that. One evening in Moore's Hotel in Cork after a coursing meeting he was introduced as a Kilkenny man by Tough Barry to Dave 'Daw' McGrath of the old Redmonds. "I've said this before, boy, and I say it again," quoth Daw. "Anybody that didn't see Kilkenny between 1907 and 1913 never saw hurlers."

The best Kilkenny team Puirséal saw in the old days he judged to be that of 1935. "That 'wet day' final was unforgettable. I can still see the shower of raindrops fly from the net at the Railway End after Martin White's bulletlike shot beat Paddy Scanlon for a vital second-half goal... Though so many of them have gone, too early, to their eternal reward, those men of 1935 will never fade from my memory but they must still rank second in my book to the consistently brilliant squads that Fr Tommy Maher and Mick Lanigan have trained and tutored so successfully these past five years."

By the time the 1975 *Yearbook* was published, 1974 had been replaced as Kilkenny's greatest year ever. All Ireland senior champions, minor champions, under-21 champions, vocational champions. St Kieran's were colleges kingpins again and Pat Ryan from – aptly – Gowran won the Féile na nGael skills competition.

They'd never had it so good. Three decades would pass before they'd have it as good again.

CHAPTER 21

Twilight

I was fading out at that stage
Tommy Maher

By rights Tommy Maher should have stepped down as Kilkenny coach on the evening of September 7th 1975 or in the days or weeks shortly afterwards. He had come, seen and conquered. He had recast Kilkenny hurling in his own cerebral image. He had taken the county from genteel poverty to Nob Hill. His mission was accomplished and his comments in the Paddy Downey interview spoke of a man whose heart was no longer in it. What was once a celestial fire was now embers.

He would stay on for another three seasons. One golden afternoon was left to him and the players. But only the one.

If the coach was becoming slightly detached from things and had no new tricks to impart, this was either not apparent or didn't seem to matter. The ship was ploughing ahead as surely and steadily as she had ever done, and while most of the officers were the wrong side of 30 there were new hands, all of them accustomed to success, coming aboard from the county's under-age ranks the whole time. Kilkenny had not achieved an All Ireland three in a row since 1911-13, and even then one of the titles was won in the committee room. The new hurling season was an unwritten narrative involving one storyline and one storyline only. Could Kilkenny make history? And if not, who the hell was going to stop them?

The great disaster of 1976 can be related partly by recourse to dates. On April 4th they met Cork in the National League semi-final in Thurles, a game that a late Seánie O'Leary penalty goal sent to a replay. On April 25th the sides met again, nine points from Eddie Keher helping his team to a 2-17 to 3-10 win. May 9th brought the county's first appearance in a National League final since the ill starred 1968 affair against Tipperary, the novelty of the pairing – Clare, their opponents, hadn't won the competition since 1946 – drawing a crowd in excess of 30,000 to Semple Stadium. A splendid contest ensued, with late goals for the underdogs by Tom Crowe and Noel Casey bringing about a 2-9 to 0-15 draw.

The replay was delayed until late June as a result of Kilkenny's impending trip to the US. When they reached southern California, Fr Maher stayed in Los Angeles with a friend, Fr Tom Healy from Coon, and brought Tom McCormack, whose mother had been a next-door neighbour of the Healys, with him. One evening by way of R & R the three of them headed to Las Vegas and let their hair down. Dinner, a couple of drinks, a Charlie Rich concert. Proceedings took a twist when the dancing girls came on. *Topless* dancing girls. Tom McCormack "turned puce". Tommy Maher, being in his own modest way a man of the world, didn't bat an eyelid. "Tom, don't worry. Behind this collar we're men too. And we'll enjoy the show!"

On the Sunday morning Fr Maher said Mass at Fr Healy's church. It was a typically swift Maheresque ceremony with a typically pithy Maheresque sermon, short and concise and to the point, no waffle or flannel or extended metaphors. As with his hurling, so with his homilies. Afterwards some parishioners were heard to say that they'd "barely got Mass at all".

The rematch with Clare took place on June 20th and attracted a still larger attendance, amounting to over 35,000 spectators, to Semple Stadium. This time around they didn't get value for their money. Kilkenny were at their fearsome best, hit three goals in the opening quarter and cantered home by 6-14 to 1-14, with Pat Delaney bagging a hat-trick. It was the 1973 Leinster final all over again and it was the last great display and the last national title of the Maher era. As in 1973, the MacCarthy Cup looked Kilkenny's and nobody else's.

Clare hadn't come to tug the forelock in the drawn game, the result being that a certain amount of timber was applied. They later heard their opponents had been so outraged at this insolence that they'd trained for the replay while in America. It wasn't true. The Kilkenny team of the 1970s didn't require grudges for fuel. Eddie Keher: "We just wanted to win games and the competitive spirit among the lads was so strong that that's what we went out to do every time we played."

But the fixtures were piling up. The league semi-final and replay. The league final and replay. Not just two unnecessary games for an ageing team: *four* unnecessary games. A fortnight after murdering Clare, the champions travelled to Mullingar for a Leinster semi-final date with Westmeath, who'd beaten an Offaly team containing Damien Martin, Pádraig Horan, Pad Joe Whelahan and a young Pat Carroll by three points in the first round in Croke Park. It was July 4th, the bicentennial of US independence, and a scorcher; the "ices, ices, anyone for the last few ices" men in Cusack Park made a fortune. A scoreline of 5-22 to 1-12 concealed some blotches, primarily a disjointed first-half performance. "It was so warm and fatigue was starting to set in," Keher recalls. "It took us until midway through the second half to get going."

Could a train be heard whistling down the tracks? Not by the county board, who fixed the next round of the local championship – at the time knockout, and therefore more attritional, rather than league – for the weekend before the Leinster final. One of the fixtures pitched the two clubs with the biggest representations on the Kilkenny panel, James Stephens and the Fenians, into mortal combat. Was anyone going to stand back and think of Croke Park the following Sunday? Of course not.

The Leinster final took place on July 18th. The outcome was unimaginable. The scoreline – Wexford 2-20 Kilkenny 1-6 – was unimaginable. The statistics – one point from play, one point in the second half, Kilkenny's biggest defeat in a provincial final since 1896 – were unimaginable. Everything about it was unimaginable.

"I couldn't see the signs beforehand," says Mick Crotty. "After five minutes I did. And being realistic about it, Wexford were bound to beat us some year, bound to get their day in the sun. Such a pity they never won an All Ireland."

"You'd wonder what might have happened afterwards had there been a back door at the time," Billy Fitzpatrick ponders. "Being beaten by so much was a surprise. Being beaten wasn't. That was always capable of happening with Wexford. Every few years they were going to beat you."

Absurd as it may sound, the winners' margin of victory would have been substantially greater had it not been for a truly epic performance by Noel Skehan, who stopped thunderbolts and fireballs and hailstones. But that was the most irrelevant of footnotes, lost amid the noise of the crash. O, what a fall was there, my countrymen!

Distance was no guarantee of insulation from the horror. Con Kenealy, the chronicler of all things St Kieran's on the hurling field, was covering the Ulster football final in Clones for the *Irish Independent* and had his afternoon made even more trying courtesy of a gleeful Michael Fortune of the *Irish Press*, who hailed from near Enniscorthy and had a radio with him, supplying all too regular updates from Croke Park. Subsequent reports had it that it took three weeks for Kilkenny regulars of Hanrahans' in New Ross to cross the Barrow and risk a visit to their local again.

The boot now firmly and belatedly on the other foot, Wexford beat Kilkenny again in the 1977 provincial decider, 3-17 to 3-14. Eddie Keher had a late shot to level it deflected over the bar by John Nolan, but the better team won. It was Keher's last championship appearance. The end of an era was descending in many shapes and forms.

Kieran Purcell broke his wrist against Clare in 1976 and never appeared for the county again after the Leinster final. Pat Lawlor banjaxed an achilles playing soccer for East End, Bennettsbridge's finest exponents of the foreign code, the following spring and was forced to retire at the age of 29, convinced he still had another three years in him. The dominoes were falling again. This time they would not be righted.

The same year brought another league showdown with Clare in Thurles, as 1978 would too. The Banner won both, to some extent because their need was greater than Kilkenny's. In much the same way it was a pity, as Mick Crotty laments, that Wexford never won an All Ireland during the period, so too Clare's inability to conquer Munster with their best team since the mid-1950s would remain a source of regret for hurling folk.

In his 15 years in the saffron and blue, Johnny Callinan was inured to the clang and chaos of Munster championship battle against Tipperary and Limerick and Cork. Gruelling as these clashes could be and would be again, they hadn't quite prepared him for the trials of facing the Kilkenny defence.

Facing the stripey men, he found in the course of the four league finals in three seasons, was more difficult than facing any other county. One word summed up the Kilkenny defence for the Clarecastle man. *Hardness.*

Physically they were hard. Mentally they were adamantine. Their resolve even extended to being tough on one another. "If I got a point off Pat Lawlor he'd get a bollocking off Pat Henderson – and you were let know that, which was part of it as well. It was almost like, 'Sorry, but am I not entitled to get a puck?' 'No, you're not!' They were incredibly jealous of any score that was given away. Any point you got you earned. Playing on them was physically demanding. That hardness about them."

The 1978 All Ireland final was the day the intercounty world ended for three hurling greats: Christy Ring, Pat Henderson and Tommy Maher. It was not the day it ended for someone who became a hurling great, although at the time it seemed like it already had. In the heel of the hunt it turned out to be nothing more than the end of a chapter for Brian Cody. For him the sun would rise again.

It was not a good time to be meeting Cork, who were chasing a third All Ireland in succession. Kilkenny were in transition, caught in midstream between the demobilisation of one double team and the creation of another. In addition, training had not gone well before the final. Matt Ruth, who'd been a sub for the county in 1975, was one who found the setup to be "very slack".

It was a match Kilkenny wanted to win but didn't. It was a match Cork could not afford to lose and wouldn't. The finals of 1939 and '47 had not been forgotten on Leeside. The final of 1972 never could be. And as well as the spur provided by the sight of the black and amber, the defending champions had another factor to motivate them. The team they'd beaten in 1976 and '77 was Wexford. Wexford. Not Kilkenny. The Cork players hadn't been allowed to forget that. Jimmy Barry-Murphy could not but be conscious of the jibes.

"With no disrespect to Wexford, who were a fine team, our team's legacy would have been tainted if we hadn't beaten Kilkenny in 1978. No question about that. You wouldn't have heard about us at all, really."

Nerves were pitched to batsqueak the week of the All Ireland final. Then, on the Thursday night, something remarkable happened. The Cork players had eaten in the large room in Páirc Uí Chaoimh when Christy Ring took the floor for the first time in his tenure as a Cork selector. Eyes popped as the living legend spoke at length. He talked about preparing for a big match and the importance he used to place on visualisation: what he'd do, when he'd do it, the player he'd be marking, where he'd run. Then he segued into a description of his famous goal in the 1946 All Ireland final against Kilkenny, the afternoon the Cloyne man went supernova. He'd won possession out the field, he'd soloed forward, he'd let fly – "and the next thing I saw was the raindrops falling off the back of the net." The players were enraptured. The tension floated away into the ether.

For all that Cork were worthy of their four-point victory the following Sunday, 1-15 to 2-8, a few Kilkenny might-have-beens persisted. The sides were level at half-time and still locked together in the 50th minute when Mick Brennan and Kevin Fennelly collided spectacularly, the sliotar running free for Tim Crowley to hit the lead point with a mighty effort from under the Cusack Stand. Paddy Prendergast subsequently flaked a sideline ball straight to Ray Cummins, who picked off an unopposed point. And then there was the substitution of Liam O'Brien.

The consensus on Noreside ever since has held that "there was no one to take the frees when Chunky went off". Sitting in the dugout with Johnny McGovern and the other selectors, Georgie Leahy, a clubmate of O'Brien's, had given the very same warning as they discussed what switch to make. But the substitution did more than cost Kilkenny their freetaker. It cost them the goal that swung the game.

Twelve minutes remained and Cork, playing into the Railway End and two points up, had a free deep inside their own half when O'Brien was called ashore, where the first man to shake his hand was Ring. On came Pat Henderson at centre-back, his brother Ger moving to midfield. As John Horgan's typically booming free landed it dropped into the space the younger Henderson, hitherto imperious in the air against Gerald McCarthy, had vacated.

An ancient soccer maxim advises against making a substitution immediately prior to defending a corner; this was its hurling equivalent. With Ger Henderson no longer there to stick his paw up, the sliotar ran free, a melee followed and Jimmy Barry-Murphy, a man whose gifts as an athlete were exceeded only by his humility as a human being, struck for what Micheál O'Hehir, by now beginning to get hazy on names but capable of recognising a moment of significance nonetheless, immediately branded "the goal that can win an All Ireland".

A scuttery effort it may have been, what with Noel Skehan unsighted by Dick O'Hara and the sliotar hopping past him in slow motion, but Kevin Fennelly's early goal at the same end had been equally sloppy and in any case it took only two minutes for Billy Fitzpatrick to repair the damage at the other end. Back to within two points with 11 minutes left, the challengers were near enough if good enough – and, clearly, not good enough. That total of 2-8 tells its own story. (Wexford had hit 4-11 against Cork two years earlier and still lost.) Interestingly, Gerald McCarthy said afterwards that Kilkenny had been more than justified in pushing Ger Henderson up the field on the basis that the forwards "were so poor".

Received wisdom can be as unreliable a narrator as faulty memory. A look at the video of the game reveals Brian Cody, the losers' full-forward, to have been nowhere near as poor as lore would have it. Raymond Smith decried his lack of mobility in the *Irish Independent* next day and there was something in that, but for Cody to be booed at the homecoming at the Courthouse in Kilkenny on the Monday night was not only unfair, it was plain wrong. Had the civic authorities chosen to hold an auto da fe rather than a homecoming, he would have been neither the first nor the only person on the pyre. Cody had a hand in Fennelly's goal, he won a free off Martin O'Doherty, he created a chance for a point that Mick Brennan drove wide and when moved to centre-forward in the second half he caught two balls in succession over the head of Johnny Crowley. All told, he didn't do enough to win his battle against O'Doherty – the full-back always has to do less than the full-forward in order to shade the duel, after all – but he wasn't cleaned out and he wasn't made to look silly. At least three other members of the attack were more ineffective. Not to put too fine a point on it, the Kilkenny forwards looked as if they'd been introduced to one another for the first time in the dressing room beforehand.

The losers' 2-8, a laughable tally when set beside their All Ireland scores from earlier in the decade, even allowing for the lost ten minutes, was comprised of four Liam O'Brien frees, 1-1 from Billy Fitzpatrick, Fennelly's goal, 0-2 by Mick Brennan – the best of the forwards – and a Joe Hennessy 70'. To put it another way, three of the forwards failed to score (all six Cork forwards scored); between them the sextet hit 2-3; and of Kilkenny's eight points, five came from placed balls. And after all those sins of omission and commission, they were still only three points behind entering injury time.

Bamboozling hurling a la 1957 it was not. This was an attacking systems failure on a grand scale, which gave rise to the biggest might-have-been of all: what if Keher had been there? Matt Ruth, the left-corner forward, walked off the field having barely broken sweat and vowing never to allow a game bypass him again. If the ball wasn't coming into his corner in future, he told himself, he'd go looking for it. As for Eddie Keher, he consoled himself that having the multitudes tell him it was a pity he hadn't stayed on for another year was a good deal preferable to having the multitudes tell him it was a pity he had.

Donal Carroll in the *Irish Independent* adjudged the losers to have been "less well serviced at selectorial level" than their opponents. There was no arguing with that from the Kilkenny camp, then or decades after the fact. To Johnny McGovern it was, like 1971, a day the management didn't cover themselves in glory. For weeks afterwards Georgie Leahy received abusive letters signed "Lory Meagher" or "Jimmy Langton". Nickey Brennan, who was a sub, sums it up best. "Cork were the better team, but that's not to say a smarter sideline might not have swung the game for Kilkenny."

Fr Maher was, as ever, philosophical, too old and wise to get worked up about what was, in the end, just one more defeat. "If we hadn't decided to build a new team we might never have reached this All Ireland," he told the media. "We achieved a lot in getting to the final with quite a few newcomers."

He wasn't simply whistling past the graveyard. Kilkenny's newcomers would enjoy brighter days and plenty of them, starting the following season. But Tommy Maher would not be there to share them. Men must endure their going hence, even as their coming hither. Nor would Christy Ring, who died suddenly the following March at the age of 58.

Two of hurling's all-time greats thus vacated the September stage simultaneously. The legacy of one was already assured. The legacy of the other would grow deeper and richer as time went by.

CHAPTER 22

Healy

And Iggy is after him now... And Iggy beats him... And Iggy gets the ball out the field, way out the field... Where Pat Delaney goes up for it and Pat Delaney grabs it... Pat's going upfield now... Three Galway men about to descend on him... Make that four... In now to Brendan Bermingham... Bermingham inside to Flaherty... Flaherty is inside and the ball is in the net and it's a goal! Offaly are in the lead! Johnny Flaherty – there he is! – Johnny Flaherty putting Offaly into the lead in the closing stages of the game...

Mícheál O'Hehir, September 6th 1981

Sheila Gallagher, later Sheila Molony, was coming home from school one day in 1976 when an individual she'd never met before stopped her on the street in Tullamore. "Would you ever tell that man to get sense?" the stranger demanded. "He'll never make a silk purse out of a sow's ear."

"That man" was her father, Andy Gallagher, recently appointed the Offaly hurling manager, and the stranger an old teammate. As for Offaly, they were a county that had never won an All Ireland, that had never won a Leinster title and that up to then had contested one provincial final ever.

Gallagher pére had hurled in goal with them from 1955 to 1969 and that hadn't been a barrel of laughs either, a near-perpetual diet of league matches against the Westmeaths and the Laoises followed by a glance at Monday's paper to see if he'd got a mention for saving most of the bullets fired at him the previous afternoon. He rarely had. "From the point of view of enjoyment it was okay," he would reflect from the promontory of half a century's hindsight. "From the point of view of winning anything it wasn't great. Collective training? Not with us. We went from match to match."

But here was the thing with Andy Gallagher, a hurling fanatic in a football town. He believed. He believed so fervently, so implicitly, so hopelessly and so publicly that strangers stopped his daughter in the street to bemoan his naivety and his colleagues at work in DE Williams delighted in calling him The Super-Optimist. "When I was hurling with Offaly and we were literally nobodies, I still had this oul' conviction that if we went the right way about it we could win something."

Division 2 matches and oul' convictions. That was their universe. That was where it began. To acknowledge the place Offaly hurling arrived at in the 1980s and '90s, one must first recognise the place from where they started out. To appreciate fully the casket of wonders the world opened up to them, one must first realise what the world used to hold for them. To understand the Brian Whelahans and the Johnny Dooleys and the Michael Duignans, one must first know the Andy Gallaghers and the Damien Martins and the Pat Fleurys.

Gallagher and his super-optimism. Martin making his intercounty debut as an 18-year-old against Wicklow in Ashford in the National League in the autumn of 1964, keeping a clean sheet, being asked by some youngster for his autograph afterwards and going home delighted with himself, unaware that not every match he'd hurl for Offaly would result in demands for autographs. Fleury making his championship debut against Kildare in 1975 and failing to finish on the winning side. That's how it was. There seemed no obvious reason why that wasn't how it would forever be.

Yet somehow there was always something that kept the flame flickering in the hearts of the Faithful few, Gallagher's old ticker among them. The "colossal effort" Offaly put in for 50 minutes against Wexford in the 1957 Leinster semi-final at Nowlan Park. Gaining promotion to Division 1 of the National League in the mid-60s. Beating Tipp in the league, a first, in November 1966, 3-13 to 2-7 in Birr. Flooring Wexford, the reigning All Ireland champions, in the 1969 provincial semi-final and scaring the wits out of Kilkenny in the final, albeit with a team that didn't possess the legs to kick on from there.

When Gallagher inevitably graduated to the manager's job, he was pleased to find not the slightest hint that the hurlers were the poor relations. If anything, Offaly's All Ireland football triumphs of 1971-72 had taught the county to think in primary colours. That was something, at least. And then, not long after Sheila Gallagher found her walk home from school so rudely interrupted, a group emerged that included Pat Fleury, Aidan Fogarty and Eugene Coughlan and that would go on to win a Leinster under-21 title in 1978.

That year's senior championship began with Offaly quietly fancying their chances. It ended brutishly in a 2-17 to 1-4 defeat by Kilkenny in Portlaoise, one of the winners' goals coming from Brian Cody. Gallagher, as perplexed as he was depressed, prevailed on Paddy Buggy, at the time Kilkenny's delegate to Leinster Council, to send up a legation of three or four of his countymen to offer advice. When 1979 brought no breakthrough either a second set of emissaries was despatched. "Don't let one defeat upset the work you're doing," was the message on both occasions. Among the members of the delegation the second year was Dermot Healy.

Two events of profound import occurred the same autumn. At the time

Kilkenny and Wexford were, as they had been for years, seeded to meet in the provincial final. Gallagher's argument to Leinster Council was that this was grossly unfair on Offaly and any other aspiring team. They might beat one or other of the province's big guns. They wouldn't beat both. His powers of persuasion, or perhaps simply that cockeyed optimism of his, worked: the authorities accepted his contention and dropped the seeded arrangement. Michael Fortune of the *Irish Press* excoriated the development under the headline, "Disastrous decision by the Leinster Council". Gallagher kept the cutting.

Some of the credit for what happened next rested with Damien Martin, who told a county board meeting at the back end of 1979 of his firm belief that Offaly had a team that could win an All Ireland but that they were stuck on the edge of a seesaw and needed a push – just a small push, but one that could only be applied by an outside manager – to tip them in the right direction. Why the delegates heeded him he was never fully sure afterwards. Possibly because potential resistance from the indigenous hurling diehards may have been diluted by the presence at the meeting of the football fraternity. Possibly because, having been around the place so long and been the goalkeeper on the first All Star team, he possessed a certain profile. Being honest about it, he didn't even know who this putative outside manager might be. He definitely had nobody in mind himself. But somewhere along the line someone came up with the name of a man in his early 30s from Kilkenny who had learned at the feet of the master, Fr Tommy Maher. The casket of wonders was about to inch open.

By this stage Dermot Healy had been coaching for ten years after learning the ropes as a seminarian in St Kieran's in the late 1960s. The first group of youngsters he dealt with included Brian Cody, Nickey Brennan and the most gifted hurler he was to encounter in four decades coaching, Billy Fitzpatrick from Johnstown. ("All the skills. Big and strong without being robust. Very athletic and a good head.") A raft of All Ireland colleges and minor titles followed.

By 1979 Healy had been there and done that, had made frequent pilgrimages to Gormanston and had his theories on the game formulated. He'd been coached by Tommy Maher and had watched him point out to players what they were doing right, what they were doing wrong and instruct them in the manner in which wrong could be made right. He'd learned that hurling was a game of skill instead of one of physical strength or force and that the way to become good at it was to practise the skills. He'd been in Gormanston the year some chap at the back of the hall stood up and asked whether putting a furm in a dressing room and jumping up and down off it 100 times would make him fit. "Yes indeed," Fr Maher replied. "It would make you very proficient at jumping up and down. But if you want to be a hurler, practise the skills." He'd discovered that All Irelands were won not by performing astonishing feats of heroism but by doing the simple thing over and over again. He was, if not actively seeking an intercounty senior role, then at any rate available to be talked into one. Whereupon Offaly came knocking.

Saying yes was no difficult decision, though he did consult with Fr Maher, who agreed it "could have potential" and gave his imprimatur, as well as looking into his own heart. Healy's heart, whatever about his head, said yes. "All the years in the '70s that Kilkenny were winning All Irelands, we'd come home on the Monday night and go to the Courthouse and mention something about how hurling needed to be spread. I'd even spoken about it myself. Now I was getting the chance to do something about it." A tacit consideration was the fact that it was Offaly, a county who had never won a provincial title, still less an All Ireland, who were courting him. Whatever Healy achieved with them would hardly come back to bite Kilkenny, he told himself – and in the unlikely event it did, the bite would not prove fatal.

What Healy discovered on decamping to Offaly was a hardcore of experienced, intelligent hands plus "two silent monsters": Eugene Coughlan in defence and the quietly effective Brendan Bermingham up front. "Often after a match people wouldn't even know that Brendan had been playing. He just did a job at centre-forward, getting the ball through and neutralising the centre-back. Centre-backs never starred when playing against Brendan Bermingham."

Healy landed on his feet in terms of his selectors too. Mick Spain, Charlie Daly, Paudge Mulhare, Tommy Erritty and Gallagher, who stayed on as manager. Wise men who knew the game and knew what Offaly were and weren't capable of. They never voted on anything. They never had to. "We'd sit down three weeks before a match and pick a team. We might tweak it after that, but mostly the team stayed as it was." That suited Healy, whose next words are *echt* Tommy Maher. "I don't believe in training a team, then picking it the night before. Players must be coached to play their position on the field."

At his first training session he put a sliotar on the ground and commandeered a hurley from someone. "This," he announced, "is how you hit a ball on the ground." Eyebrows were raised by those panel members from north Offaly who prided themselves on their ground-striking ability. Was this guy trying to teach his granny how to suck eggs? Not quite. He was a party leader setting out his manifesto at the launch of a new campaign. Right from the beginning it was obvious that this was a manifesto into which all the members could buy.

His new charges soon became acquainted with what Pat Fleury terms Healy's "mottos and mantras": a mistake is an opportunity to put things right, defenders be first out to the ball, and so on. Training was switched from Birr with its boggy pitch to Tullamore with its faster sod and the importance of keeping mistakes to a minimum – "the cause of a lot of our problems up to then," according to Fleury – constantly stressed. Healy: "Offaly had been doing well in the league every year and doing respectably in the championship, so it was clear there was something to work with, but what I discovered when I got there was that they were doing plenty of physical stuff. So I reduced the physical and increased the skills training. And gradually matches they'd been losing by two or three points they began to win by two or three points."

A favourite Maher drill, adopted by Healy, had four players in a row hitting the ball to each other. Healy enumerates the skills it honed. "If you did only that one exercise you'd be working on many aspects of your game. It developed ground hurling. It developed running to the ball. It developed striking left and right. If that line drill is properly coached it also develops anticipation because I'm moving to the ball even before you hit it. How often do you see a corner-back waiting for the ball? And the drill also taught players that if you ran to a ball and missed it you didn't pound the ground with the hurley in frustration – you got back and got it right with the next ball."

The shallowness of the pool of players at the management's disposal was not the drawback it may have appeared. "If a corner-back is being beaten and you've nobody to replace him, you have to leave him there. So he begins to think he mustn't be too bad after all and grows in confidence. And you coach him and coach him and coach him. And he improves. Sometimes you sacrifice a battle to win a war. You play the cards you've been dealt. There's no such thing as an impossible task. With hard work and by doing the right things you can make good players. But you have to be a super-optimist. Crises come. You have to be able to look past them. 'Right, lads, back training tomorrow evening.' You have to view crises as opportunities."

The goalkeeper wasn't forgotten about either. Sometime in the mid-1960s Fr Maher had paid a visit to Offaly and spoken about the various qualities a top-class goalie needed, among them quick wrists, lightness on his feet, courage, a good eye and – staggering to Damien Martin, who'd never heard of the term before – peripheral vision. When Healy took over as coach he initiated a drill that entailed three or four players lining up on the 21, each equipped with a sliotar, and Martin standing on his goalline with his back turned. Just before striking the ball each player would shout to him. Martin would turn and try to save.

He didn't succeed every time – "the ball was always in a hurry" – but it sharpened his reflexes and taught him to expect the unexpected. "Anybody can stop a ball if they can see it. A ball coming out of nowhere is a different matter." And years later, around 2009, when Martin was asked to draw up a training programme for young goalkeepers in the county and contacted Ger Cunningham to pick his brain, he discovered that what they were doing in Cork was no different to what they'd been doing in Offaly under Dermot Healy three decades earlier.

The diet of skills drills, unceasing but never boring, developed the players' comfort with the basics, which in turn helped to increase their confidence. To Pat Fleury they were a better side than they'd looked in the late 1970s anyway, but the wait for jam tomorrow could not continue indefinitely. "Our championship results weren't showing much in terms of progress, but we'd come up from Division 1B in the league and that was important in terms of giving us matches against the top teams. In 1979 we ran Wexford to a point in the Leinster semi-final in Athy. But some of us had been around long enough to know that we couldn't be waiting forever."

It wasn't all about the skills. Healy knew that. In fact he knew that sometimes, other things being equal, it wasn't about the skills at all. One year he'd organised a coaching course in St Kieran's and persuaded Kevin Heffernan to come down and speak at it. What do you want me to talk about, Heffernan asked him. The psychology of coaching, Healy replied.

"Isn't coaching all about psychology?" Heffernan shot back.

"You know that," Healy nodded. "I know that. Now tell these people that."

There was no overwhelming reason for Offaly to win the 1980 Leinster title, not only because they were Offaly and Kilkenny were Kilkenny but also because they'd been no more than adequate in beating Dublin by 0-18 to 0-10 in the curtainraiser on provincial semi-final day. By contrast the MacCarthy Cup holders had seen off Wexford by 4-16 to 3-14 in a cracking main event. Nor was it any surprise that the decider attracted a paltry crowd of 9,631 spectators, the smallest attendance since the Emergency. Kilkenny versus Offaly, remember. This particular Goliath hadn't been in the habit of losing to David since around the time of the same Emergency.

The Offaly panel were standing around the mouth of the tunnel watching the minor match when RTE's Mick Dunne materialised. "Another trouncing?" he enquired of Healy in jocular fashion. "No," Healy replied, "we're going to win." Dunne, stunned by such chutzpah, made a beeline for John Dowling, the Offaly county secretary and future GAA president, and gasped. "Healy's mad!"

But Healy was confident. He had to be. He *knew* he had to be. Optimism, even blind optimism, was the day's imperative. "We were playing the All Ireland champions. We had to be totally convinced. If not we'd have been caught in the last 10 minutes, which is what happens to a lot of teams in that situation. They don't fully believe. I had Offaly brainwashed for a month beforehand that they'd win. I had myself brainwashed."

On the balance of play the underdogs, who led by 1-4 to 0-1 after eight minutes, should not have gone in at half-time trailing by 3-6 to 1-10. But that was no bad thing; a lead might have given them pause for thought whereas arrears ensured they had to concentrate on the job in hand. The angle of the slope was eased when Kilkenny, in one of the most stupefying moves ever enacted by a management team from the county, withdrew Frank Cummins at the break. If Offaly had hurled well in the first half they hurled even better in the second half, determined and purposeful and ever willing to shoot from out the field. It looked like a case of the same old story when a goal by Mick Crotty and a point by Billy Fitzpatrick put the champions 4-10 to 1-16 in front, but Offaly hit back with goals by Brendan Bermingham and a handpassed Johnny Flaherty effort to win by 3-17 to 5-10. They were the first first-time Leinster champions since Laois in 1914.

Ah yes, Johnny Flaherty. Whether or not it's strictly true, or even half true, the following tale demands to be printed. The story goes that Healy, not long in Offaly, was on his way out through the hotel bar following the post-training meal one night when he encountered a smallish man having a pint at the counter. An exchange of pleasantries led to a long conversation which finished with Healy deciding that if his new friend could hurl even half as good a game as he talked, he'd surely be worth a place on the panel. The name of the stranger, who had spent most of the 1970s in New York, was Johnny Flaherty. Within a year Offaly had won their first Leinster title. Within two years they had become the most recent county, and the only new one in the second half of the 20th century, to add their name to the MacCarthy Cup roll of honour.

Back at work in the *Kilkenny People* newsroom the day after the GAA upset of the year, Healy received scores of phone calls from friends and acquaintances congratulating him. He had put his faith where they'd been putting their mouths. His adopted county might have gone all the way to Croke Park that September, but after Flaherty had come out in hives the week before the All Ireland semi-final against Galway they walked out of the traps and, amid claims that JJ Landers from Waterford had ended the game a couple of minutes early, came up two points short.

Not to worry. They'd done more than enough for one year, while the sight of Galway beating Limerick in the final only sharpened their appetite, according to Flaherty. "Galway had been around longer than we had and were a very stable team. Seeing them win the All Ireland gave us a huge confidence boost and led us to believe we could come back in '81, win Leinster again, reach the All Ireland final and perform in it."

Exactly, says Andy Gallagher, who agrees that not reaching an All Ireland final at that point in the team's development may have been a blessing. "You never know how we might have reacted. Had we got a hammering from Limerick it would have set us back. As it was, we were happy to have won what we'd won and we had everything in our favour looking forward to 1981."

They had. They would have the luck in their favour too. Witness the goal that never was by Pádraig Horan – it hit the side netting, but the umpire had turned his back and on seeing the sliotar nestling in the rigging concluded it had to be a goal – that enabled them to scrape past Laois in the provincial semi-final. Wexford were seen off by two points in the Leinster final. This gave Offaly a bye to their first All Ireland final.

If nothing else, the hiatus between the provincial decider and the first Sunday in September served to keep the hype on a leash. "People mightn't believe it now the way things have gone," Gallagher says, "but we broke up for a month after the Leinster final and had a three-week run-in to the All Ireland. So whatever excitement there was after the Leinster final had died down by the end of August. There was no massive excitement coming up to the All Ireland final the way there would have been had we won the Leinster final and then won an All Ireland semi-final. The break allowed us to simmer."

Chris Dooley, on placement from journalism school in Rathmines in Dublin, interviewed a number of players for the *Midland Tribune* in the run-up to the All Ireland final. The one conversation that stuck in his mind was his chat with Johnny Flaherty. "My questions were less than inspiring and I was routinely asking things like, 'And who do you fear most on the Galway team?' Flaherty nearly exploded. 'Fear?! Fear?! I don't fear anybody!' I think he was having a bit of fun at my expense, but I also think the answer was indicative of an inner belief the players had in themselves – or perhaps more true to say that Dermot Healy had instilled in them. Flaherty would definitely have been one of the strongest characters in the team as well as maybe the most gifted."

As an ordinary Offaly supporter, Dooley had been in O'Moore Park in 1978 for the trimming by Kilkenny. "Who'd have thought that within two years they would beat Kilkenny in a Leinster final? The transformation in the team and in their self-belief when Healy took over was instant."

Anxious lest a bad start against Galway dampen spirits, Gallagher and Healy told the players time and again beforehand that if they were within six points of the holders entering the closing 10 minutes they'd win. It was part mind games, part common sense. Offaly had a more economical style, spare and spartan, than the holders. They'd keep the ball moving, even if it was only to flick it two yards sideways to a colleague; Galway would run 20 yards and handpass it to achieve the same result. Gallagher: "Our lads didn't physically kill themselves trying to go round an opponent. So we were fitter in the last 10 minutes." Besides, Offaly had almost caught Galway in the 1980 semi-final after giving them a big lead early on, so a half-time deficit of six points was nothing daunting.

Liam Hogan from Coolderry, one of the subs, was struck by Healy's poise in the dressing room at the break. "He was cool, calm, calculated" – just like, had Hogan known it, Fr Tommy Maher at half-time in the All Ireland colleges final 24 years earlier. The coach's tranquillity transmitted itself to his flock. On retaking the field Offaly continued doing what they'd been doing in the first half. So taken was Hogan by Healy's calmness – here was a novel creature, a coach who didn't in go for roaring and shouting – that he filed it away for emulation at a later date. When Ballyboden St Enda's won five consecutive Dublin senior hurling titles between 2007 and '11, Hogan, their coach, made sure not to raise his voice in the dressing room at any stage.

By degrees, and by keeping the ball moving as they'd practised so often, Offaly chipped away at Galway's lead. It is not feats of heroism that win All Irelands but the basics done properly, over and over and over again. Andy Gallagher can still picture Damien Martin making an improbable save from Noel Lane with the issue in the balance, can still visualise Pat Delaney driving up the field in the prelude to Johnny Flaherty's decisive goal ("I'd been out giving advice to one of the players and was going back to the dugout but wasn't yet in it"), can still see Mick Verney, the elderly treasurer of the county board, clapping his hands and dancing a jig behind the goal after Flaherty palmed himself and his county into history. For a couple of hours afterwards Gallagher wasn't entirely sure whether he was awake or dreaming.

"I kept thinking, when am I going to come back down to earth and realise this is happening? What was very satisfying afterwards was the reaction from genuine hurling people around the country. They were delighted to see a new county on the roll of honour."

Flaherty's goal was not quite the glorious piece of extemporisation it appeared. One of Healy's drills in training was a handpassing exercise that involved bringing the full-forward line out to the 40 and having them work their way in, palming the sliotar to one another as they went. When they reached the edge of the square, the man in possession handpassed the ball to the net. "They did it for ten minutes every evening. Hence Johnny Flaherty's goal. It was the 1,000th ball he'd handpassed into the net that summer. Only for that he'd have tried to use his stick, would've been hooked, wouldn't have scored and Offaly wouldn't have won the All Ireland. It all began in Fennessy's Field." Thus was a skill practised until habit became instinct and instinct won an All Ireland. Dick Dowling in 1957. Johnny Flaherty in 1981.

To Healy there was no contradiction between ground hurling and the use of the handpass because each was deployed with the same objective in mind: to move the sliotar as efficiently as possible depending on the prevailing wind. "For example, a player grabs a high ball but is unable to swing the hurley to strike it, so he delivers it via handpass. Tommy Maher's philosophy was to perfect all the skills of the game so that players would have an armoury to deal with any given situation at any given time."

Seamus Dooley, later the Irish organiser for the National Union of Journalists, did the post-match interviews for the *Midland Tribune*. In order to negotiate his way through the crowd and do battle with Croke Park's men in blazers he headed for the dressing rooms before the final whistle, consequently missing Flaherty's goal. "I thought I was going to the losers' dressing room and was ready with my funeral face when I heard the cheers." The following week's edition of the *Tribune* featured two deathless headlines, both the work of Jimmy Fanning, the editor/proprietor: 'Glory O Glory O to the Bold Offaly Men' and 'From the Fury of the O'Flahertys Deliver Us', the latter reputedly a line from a monument in Galway.

The heroes returned by train to Tullamore on Monday evening before moving on to Blue Ball, Kilcormac and Emmet Square in Birr. The natives were hanging from rafters, rooftops and windows. Damien Martin didn't believe there could be so many people in Offaly.

"Wasn't it all worthwhile?" his fellow veteran Pádraig Horan turned and said to him at one stage.

"It would have been all worthwhile even if we didn't win," Martin responded.

On Tuesday the cup was brought to Banagher, home of St Rynagh's, on the border with Galway. A banner hung from Nallens' shop in the town that read, "Sorry Galway, better luck next time." The *Midland Tribune* quoted this and implied that it had been erected by Gerry Nallen, a leading St Rynagh's clubman. Uproar ensued with the publication of the paper on the Wednesday night. Nallens' Galway customers cancelled their orders and the *Tribune* had to print a clarification stating that Gerry Nallen had not put up the banner. Order, harmony and milk orders were restored.

So many wellwishers gathered to see the team off at Heuston Station on the

Monday that Seán Mac Connell of the *Irish Press* was lucky to make it aboard the victory train at all. After phoning in his copy from Tullamore he made it over to Birr sometime after 11pm. Along the roadside danced the embers of fires lit to welcome home the champions.

Mac Connell spent the rest of the night making it up as he went along. Fighting his way through what seemed like most of the population of the midlands in order to get into Dooly's Hotel. The victory dinner served at 1.30 on Tuesday morning. Fans finding ladders, climbing up the outside of the hotel extension and getting in the windows, which were at least 12 feet above ground level. The front door breached and hundreds of people pouring into the hotel, filling the ballroom, the bar and the corridors. Mac Connell attempting to make his way back to his bedroom when the speeches ended around 4am and failing. Beating his way back to the ballroom and waiting there until the crowd had thinned out.

"I managed to make my way to the reception desk by 7.15am and filed a story to the *Evening Press* about the craic the night before, phoning it in from the cubby hole behind the desk. Someone on the staff eventually got to my room, rescued my unopened bag and I thought it best to blow Birr and try and get home.

"I went out on the road and began to thumb. A lorry driver who was going to Dublin to catch a ferry stopped and picked me up. Had I been at the reception and was it not great fun, he asked. After about ten minutes he suddenly came up with a bright idea. 'We should go over to Portlaoise and see how the Laois lads are taking our win.' I was in no mood to argue and sometime later we arrived in Portlaoise, where he knocked on the door of a pub that contained ten Offaly men who had made their way back there. Suffice to say I was encouraged to join in the celebration and it was late that afternoon when we got back to the lorry.

"'Arrah, I've missed two ferries already,' he said. 'We should go back over Kinnitty side to see how they are getting on.'

"At this stage I was getting into celebratory mood and we headed back over towards Kinnitty. We made a few stops on the way in various villages, and not in the local churches either. It was very early the following morning before he dropped me off near my home and headed for Dun Laoghaire and the boat. That was how I covered and celebrated the historic Offaly win and I will never forget it until the day I die."

The taste of ambrosia, delightful but intoxicating, affected different people in different ways. The late Noel Magee, a barber on the main street in Tullamore and one of the town's most colourful characters, appeared in the Manor Lounge a day or two later with hands trembling from lack of sleep and excess celebrations. That would have been okay, even for a barber, had not a priest decided to drop into him for a shave. Noel was barely able to hold the razor and drew blood. Before the priest could say anything, Noel, according to himself, decided to get his retaliation in first. "Ah Jaysus, Father, doesn't alcohol make the oul' skin very tender?"

All of this would have been remarkable enough in and of itself. What was no less astounding about the Offaly story was that 1980-81 proved to be a beginning rather than an end. Instead of vanishing into some midlands twilight and commemorating 1981 for ever more they stayed around for the next 20 years, annoying Kilkenny and confounding Wexford and rendering Laois redundant and winning provincial titles and reaching All Ireland finals.

The 1982 team were more accomplished than the '81 edition but were mugged by Liam Fennelly and Matt Ruth in the closing stages of the Leinster final and Damien Martin went home to Banagher to spend the summer keeping the rooks out of the corn. Kilkenny, en route to a double double of league and championship in successive seasons, beat them again 12 months later and Cork proved altogether too much for them in the centenary All Ireland final in Thurles. Offaly didn't hurl as badly that day as the scoreline of 3-16 to 1-12 suggested, but they squandered a couple of good chances in the first half and Seánie O'Leary, that most artful of dodgers, picked Martin's pocket for one of Cork's goals. At the homecoming in Tullamore the following night Pat Fleury, the losing captain, apologised to the crowd for letting them down (shouts of "No! No!") and promised that Offaly would make amends in 1985. Such promises are easily made and usually repented at leisure. But not this promise.

By 1985 they'd evolved from the breakthrough combination of 1980-81 into a smoother entity. They were older. They were wiser. They were defending as methodically and watchfully as they ever had and they'd become handier at firing over points from out the field. They came from nine points down to draw with Kilkenny in the Leinster semi-final (Andy Gallagher: "When did any team ever do that against Kilkenny?") before beating them comfortably in the replay. They put five goals past Laois in the provincial showpiece. And Dermot Healy had added to his grab-bag of psychological tricks. In conversation in the Anner Hotel in Thurles with Fr Michael O'Brien, an old foe from the colleges arena, on the night of the 1984 All Ireland final, he learned that the latter had employed Cork's commercial woes – Ford's and Dunlop's had closed their doors during the course of the previous 12 months, tearing the heart out of the city's traditional industrial base – as a motivational tool in the buildup to the game.

Being neither too proud nor too foolish to borrow from others, the Friday night before the 1985 All Ireland final Healy spoke at length after training without once mentioning hurling. That summer had been wretchedly, unceasingly wet. Every time he reached Killeigh on the way to Tullamore it was raining. Half of Offaly was under water. Think of what winning on Sunday would do for the county, Healy declaimed. Think of the way it would lift the community. Think, even, of the suicides it might prevent.

They didn't hurl brilliantly against Galway on the Sunday but they got there in the end, 2-11 to 1-12. Chris Dooley, now out of college and doing a colour piece for the *Irish Press*, wound up in the dressing room afterwards and was struck yet again by how grounded a bunch they were. "They were so quiet and self-effacing about the whole thing. You'd think they had just won the Walsh Cup rather than the All Ireland. Dermot Healy made a speech to them in which he said something like, 'It may not have sunk in yet, but later you'll realise what you've achieved today.' A year later I was in the dressing room with the Cork team after they had beaten Galway in the final and they were shouting and roaring, giving their manager Johnny Clifford the bumps and so on, and I remember thinking, 'Now these fellas know how to celebrate an All Ireland.'"

To Andy Gallagher the hallmark of Offaly's breakthrough team was "a fierce togetherness". In 2006 they celebrated the silver anniversary of their first All Ireland victory by heading to Italy for a holiday, and they were happy if less than surprised to discover that "the togetherness still existed". Long before then he'd experienced at first hand the "immense joy" the success of the hurlers gave to the Offaly exiles they encountered on All Star trips to New York and San Francisco. "Making the breakthrough made us known. It gave Offaly people living outside the county a great sense of achievement and pride."

The breakthrough would be built on. The 1990s brought further success and success that was more spectacular. The armed robbery against Limerick in the closing five minutes of the 1994 All Ireland final, the sublime dismantling of Kilkenny in the rain the following season (has Croke Park ever witnessed a finer exhibition of pure hurling?), the history-making backdoor All Ireland of 1998. But the 1980s was where it began.

There have been better teams than that Offaly outfit. There have been flashier teams. There have been higher scoring teams. But there have been few teams that stayed in their own movie so neatly, that lived within their means so economically, that knew their own game so intimately, that adhered to it with such flinty resolve and that won their matches by doing the simple thing so clinically, so patiently, so well and so often.

The ultimate Tommy Maher team was one he never coached at all.

CHAPTER 23

Mullinavat

Now I've sung my song and I'm going away to have a quiet jar
But before I do I must salute you, Fr Tommy Maher
You had the lads at fitness peak and when limbs were tired and sore
Your training skills were there to see, just like the days of yore
From *The Great Rod Iron Men – A Tribute to Mullinavat, Kilkenny*
***Centenary Junior Hurling Champions 1984* by James Murphy**

Fr Tommy Maher was appointed president of St Kieran's College in the summer of 1976. One version of the story had it that he was not the first-choice candidate and that Bishop Birch had intended appointing a younger cleric to the post, only to be talked out of it by a number of hurling-loving canons and PPs around the county who convinced him that such a course of action would be an insult to Fr Maher. Whatever the truth of the matter, his presidency would not be an easy stewardship.

His tenure coincided with a coming together – "forced marriage" would be a more accurate term – of the college secondary school and Kilkenny City Vocational School 200 yards down the road, two very different educational establishments. Both schools wanted to expand; the Department of Education's answer was a new building on the grounds of the college to be shared by the two schools, accessed at one end by the boys from St Kieran's and at the other end by the boys and girls of the Tech. It was a solution-by-committee that pleased nobody, not least the respective teachers: different staffs, different qualifications, different teaching unions. Fr Maher, being charitable and liberal and full of the milk of human kindness, at any rate up to a point, saw it as incumbent on the college to extend a hand of friendship to a less privileged school community. A number of his teachers believed otherwise and were completely opposed to common enrolment. For a period the tension in the St Kieran's staff room was palpable.

Negotiations dragged on for years. The CEO of Kilkenny VEC was Brendan Conway, a native of Feakle, who often travelled with Fr Maher to meetings with departmental officials in Dublin. The only subject ever discussed in the Conway car was hurling. Never the merger, always hurling. It was a topic of inexhaustible interest because the man driving the car was as much a hurling fanatic as his passenger. After all, An tÚasal Mac Con Bhuí had hurled for club and county, had been coached in St Flannan's by Tull Considine, and his former next-door neighbour at home in Feakle, Kevin Hogan, had been a contemporary of the young Maher's in Maynooth. What did he glean from those trips to Dublin?

"Fr Tommy said he wasn't physically strong as a young man. Not tall. And being in Maynooth meant he had no chance of playing National League, of course, so his playing career with Kilkenny was always going to be limited. But he had a great sense of seeking to impose his physics and science on hurling. The ball, he often said, was 'an awkward cuss of a thing to control', so the less often you touched it, the less you were likely to make a mistake. And though I'd taken the frees for Flannan's and Feakle, one thing he said had never struck me before. When you're taking a free, connect with the ball in front of your eyes because you have more control on a horizontal stroke."

That Tommy Maher was born to be the kindly but imaginative country parish priest he ultimately became is inarguable. That he felt constricted as president of the college, bound by rules and pieties, became the conventional wisdom, and in this instance there is no reason to doubt the conventional wisdom. Put simply, being president of St Kieran's wasn't really for him in the same way that being junior dean hadn't really been for him. Too bureaucratic, too official, too hidebound, too remote. His time coaching Kilkenny was spent working with people and getting inside their heads as well as improving their technique. The college presidency provided scope for neither.

Another report claimed that when the post of principal of the secondary school became vacant in 1977 he offered it not to a cleric but to a lay member of staff, an unheard-of move at the time. While the report was unconfirmed and in the end a priest was appointed, even the possibility of a leap of imagination like that – a decade before lay teachers began to replace priests and nuns as school principals nationally – does not come as a surprise. Tommy Maher had been making such leaps for most of his life. As an educator he was full of ideas and ideals, convinced of the merits of co-education.

On college sports day he was both handicapper for and participant in the teachers' race. He was not averse to giving himself a generous start and, if no longer the 'flier' of Bobby Rackard's memory, for a man in his mid-50s was still notably fit. He returned as often as he could to Whitepark to help out on the farm, Johnny McGovern regularly encountering him there in his day job delivering oil. And even as president of St Kieran's, with all the cares it entailed and the visiting dignitaries to be entertained, there was nothing he liked better than taking a stroll around the college farm to inspect a new bull. Activities on the farm were a source of abiding interest to him, to the extent that he frequently returned to the college with muck on his wellingtons. Not in keeping with the dignity of his office, perhaps, but that didn't bother him in the slightest. Fussiness, fustiness and formalities may have been for other clerics. They weren't for him.

The high point of the Maher presidency was the college bicentenary in 1982. Two hundred years had passed since the opening of St Kieran's College, the first Catholic school to be established in Ireland after the relaxation of the Penal Laws. The anniversary was marked thoughtfully and in style. The planning for it saw Fr Maher at his imaginative, organised best.

An overseeing committee came together at his behest in early 1981. A slew of sub-committees – catering, liturgy, entertainment, fundraising, research and publicity – followed. A representative of each class year dating back to the late 1930s was appointed. A bicentenary crest was designed and appeared on ties, scarves, postcards, copper etchings and other souvenirs. Fr Fearghus Ó Fearghail from Johnstown was inveigled by the president into interrupting his scriptural thesis in the Irish College in Rome and returning to write an updated history of the college, less weighty than the 1951 Birch tome and illustrated. Articles on St Kieran's appeared in *The Word, Africa* and the *Far East*. Tom Kilroy from Callan, a student in the early 1950s, returned and did a reading from chapter two of his award-winning novel *The Big Chapel*. And much, much more.

The official opening of the bicentenary celebrations took place on St Kieran's Day, March 5th, a Friday. The day began with prayers on the front lawn and the raising of the tricolour. The student body were dismissed to spend the morning on town walks or games, after which they were treated to lunch in the college gym. Bishop Laurence Forristal, the new Bishop of Ossory in succession to Peter Birch, who had died the previous year, was the chief concelebrant at a special Mass in St Mary's Cathedral in the afternoon.

The other showpiece event was the layside reunion, which took place on the last weekend of September and was attended by nearly 2,000 past pupils as well as President Patrick Hillery, Cardinal Tomás Ó Fiaich, Jack Lynch, Liam Cosgrave and the former Minister for Education John Wilson, another contemporary of Fr Maher's in Maynooth and a teacher in St Kieran's from 1947 to 1950. Wilson played at right-half back for Cavan against Kerry in the 1947 All Ireland football final at the Polo Grounds and managed to get back from New York in time for school the following Monday week. "Christ, I wasn't expecting you back for a month," was his greeting from Fr Dunphy, the senior dean.

Naturally there was a hurling match. Three weeks after Kilkenny had overturned an unbackable Cork team in the 1982 All Ireland final, an ex-St Kieran's selection took on a Kilkenny XV on the back field. Anything other than a victory for the hosts was clearly inconceivable and they duly beat their opponents by 0-18 to 2-10. The St Kieran's team was: Pat Dunphy; Joe Doran, Frank Holohan, Richie Reid; Brian Cody, Paddy Prendergast, Nickey Brennan; Ger Fennelly, Kieran Brennan; Billy Walton, Billy Fitzpatrick, Harry Ryan; Mick Crotty, Christy Heffernan, Eddie Keher.

Nothing could have been more fitting had the bicentenary been marked by an All Ireland colleges triumph. Nothing could have been more unlikely either. The state of hurling in St Kieran's was not so much at a low ebb – viz Con Kenealy's dictum about its cyclical nature – as in the gutter with no stars to be seen anywhere; they had long since done their Leaving Cert and left the school. The college went from 1977 to '84 without winning a Leinster title and in 1980 hit an all-time nadir when losing by 2-17 to 1-2 to Birr Community School in Rathdowney. No, the scoreline is not a misprint. It makes it clear, moreover, that time spent in the black and white hoops was not always either a golden ticket to success in the here and now or a presage of future glory in black and amber stripes. Kenealy's last journalistic marking, as it happened, was in the spring of 1981 and involved another defeat for his alma mater against Birr, who boasted a man-mountain called Ken Hogan at full-back.

The 1982 team made their exit from the provincial championship in Bagenalstown the Sunday after St Kieran's Day. Eschewing the usual official buses, a number of students travelled by train without bothering to buy a ticket, their rationale being that the worst that could befall them would be to be thrown off at the first stop – ie Bagenalstown. The St Peter's supporters sang "Happy birthday, dear Kieran's", although whether they were being sincere or sarcastic nobody could quite tell. The game finished 0-12 to 0-5 in favour of a St Peter's outfit that included Tom Dempsey, a man who would endure a lifetime of travails in the purple and gold before finally winning a richly deserved All Ireland medal in 1996. But a couple of the losing players would be heard of again, primarily Pat Dwyer and Eamon Morrissey. And in 1988 St Kieran's were at last All Ireland champions once more with a team that included Adrian Ronan, Pat O'Neill and DJ Carey. And for the next 20 years and more they wouldn't stop winning All Irelands. Winter, and Rathdowney in 1980, had been left behind.

Thoughtfully planned and energetically enacted, the bicentenary celebrations proved a signal success. His job done, Tommy Maher was made a monsignor and despatched far from the madding crowd to Mullinavat, 20 miles from

Kilkenny on the main road to Waterford and his first and last parish. Well done, thou good and faithful servant. First a hurling visionary, then a parish priest: his life's dual destiny.

Being a coach had engaged Tommy Maher's intellect; being a parish priest would engage his heart. Being president of St Kieran's had been about bureaucracy; being in Mullinavat would be about people.

Knowing – few knew better – how the human mind worked, he had mastered the trick of leading from the front while appearing to be trudging along at the back. When there was a task to be undertaken or a problem to be solved, he'd call a parish meeting and outline the situation. After a little subtle guidance on his part, the parishioners would arrive at the solution he'd wanted them to arrive at all along. His idea became their idea. Honey catches flies sooner than vinegar.

When it was decided the graveyard had to be cleaned up and a ditch removed, he arranged the plan of campaign with the thoroughness of an old general with a thousand battles behind him. A meeting was called and people from different areas of Mullinavat given specific tasks: the faithful from one end of the parish to bring billhooks and slashers and chainsaws, those from another end to bring tractors and trailers, someone else to find a digger. They gathered at nine o'clock one morning and between them had the job done in jig time. (Oddly enough, he hadn't seen fit to gather his team together the night beforehand and put them through their paces, possibly correcting a grip on a billhook here or tightening someone's swing of a slashers there. Tut.)

In the mid-1990s the local voluntary housing association decided to build homes for the elderly in the grounds of the old boys' national school. They didn't have far to go for assistance. Fr Maher went through the diocese to obtain the land and to a former St Kieran's student of his, now high up in Kilkenny County Council, to set the process in motion. When the eight houses for the elderly were completed, there was only one name that could possibly be bestowed on the development. Fr Maher Place is a small oasis of peace and quiet tucked away from what used to be the main Kilkenny-Waterford road.

In the words of Tommy Duggan, a stalwart of the local GAA club, he "was a great PP". Always a word for everyone, always a few sweets in his pocket. If Declan and Tony Duggan were pucking around at home when Fr Maher called to see their father, he'd join in and pass on the occasional tip ("here, try it this way, it's better"). One time in Croke Park at a Kilkenny match, Tommy Duggan found himself in the front of the upper deck of the old Hogan Stand, one row behind the RTE cameras, with Fr Maher on one side of him and Nicky Purcell, the former Kilkenny county board chairman, on the other, analysing and deconstructing the proceedings between them. On arriving home that night he had no need to listen to the experts on *The Sunday Game*.

And yes, the Mullinavat lads persuaded him to help out with the team as well. Of course they did. He didn't say yes immediately. Hurling, after all, wasn't what he had come there for. But the club elders kept asking and in the end he agreed, as they had sensed all along he would. It was raining outside at the time. Someone wondered aloud when the first training session would be held. By way of response, Fr Maher stood up and drew back the curtains in the parochial house. "I wouldn't like to be out in that and I don't think the players would either."

In throwing in his lot with the men of Mullinavat he wasn't doing it for the glamour. If Nowlan Park was Broadway, then Mullinavat did their thing not so much off-Broadway as somewhere in the Ozarks. Most of their matches they played in Piltown. Sometimes they played in Thomastown. That was as glamorous as it got.

The last time they'd won anything, the county junior title in 1939, Tommy Maher was a student in St Kieran's. They'd reached a couple of southern junior finals in the 1970s and another one in 1981, and Mossy Murphy, Kilkenny's pointscoring substitute against Cork in 1972, was still knocking around and taking the frees despite being, in his own words, "bet at that stage". But there was no good reason why the Centenary Year of the GAA would also be a year of glory for Mullinavat. Well, no good reason apart from the identity of their coach. That, it transpired, would be reason enough.

What most struck Tommy Duggan, one of the selectors, was the sheer simplicity of Fr Maher's methods. "A child could pick it up, the way he taught it. He was like a schoolteacher, which he had been. He never raised his voice or fell out with anyone. People around here would stand on their heads for him."

He may have been long gone from the intercounty arena, but the human touch had not deserted him. It never would. One player turned up late for training one evening and was slagged by his teammates. In stepped the coach. "Hang on, now, hang on. This man is after a hard day's work on the farm. Bringing in hay, piking bales. He's done a lot more today than most of you. He doesn't need training."

Another night he refereed a match in training and kept blowing a particular player. The player, fed up, got the ball, belted it into the next field and stormed off. He wasn't seen at training for days afterwards. Eventually the club chairman went to Fr Maher and asked if the player could come back. "Where did he go?" was the response. "Sure I didn't send him anywhere or stop him coming back."

Individual coaching was not neglected, naturally, particular horses being specifically prepared for particular courses. An example. Harry Waters, one of the corner-forwards, was a great man to snap up possession and shoot on sight, no matter where he was positioned or how many defenders surrounded him. Fr Maher devoted an entire session to coaching him to look up, take the four steps and make room for himself. Waters duly scored a goal in the southern final. A *handpassed* goal.

Mullinavat's road to glory in 1984 involved a dozen games in the southern championship alone, culminating in a 2-12 to 2-6 win against Dunnamaggin in the divisional final in Piltown. En route they saw off Thomastown, Mooncoin, Kilmacow, Rower-Inistioge, Tullogher-Rosbercon, Carrigeen, Slieverue, Ballyhale Shamrocks and John Lockes (twice). Their only defeat was sustained at the hands of Dunnamaggin but avenged in the final. And as with the Kilkenny team of 1957 before them, they made an interesting discovery on the journey. The more they practised and played, the better they became.

As Nowlan Park was being redeveloped, all roads led to Callan on October 21st for the county final against Emeralds of Urlingford. The day was misty, the sod greasy, the first half sluggish. Mullinavat, under the captaincy of Tommy Frisby, led by 1-3 to 1-2 at its end. Both sides needed a break. The southerners got one when Mossy Murphy – not quite so bet after all, evidently – sent in a dangerous ball from out the field and Michael Law got a touch that deceived David Burke, a future Kilkenny and Wexford goalkeeper, on the Emeralds line. From there Mullinavat coasted home by 3-9 to 1-5. The parish had a new set of heroes to join the men of 1939. Foremost among them was Mossy Murphy, who finished up top scorer in the final with seven points.

"As close and all as the hurling was," the *Kilkenny GAA Yearbook* noted, "you could see the Maher influence on the Mullinavat team. The ball was moved quickly. The basic handpass was a gambit used effectively, and regularly, but not too often at the same time." Among the spectators was the late Fr Donie O'Brien, a Mullinavat native ministering in the diocese of Hexham, a Newcastle United season-ticket holder and a hurling fanatic. Fr Donie drove back for the match, went straight to Nowlan Park and had to rush out to Callan on learning it was being held there instead.

"Did we have players who were going to win a county title anyway?" Dan Power, the Mullinavat centre-back, muses. "I'm honestly not sure. But did Fr Maher make a difference? Without a doubt."

Apologies for the cliché, but to Power the coach was – yes – a breath of fresh air. "He got the simple things right, he put no great emphasis on physical training and he was way more interested in the ball and how to use it. You've often heard it said, but he really was years ahead of his time."

He was ahead of his time from a psychological viewpoint likewise. Mullinavat had had trainers who preached the gospel of fire and brimstone, threatening eternal damnation for players who went drinking the night before a game. As befitted a man who enjoyed a drop of whiskey himself, the Maher sermon for the weekend of a game didn't come from the Book of the Apocalypse. You normally have five pints on the Saturday night before a match next day? Then have two pints. That way you'll get a night's sleep and won't be a total bag of nerves on the Sunday morning.

During the puckaround before one of the matches in the southern championship Power, who at school inside in De La Salle College in Waterford had partnered Ferrybank's Shane Ahearne at midfield, looked down the far end of the field, "as you do", saw the opposition centre-forward and did a double take. The centre-forward might have come straight out of the mists of time and off the Wexford team of the 1950s: 6'3 in height, tanned legs like tree trunks, driving balls over the bar from all angles. Power was "planking it". Spotting his anxiety Tommy Maher, who may or may not have recognised something of Ned Wheeler in the stranger, ambled over, hands in his pockets, kicking stones out of his way.

"Who's yer man?" he asked. "The number 11?"

"I don't know."

"Hmm. Me neither. But someone built like that, if he was any good he'd be on the county team and we'd all know about him." That was enough for Power. Problem solved. Sure enough, the centre-forward turned out to be a triumph of show over substance and Power hurled the ears off him. He had another high day in the county final, which was followed by celebrations that he calculates lasted "about a month". He's never quite worked out how many of Mullinavat's publicans were able to retire afterwards.

One of Tommy Maher's oldest and happiest friendships had been sundered in the spring of 1976. Nicky Rackard died in St Vincent's Private Hospital in Dublin on April 10th, having conquered alcoholism only to encounter an even more implacable foe in cancer. The man whose "whole life was a close-in free", as his brother Billy so aptly put it, called to St Kieran's to visit his former classmate shortly before going into hospital for the last time. Rackard was dying, but he was dying at peace with himself and with the world and with his maker, a very different Rackard from the Rackard who a decade earlier had regularly been seen drunk on the streets of Bunclody, a stumbling, shambling shell of the hero of yore. He'd turned his life around and become a latterday apostle of temperance. Tommy Maher felt humbled afterwards.

"I can truly say that on that occasion I met a man who was happiness personified. I have many memories of him, both on the field and off, as man and boy, as teammate and opponent, but the greatest memory I have is of his last visit here. I could never envy that man anything, but I must admit that I was tempted to envy him this peace and serenity which was surely heavenly."

They buried Rackard in Bunclody, by the gentle Slaney under the Blackstairs. Ten thousand people attended the funeral. The coffin was draped in two number 14 jerseys: the purple and gold of Wexford and the black and amber of Rathnure. It is safe to assume that when Nicky Rackard died, a part of Tommy Maher died with him. But the memories could never fade, and every so often a voice would come whispering out of the past to him, far away yet so very near. "Arrah, come on, Maher. Tog out and we'll go for a few pucks down Fennessy's."

Around the same time, with Northern Ireland in flames, Des Ferguson, his confrere from the Gormanston course, was imprisoned. Fr Maher was outraged at his sentence, briefly entertained wild ideas of a protest in Croke Park and finished up having to settle for going to visit Snitchy in Portlaoise Prison with Bishop Birch, the wonders of the phantasmagorical world long swapped for the cares of this world, in tow. They weren't allowed in.

So life went on, for Tommy Maher and for his family. The Mahers moved with it as they could and as they chose to. Tim settled in Kilkenny city, Johnny in Waterford, Dan in Dublin. Willie lost his sight in his early 20s, possibly from the diabetes he was subsequently diagnosed with, but through memory he was still able to walk the roads of the neighbourhood. In time he went to live with Mary Kate, who had married Martin O'Shea, a farmer nearby in Raheenroche. Tim and Johnny acquired wives. Tommy became an uncle several times over.

He was not a constant in the existence of his nieces and nephews as they were growing up. He had his life and they had theirs. On the occasions they did see him he was brisk and practical rather than loving and indulgent, but he was always good for ice cream and sweets and he was always useful for advice.

The work ethic acquired in childhood at home in Whitepark never left him, as his niece Stacy discovered upon writing to him from boarding school in search of tips for an upcoming exam. "There is no such thing as tips for an exam," he wrote back. "You have to study." Typical Tommy Maher; would he have sent Kilkenny out for an All Ireland final without coaching them? Still, Stacy, initially irked, was more than mollified by the ten-shilling note he enclosed with the advice.

The same work ethic was in evidence one time he had two lads working on a Fás scheme in Mullinavat. One morning one of them was out sick, leaving the other to assume the parish priest would give him the day off. What a misguided notion that was. Monsignor Maher stepped into the breach himself and the pair of them were still labouring away at teatime. There was a job to be done and that was that.

In his personal habits he was spartan, his sweet tooth (Scots Clan toffee was a favourite) and partiality to a drop of whiskey or gin aside. Foodwise, enough was as good as a feast. He was asked on one occasion how he kept his figure. "By pushing back from the table," he replied. In contrast to his brother Johnny, who was apolitical, and Dan, who as a civil servant in Dublin developed a visceral and well grounded antipathy to CJ Haughey, he remained a Fianna Fáil supporter.

In common with hundreds of clubs around the country, Mullinavat brought out a club history in 1984, the GAA's Centenary Year. In their case publication was delayed till the end of the year in order to take account of the momentous events of the summer and autumn. The parish priest contributed an essay entitled 'The Church and the GAA' written in his clear and straightforward prose style, devoid of rhetorical flight or literary allusion.

In the article he recalled his encounter with Bishop Collier at Nowlan Park prior to the 1945 All Ireland final and referred to the culture of nods and winks which surrounded the ban on clerical students playing game – hence the basis, one can infer, for his advice to Tom Murphy in 1964 not to ask for permission to travel to Dublin for the All Ireland final. He also quoted Dan Kennedy, Kilkenny's captain in 1947 and a Thomastown teammate, objecting to men of the cloth playing hurling on the grounds that he "couldn't pull into them as I would pull into one who was not a priest". Maybe, the monsignor concluded, those priests who never played for their county but who were keen followers of the game and who helped provide facilities for the local club and community rendered the best service of all to the Association. After which came a little dig, precision-targeted and neatly delivered.

"Sad to say most colleges run by priests of the religious orders, especially those within the Pale, lost their enthusiasm for Gaelic games and ceased to play them by 1936. The reason given...was the Ban. Some would say the Ban was merely an excuse. The schools run by diocesan priests remained faithful to the games and ideals of the Association." Why did he mention 1936? Easy. That year's

Leinster colleges senior hurling championship was won by none other than Blackrock College.

Gradually, and inevitably as the youngest member of the family, he began to lose his siblings. Willie and Tim both died in 1976. Din – the other good hurler in the family; he played with the Blacks and Whites and was the full-forward and scorer of one of the goals in Kilkenny's 1946 All Ireland junior success – passed away in 1982. Dan, once described by a colleague in Dublin as being "a reasonable man in everything except when it came to Kilkenny hurling" and who had come back home to live in Whitepark on his retirement from the civil service, died in 1995 and Mary Kate three years later.

But the Maher nieces and nephews begot a generation of grandnieces and grandnephews. One of them was Niamh Herlihy, Stacy's daughter, from Waterford. Mother and daughter dropped in to see the monsignor in Mullinavat after Niamh had been called up for one of the Irish under-age hockey squads. He may have pretended not to be impressed, muttering something about "Protestant hurling", but he was. His grin and the £100 he handed Niamh gave the game away.

The years went by. Monsignor Maher became an integral part of life in Mullinavat, ministering and succouring and overseeing Fás schemes and attending matches, a quiet but watchful shepherd. When he spoke about "going home" after a day out somewhere he meant returning to Mullinavat. He announced his intention to be buried there and he chose a plot.

The only time he'd be less than welcoming was if someone decided to call in on a Sunday afternoon to watch the big match of the day on television with him. Much to his irritation, they'd feel it necessary to try and dazzle him with the perspicacity of their observations. "One commentator is enough," he remarked acidly.

And then came the day after which there would be no more big matches or Sunday afternoons. He travelled to the 1999 All Ireland final, Kilkenny versus Cork in the rain, with Tommy Duggan and seemed oddly strained throughout. After they arrived back in Mullinavat that night he admitted to feeling tired. Duggan brought him into the parish house, put on the burglar alarm and said goodnight. Next morning he called up to see him, got no answer and assumed he was out somewhere. Around midday he heard the news. Monsignor Maher had had a stroke and been taken to Ardkeen Hospital in Waterford.

He would survive. But his ministry was over.

CHAPTER 24

Aftermath

Offaly 2-16 Kilkenny 2-5
1995 Leinster final

Tommy Maher departed but the lovely river flowed on. Of Kilkenny's 13 All Ireland titles over the course of the following 33 seasons, each was won under the stewardship of a former player of his. Pat Henderson, Eddie Keher, Ollie Walsh, Brian Cody. The fountainhead and the streams.

The baton was passed on from the gun without a missed stride. Twelve months after the disappointment of 1978, Kilkenny were back in the All Ireland final with Henderson and Keher as joint-managers. Noel Skehan saved a penalty from John Connolly seven minutes from time with Galway trailing by two points and Chunky O'Brien returned from the Reichenbach Falls to hit 1-7 and be named man of the match. Donal Carroll in the *Irish Independent* next day was moved to expatiate on "how wrong it was" that the James Stephens man had been called ashore the previous year and to single out Nickey Brennan, a starter on the big day at last, as the winners' best performer after Ger Henderson.

The rise of Offaly under Dermot Healy provided the county with new opponents in Leinster, ones whose threat it took them a long time to fully recognise and longer still to come to terms with. But 1982 brought the emergence under Henderson of one of the truly great Kilkenny teams, a side that did the league and championship double in successive seasons. Occasionally Henderson would pause and wonder how coaching seemed to come so instinctively to him. It didn't take him long to find the answer. Fifteen years under Tommy Maher had prepared him for it. He was similarly blessed in his on-field leaders, old colleagues like Frank Cummins and Noel Skehan. "They couldn't have made it easier for me."

The captain in 1982 was Brian Cody, four years on from his 1978 Croke Park agony in the garden. There are no second acts in American lives? There can be second acts in Irish sporting lives, and in this case there would be a long-running third act. One of the stars in the All Ireland final was Christy Heffernan, who hit 2-3 in the hammering of Cork. Another was Skehan, now 36 "and training three times harder" than he had done a decade ago, who made a string of improbable saves and walked off munching the apple thrown to him by an admirer on the Canal End. In view of various events that were to take place on Leeside two decades later it is only fair to quote the tribute paid to Skehan, who was winning his eighth All Ireland medal, by the Cork county secretary Frank Murphy, a brilliant and complex man, on what must have been a ghastly afternoon for him. "You have given great service to your county and to hurling and no better goalkeeper could achieve what you've done."

Cork were seen off again in 1983, this time by a rapidly diminishing two points instead of 11. It was the afternoon Billy Fitzpatrick, in his sixth All Ireland decider, finally attained his majority, man of the match with 0-10 of the winning total of 2-14. Not a fan of ground hurling and not particularly good in the air, Fitzpatrick liked to get the sliotar up and into his hand ("that way you were in control"), and his left was nearly as strong as his right. Half of his total in the 1983 final was sourced from play; one of the frees was narrowly wide but the umpire waved the white flag regardless, as if to atone for the divine effort featuring a dummy handpass Fitzpatrick had had wrongly disallowed by Noel O'Donoghue against Cork 12 months earlier. The RTE cameras caught him giggling to himself as he trotted back out. "I never admitted it was wide. But it was. About half a foot wide."

But there would be bad days too, and plenty of them. Days when the falcon could not hear the falconer, or the falconer wasn't up to the task, or the falcon was not the creature of beauty like previous falcons. Kilkenny lost matches under Fr Maher and they would lose matches long after he was gone.

One year they were reduced to paralysis and peremptory defeat when the opposition unveiled a three-man midfield in an All Ireland semi-final; another year one of their players threw a punch at a colleague during a National League match. One year they drew with Kerry in the league; another year the minors were knocked out of the Leinster championship by Antrim. And one management team resigned after a league semi-final defeat at Nowlan Park in which the tannoy announcement of the substitution of the manager's brother was greeted with cheers.

Offaly hurled them out of it in the wet in the 1995 Leinster final with the kind of hurling Kilkenny had played in 1957, clean and astringent, never taking three touches where two would do, never taking two touches where one would do. The rain put a premium not just on efficacy of first touch but also on efficiency of ball movement. Kilkenny had one of those items; Offaly had both. Eleven points was the difference between the sides at the final whistle, and that was with two late goals from DJ Carey failing to take the bad look off the scoreline.

DJ, who learned his freetaking technique from Eddie Keher, had had moments that were more obviously important and he would have them again, but this was a manful intervention on a team being beaten out the gate. He would have poor All Irelands too, for a variety of reasons, but it has been stressed neither often enough nor loudly enough what a brave hurler DJ Carey was. In time his stock would be surpassed by Henry Shefflin. Yet there has never been a more electrifying Kilkenny player.

Four years later they foundered again on soft going, Cork catching them in the final furlong on All Ireland day. The turnaround led Justin McCarthy, still one of hurling's deepest thinkers, to criticise Kilkenny's preference for taking the ball to hand instead of, in view of the conditions, moving it first time. It was a fair and accurate point, and one that would have been echoed by his old friend from the Gormanston days.

Nor can every misstep and blunder be dismissed as relics of a less streamlined age, for as recently as 2007 the Kilkenny minor manager of the day, on seeing his team beaten by the reigning champions in an All Ireland semi-final, blithely attributed the reversal to the notion that "Tipperary are used to winning and we're not". And while Tommy Maher's alma mater proceeded to win colleges titles with clockwork regularity once they rediscovered their heritage in 1988, 2007 also featured a city derby at Nowlan Park in which St Kieran's took on Kilkenny CBS with Richie Hogan deployed at centre-forward and TJ Reid 20 yards behind him at midfield. Unsurprisingly, they lost. Never make the mistake of assuming that Noreside provenance renders a team all-talented on the field or all-seeing on the sideline.

A Maher legacy there was, however, albeit one that passed largely unmentioned in the normal run of local public discourse. The possibility of him being made a freeman of Kilkenny, for instance, never arose. But in the winter of 1998 the county board appointed a manager who would be.

CHAPTER 25

Legacy

It's not today's men who have made Kilkenny famous. It's the men of years ago
Paddy Grace's old friend Bill Sullivan to fellow regulars in the front bar in Langton's on the Sunday night before the 2010 All Ireland final

It began in rain and misery and it ended the same way. It began with Kilkenny supporters trudging down Jones's Road in the drizzle in 1999 with the words of Mark Landers – "Welcome back to Leeside, Liam MacCarthy! We've missed you a lot!" – echoing in their ears. It ended with Kilkenny supporters trudging down Jones's Road in the drizzle in 2010 with the strains of Pat Kerwick singing 'The Galtee Mountain Boy' echoing in their ears.

What happened in between – well, what happened in between was a slightly different story. What happened in between the showers was a decade of endless summer. What happened in between was the noughties. And the noughties were painted in black and amber stripes, like no decade had been painted in any county's colours before.

One decade. One county. One manager. Ceaseless triumphs. By the facts and figures in the first instance shall ye know them. Apologies if the following paragraphs induce dyspepsia in readers from other counties.

In 2000 Kilkenny captured the county's 26th All Ireland senior title by defeating Offaly in a game they could not afford to lose, having been beaten in the previous two finals.

In 2001 they won nothing.

In 2002: All Ireland senior and minor double plus the National League.

In 2003: All Ireland senior, minor and under-21 treble plus another National League title.

In 2004: All Ireland under-21 title. This was not quite the comedown it might at first glance have appeared, for if 2003 had seen three Kilkenny teams win their respective championships, 2004 saw the three teams reach their respective finals once more, a scarcely less worthy achievement.

In 2005: National League title plus All Ireland club success for James Stephens.

In 2006: All Ireland senior and under-21 titles plus the National League.

In 2007: All Ireland senior title plus All Ireland club success for Ballyhale Shamrocks.

In 2008: the jackpot. All Ireland senior title for the third year in succession, the county's first three in a row since 1913 and technically speaking their first 'proper' three in a row (no All Ireland final took place in 1911, Kilkenny being awarded the crown after Limerick refused to play a refixed decider in Thurles). All Ireland minor title. All Ireland under-21 title. All Ireland intermediate title. Tutankhamun's tomb. Everywhere the glint of gold.

In 2009: All Ireland senior title for the sixth time in eight years and the fourth year in succession, plus the National League title. The defeat of Tipperary marked only the second time in history that four consecutive All Irelands had been won, and in this case the feat was achieved without the asterisk of the 1941 Foot and Mouth affair that accompanied the first leg of Cork's four in a row.

Seventy years on from the Thunder and Lightning final Tommy Cummins, now rising 85 as opposed to celebrating his 15th birthday, made it back to Kingsbridge – or Heuston Station as they called it these days – in time to have a drink before catching the train home. And when he arrived back in Kilkenny, the city was not in darkness.

Fr Tommy Maher had taken a grand but decaying old house, put in new foundations and rebuilt it from the bottom up. Brian Cody added the new wing, the outdoor pool, the customised gym, the heated driveway and the boutique winery out the back.

But the bare statistical bones told only half the story. It wasn't just what Kilkenny did, it was the total and utter ruthlessness with which they did it. The four in a row. The 21-match winning run that brought them to within one victory of five in a row. The average score per game of 2-22 in the course of the four in a row, the average winning margin of ten points, the average winning margin against Munster opposition of 8.5 points. Opponent after opponent unseamed from the nave to the chops; no fuss, no mercy, nothing personal, just business. One defeat in 26 games between 2006 and 2011, with Kilkenny leading at half-time in no fewer than 24 of the 26 encounters. Liam Griffin was coming out of Croke Park one day when he overheard a disgruntled Offaly supporter saying, "Feck those Kilkenny lads, they want to win everything!" That summed it up perfectly.

In doing the All Ireland senior and minor double in 2002, Kilkenny beat Clare and Tipperary by an aggregate of 21 points, leading the TV columnist of *The Irish Times* to make a reference to "Kilkenny arts week" the following Saturday. The treble of senior, minor and under-21 honours the season afterwards prompted the *Irish Examiner* to put a picture of a black and amber jersey – DJ Carey's, as it happened – on the front page of their sports supplement atop the headline "Too good?" When the under-21 title was retained the following season, it was done so by way of a 3-21 to 1-6 evisceration of Tipperary at Nowlan Park. The consummation of the three in a row against Waterford in 2008 was soundtracked by the noise of all manner of records, ancient and modern, being smashed, from the score Kilkenny hit (3-30) to the winning margin (23 points) via the highest number of scores in a final (47) and the dead-eyed assassin's accuracy of their shooting: 37 attempts on goal, two wides, one shot saved, one shot back off an upright, 33 scores.

Their smallest winning margin in the 2008 championship was the nine points they had in hand against Cork in the All Ireland semi-final. Their average winning margin was 17.25 points. One could not but think of the Irish National Hunt handicapper of the 1960s, that gentleman who was forced to design separate steeplechasing handicaps, the first framed for races where Arkle was entered, the other for races where he wasn't. And for backers of favourites Kilkenny were a dream, shattering the spread match after match. They didn't so much rewrite the record books as tear them up, set fire to them, throw away the ashes and sit down to compose their own volumes.

Earlier the same afternoon against Waterford, just to prove that Kilkenny teams didn't even need to be the better side in order to win, the minors, hitherto scoreless in the second half, hit a late goal and point to mug Galway. Activities the following spring, as if *pour encourager les autres*, included ritual disembowellings of Tipperary (18 points) and Cork (27 points) at Nowlan Park in the National League. Faster, pussycat, kill, kill. Brian Cody's charges concluded the competition by pulling away from Tipp in extra time in the final in Semple Stadium despite having only seven of the team that had started against Waterford the previous September still on the field.

There had been superpowers in hurling and Gaelic football before. Under Cody, Kilkenny became the GAA's first hyperpower. In retrospect the Hades of the 1999 All Ireland final turned out to be a small price to pay for passage to Elysium.

Nor was it simply a matter of winning trophy after trophy, uttering some polite, meaningless words, going home to celebrate and starting all over again come January. Every success meant something, and some of them meant more than others. To single out one individual from the happy multitudes: Dan Butler, who we met in the opening chapter when he didn't fancy Kilkenny's prospects in the 1957 Leinster final and so remained at home.

The same Mr Butler didn't pass up too many opportunities to follow his county to Croke Park and elsewhere over the next half a century, a habit that reached its apotheosis when he saw Tipperary defeated on September 6th 2009. At one point in the long, luxuriant winter that followed he announced that he'd "now die happy". One can safely assume he was not the only Kilkenny man of uncertain age who was saying the same. And two years later he was able to say it all over again. For the record – and even if Dan Butler was just another Kilkenny supporter, such minutiae deserve to be recorded, because what is success if it is not, among other things, the songs of the victors' supporters? – the best player he saw during those 50-plus years was Henry Shefflin, shading Eddie Keher. His favourite player was Mick Crotty for the unseen work he did and his favourite All Ireland final that of 2011.

The team of the noughties were different to any Kilkenny team Dan Butler had watched before then and they were in many ways the same. *Briseann an dúchas tré shúile na Cait.*

Like the team of the 1970s they had a rod of iron as a spinal cord. For Dillon/Orr, Henderson, Cummins, Delaney and Purcell read Hickey, Barry/Hogan, Lyng, Shefflin and Comerford.

For Noel Skehan read James McGarry, a goalkeeper in the finest Bennettsbridge/Thomastown tradition and one who in six All Ireland starts conceded the sum total of three goals.

The team of the '70s had Frank Cummins, a man not so much born as quarried, in the middle of the field; the team of the noughties had Derek Lyng. Cummins was partnered for three All Ireland victories by Chunky O'Brien, all touch and flair and solo runs; Lyng was partnered for three All Ireland victories by Cha Fitzpatrick, a Féile na nGael skills champion.

The team of the '70s had Eddie Keher, who for three decades after his retirement remained hurling's all-time top scorer; the team of the noughties had Henry Shefflin, the man who took that mantle from Keher.

Where the forward line of the '70s possessed hardworking domestiques in Mick Crotty and Mick Brennan, the noughties equivalent had Martin Comerford and Aidan Fogarty. And with the forward line he played behind in the '70s, Pat Henderson had the luxury of being able to "put the ball down on their heads", a luxury familiar to the Kilkenny defenders of three decades later. One of the most percipient observations about Cody's side was made by Adrian Fenlon, a Wexford hero in 1996, who observed them at close quarters in his capacity as a waterboy for his county in 2007. "That wasn't a high ball in," he announced after one long delivery from Cha Fitzpatrick at midfield to Henry Shefflin on the edge of the square. "That was a pass."

Not unlike the team of the '70s, the team of the noughties had a core of superstars surrounded and complemented by a wealth of very good players. The latter iteration had more depth on the bench, and another of their blessings was the presence of a couple of forwards, usually Eoin Larkin with points and Eddie Brennan with goals, who supplemented the staple diet of Shefflin scores, with Comerford having his regular-occasional scoring days and Fogarty chipping in more frequently than was realised.

Admittedly the team of the '70s didn't have a parallel to Tommy Walsh, the boy wizard without the scar on his forehead. No hurling team in history did. But when Walsh hit the opening point of the 2003 All Ireland final inside ten seconds, a mighty effort off his left from the touchline under the Hogan Stand, it was no leap to imagine the ghosts of his fellow Tullaroan men Lory Meagher and Paddy Phelan hovering on the Railway End and guiding the sliotar between the uprights.

And then there was Shefflin. King Henry. Perhaps not *the* man, but unquestionably the main man. The alpha male, the hunter gatherer, Aragorn. Simultaneously the battalion commander, invariably first over the top and into battle, and the field marshal. The older Shefflin got, the more he seemed to hurl the game in an extra dimension inaccessible to lesser mortals. It was as though he was both in the trenches and at the same time viewing the action from somewhere among the clouds above. What was a field to others was a chessboard to him.

The 2001 All Ireland semi-final was the first time a championship match bypassed him. It was also the last time. When Kilkenny were beaten thereafter, it may have been on days when Shefflin was indifferent but it was never on days when he was irrelevant. Through force of will and determination – it was nothing to do with skill or even size – he made himself the axis on which the team spun. Occasionally he even made himself relevant by making himself irrelevant. A more insecure or lesser player might have taken Waterford's disarray in the 2008 All Ireland final as a pretext to go to town on them, but Shefflin, never one to obtain his kicks from the prospect of a turkey shoot, was content to do no more than his bit when no more than his bit was all that was required.

It may seem odd, even obtuse, that the finest Kilkenny score of the generation did not involve a single touch from the finest Kilkenny player of the generation. But there was good reason for that. Richie Hogan's goal against Tipperary in the 2011 All Ireland final came about partly because Shefflin was keeping Pádraic Maher company miles away under the Hogan Stand. That was *echt* Henry, a man frequently more dangerous when he didn't have the ball than when he did, not mastered by the compulsion or the misplaced ego to insist on doing everything by himself, grandmastering matters from wherever he chose to take up station. A 15-man game, and he didn't forget it. It was only by a quirk of spelling that there was an i in Shefflin.

Brilliance is not a synonym for greatness. There have been wristier Kilkenny hurlers. There have been faster Kilkenny hurlers. There have been more skilful Kilkenny hurlers. There have been Kilkenny hurlers who struck the sliotar more sweetly. But never has there been a Kilkenny hurler who aggregated so many of the game's gifts to and in himself. And never has there been a more durable or resilient Kilkenny hurler. Shefflin began life as a championship player the same day Brian Cody began it as a championship manager, on June 20th 1999 against Laois in the Leinster semi-final. It was the start of a beautiful friendship that endured through success and failure, through arrivals and departures, through marriage and babies, through loss of form and through two cruciate injuries. When Kilkenny took the field at Croke Park on September 4th 2011, it was Cody's 56th championship match as manager and Shefflin's 56th as player. Staggering.

What was it like to be a member of such a group?

"An amazing privilege," says Derek Lyng, who began his intercounty career as a junior clubman and finished it a six-time All Ireland medallist. "The commitment, the hard work, the things you learn from being part of a team. And it doesn't do you any harm outside hurling. You're constantly trying to prove yourself. You learn to take the rough with the smooth. All those experiences stay with you in some shape or form."

The eternal question. How did Cody do it?

"It's hard to explain. He got that respect from players. When I came in in 2001 I saw him make big calls, drop big stars. He judged you by how you were going in training. Everybody can buy into that. It's fair. And when you came back in January, you might have six All Irelands but you were still trying to prove yourself as much as a guy without any. Lads knew where they stood."

Ask Lyng to nominate an incident from the training ground or dressing room that for him serves as a freeze-frame of the group's togetherness, their sense of purpose, and he is unable to do so. There is no stand-out moment for him because, in a sense, every moment was a stand-out moment. All of them mattered in some shape or form. Pressed, he does cite the bus trip to Thurles for the 2004 qualifier against Galway.

"We'd lost to Wexford in the Leinster semi-final. We'd taken some flak. That evening you could see the spirit and the unity. The dressing room was very tense. It's difficult to describe. But when you go into something like that and you come out the other side, imagine how much it bonds a team. There were so many occasions like that."

A word here about two men who contributed immensely if unspectacularly to such days. Famously, James McGarry never did receive an All Star award, but All Stars are subjective. If anything needs to be appended by way of a coda to his All Ireland record and medal haul, it is that no Kilkenny goalkeeper ever organised his defence as quietly commandingly as he did. As for Peter Barry, the rock on whom Cody built his church of 2002-03, the county have had finer hurlers at centre-back over the years. They have rarely had finer men.

"Two brilliant leaders," Lyng acknowledges. "They were held in very high regard within the panel. James and Peter were two of the first out training every night, the kind of guys who didn't care what people outside thought of them. They never really went in for that kind of thing. Once they were driving things on, that's all that mattered to them. They brought us along and told us when to buck up and step up. They helped Brian set the template for the four in a row."

A word too about Mick O'Flynn, who did the physical work with the teams of 2000 and 2002-03 and was, according to Lyng, "ahead of his time". And a similar shout-out for Noel Richardson, who followed O'Flynn and who over the contours of five years and 22 championship fixtures as trainer measured out the petrol with such care and precision that not once were Kilkenny found wanting physically.

The week after the 2011 All Ireland final, one of Georgie Leahy's cronies hopped a ball as to how many members of the Kilkenny team of the noughties would have made it onto the Kilkenny team of the 1970s. Call Georgie biased, a charge he wouldn't dream of denying, but his amalgam of the two sides would contain more men from the '70s team on which he was a selector than from their successors of the noughties.

Skehan, Henderson, Cummins, Delaney, Purcell and Keher are shoo-ins on a Best of XV. The same goes for Hickey, Walsh, JJ, Henry and, for his goalscoring feats, Eddie Brennan. After that, beauty is in the eye of the beholder.

Therein lies both the frustration and the attraction of the exercise. It is different in other sporting spheres. We know that Arkle was the greatest steeplechaser ever and that Sea The Stars, brilliantly though he swept all before him on the Flat in 2009, was not quite the equal of the mighty Sea Bird four decades earlier. The *Timeform* ratings tell us this in black and white. There is no room for argument, still less for disagreement.

In hurling we have the freedom to argue and disagree till the cows come home. We guess and we surmise and we what-if according to prejudice and provenance. Keher or Carey? Ollie or Skehan? Mackey or Ring? As an aside, Tommy Maher was firm on the latter count. Ring by a distance. He didn't rate Mackey particularly highly on predictable technical grounds. Ring he viewed as brilliant if occasionally unnecessarily physical.

One difference between Kilkenny's shock troops of the 1970s and their noughties descendants was that the latter won more and won it more commandingly. What added a gloss finish to the four in a row was the fact that it was achieved in the era of back doors and provincial cross-pollination. Had the Kilkenny team of the '70s managed a four in a row, they could theoretically have done so by beating only two Munster outfits along the way. The team of the noughties met Munster opponents on a regular basis and destroyed them on a regular basis.

The 2008 All Ireland final was their equivalent of the 1973 Leinster final, the injury-addled 2010 All Ireland final their 1973 All Ireland final and the 2011 All Ireland final their 1974 All Ireland final. And no, they didn't manage five in a row, but they did something which was even greater and more satisfying: they came back the following year to win a fifth title in six.

An obvious similarity between the two teams was the thunder from the basslines. There may have been subtler Kilkenny XVs than the 2006-09 version; there was none as hardwearing. Were they a car they'd have been a Volvo with sundry optional extras. Not one of the players provided artistry in isolation. While all of them could hurl, each first had to be prepared to work.

Henry Shefflin was a lead guitarist who hurled like a bassist, Eoin Larkin a marksman whose primary duty was to forage, Richie Power a stylist who slowly and sometimes painfully learned the virtues of conspicuous self-sacrifice. Eddie Brennan may have been the resident triggerman, but as big a talking point as the two goals he scored in the 2007 All Ireland final was the ferocity with which he threw himself at the Limerick defence. And knowing what we know of his beliefs and preferences, it is not too much to infer that Tommy Maher's favourite member of the troupe would have been Cha Fitzpatrick. The powers of anticipation, the perfection of touch (was there a single ball the Ballyhale man did not kill first time during his 2006-08 rapture?), the tightness of swing, the determination to move the sliotar quickly, the aversion to taking four touches where three would suffice, the readiness to identify and fill gaps in his own half of the field. All that gorgeous minimalism.

Some things were different to the way they'd been even a few years beforehand. When James McGarry joined the panel in 1998, he revealed on KCLR 96FM the day after the 2008 All Ireland final, "about eight or nine" of the players trained the way they played, most notably Willie O'Connor, whose application of a Nowlan Park evening was legendary. After a couple of years of Brian Cody that number had increased to 11 or 12. Since then, McGarry elaborated, the light had dawned fully. "Now everyone trains the way they play." The manager's work ethos writ large.

In a corner of the Ards peninsula they still reminisce about the day they travelled from Ballygalget to Nowlan Park for the 1976 All Ireland club semi-final with James Stephens. The visitors' captain was first into the middle for the toss. Brian Cody, the Stephens captain for the day, was slower to materialise but shouted 'heads' from 20 yards away as he made his way up the pitch. When the captains shook hands there was, to the surprise of the Ballygalget man, no small talk from his opposite number. No "Welcome to Kilkenny". No "How did ye get here?" Not even a "Did ye come by pony and trap?" Total focus. Absolute single-mindedness.

The same focus and single-mindedness would be in evidence in a different setting one day 23 years later. Shortly after he became county chairman early in 1999, Ned Quinn dropped in to see Kilkenny's new manager in St Patrick's de la Salle. It was more than a courtesy call on Quinn's part; it was a necessary visit. The truth of the situation is that while nobody in the county had had anything much against Cody when he was appointed as Kevin Fennelly's successor a couple of months earlier, nobody had had anything much *for* him either. He was the ultimate unknown quantity.

Neither man ever publicly broadcast the details of their conversation, which lasted for over two hours, but by the end of it Cody was no longer an unknown quantity in Quinn's eyes. Cody had a vision for Kilkenny hurling which cohered with Quinn's own. He'd realised from watching Ger Loughnane's Clare that the rumour of native Kilkenny craft, passed down from generation to generation, was not enough and that being content with winning two All Irelands per decade was unacceptable. He spoke, as someone who'd known unhappy dressing rooms himself, of his determination to create a happy camp and an unbreakable spirit.

He succeeded. He succeeded wildly. Under Cody the county would lose games, would lose players, would lose captains. But they never lost their focus, they never collapsed under the weight of their own mental fragility or internal contradictions, they never died without their boots on and only once did they lose a game they should have won. Cody recast the county's image in his own iron mentality.

In 1994 the possibility of a three in a row was squandered early in the season; that didn't happen under Cody. Being satisfied with two All Irelands per decade? The man would have been barely satisfied with two All Irelands per year. And when the most appalling tragedy befell one of the most popular members of the panel the Thursday before the 2007 All Ireland quarter-final, the bonds were not shattered.

But none of this was self-fulfilling. None of it. Had it been announced on December 31st 1999 that hurling in the forthcoming decade would be dominated by one county, and dominated to an unprecedented extent, Kilkenny would not have been the obvious choice. They wouldn't have even been the first choice. Cork had won the 1999 All Ireland with a young team. Tipperary had been All Ireland minor champions in 1996 and would shortly be unleashing a youngster from Mullinahone called Eoin Kelly on a suspecting world. Galway were churning out successful under-age outfits on a near-annual basis. Kilkenny, by contrast, hadn't won a minor All Ireland since 1993.

And think back on some of those scorelines from the recent past. Wexford 2-20 Kilkenny 1-6 in 1976. Antrim 2-9 Kilkenny 1-11 in the first round of the 1980 Leinster minor championship, and at Nowlan Park to boot. Birr Community School 2-17 St Kieran's 1-2 the same year. Offaly knocking Kilkenny out of the provincial senior, minor and under-21 championships in 1989. Offaly 2-16 Kilkenny 2-5 in the downpour in 1995. At times the sight of the primrose path of the noughties engendered amnesia outside the county borders. It was as though non-Kilkenny folk appeared to believe that umbrellas had never been sold in the Marble City, ignoring the reality that regular tacky defeats had provided the backbeat of the preceding two decades.

Brian Cody never saw himself as being a coach; Tommy Maher never saw himself as being anything other than one. (Just imagine how much the latter would have relished the additional scope for coaching that the full-time intercounty season of today offers.) When Cody declared in the middle of the noughties that he "didn't do tactics", he was speaking nothing less than the truth. The announcement shouldn't have come as a surprise.

This, after all, was a man who before he turned 22 had won All Ireland medals at senior, minor, under-21, colleges and club level and been honoured by the All Star selectors; who had hurled with Eddie Keher and Pat Henderson and Frank Cummins; who had managed DJ Carey and Henry Shefflin and Tommy Walsh. What did Cody need to be worrying himself about tactics or any of that oul' nonsense for? What else, given that he had a half-forward line capable of winning their own ball, was there for him to do but let his players get on with it? Why would he want to be complicating life for them? Shag the ball down the field as fast as possible and let Henry do the rest. Demolition-derby hurling.

But at length the day came when letting them get on with it wasn't enough any more. The day in question was the day of the All Ireland semi-final against Galway. Not the 2001 semi-final, however, that game so endlessly written about and parsed from all angles for years afterwards. No: the 2005 semi-final.

It was an afternoon that might have been scripted by Raymond Chandler. *When in doubt, have a man with a gun in his hand walk through the door.* It was the afternoon that John Tennyson was left naked in front of goal and taken for a hat-trick by Niall Healy. It was the afternoon that Tommy Walsh won and processed an ocean of possession at midfield, yet in trying to make every ball a telling ball gave David Tierney the leeway to institute a couple of incisions that led to Galway goals. It was the afternoon that Kilkenny hit 4-18, sufficient to win any normal encounter but insufficient to win this glorious freak of a game.

Noel Hickey was absent through illness. Galway scored five goals. These occurrences were not unrelated, for Hickey was one of those sedate country lads, with good manners and winter in their eyes, on whom Kilkenny built and perpetuated their empire. One moment crystallised the team's disarray. When Healy beat Tennyson to kick the fifth goal and the one that put Galway out of sight, the nearest Kilkenny defender was out beyond the 45-metre line. Fill all gaps? Tommy Maher would have had a fit.

"It was a really big lesson for us and it led to a lot of soul-searching," Michael Dempsey reveals. "How we were beaten, the way we were exposed, the space Galway created in front of our goal. The first thing you have to be is hard to break down. It opened our eyes in terms of tactics."

The game stands as the most important and loudest resounding hurling match of the noughties. Off went Cody to ponder space, tactics and other such things in his heart. Among his most impressive achievements in the subsequent four years was to ensure that his team did not appear in a single championship fixture that spiralled out of control on them. Games played in winning four All Irelands in a row: 18. Goals conceded: 20. The 2005 semi-final was never repeated but never forgotten.

If defeat to Galway in 2001 taught or reaffirmed to him the importance of attitude and hunger, of the need to have the troops primed for battle, defeat to the same county in 2005 taught him the importance of logistics, of the need to fight the battle on the terrain of one's choice as opposed to being forced to fight it on the terrain of the enemy's choice. After the 2001 semi-final Kilkenny would not fail for lack of fighting spirit; after the 2005 semi-final they would not fail for lack of tactical sophistication. Defeat in 2001 was the springboard for victory in 2002-03; defeat in 2005 was the springboard for four in a row. And the new direction that Cody struck off in after 2001 lasted two full seasons until it met roadblocks erected by Wexford and Cork in 2004; the post-2005 dispensation lasted for 21 games and nearly five full championships until Tipperary saw and raised Kilkenny in 2010.

The 2001 All Ireland semi-final, with the lessons it taught about the dangers of growing soft and falling asleep at the wheel, marked the first sharp turn in the road Cody travelled. The 2005 semi-final signalled the end of demolition-derby hurling and initiated a change of direction that proved even more pronounced and even more successful. And if there would have been no seven All Irelands in ten years without Brian Cody, there could in turn have been no four in a row but for Mick Dempsey and Martin Fogarty, the two men he encountered on the road to Damascus.

The decision that Tommy Walsh would become a card-carrying right-half back rather than a chess piece to be shoved from Billy to Jack as the need arose comprised a key piece of the new jigsaw that was assembled. The reinvention of Cha Fitzpatrick, a catwalk queen who didn't quail at breaking a nail, as a defensive-minded midfielder was another. The tactical configuration drawn up to stymie Cork's possession game in the 2006 All Ireland final endured, with bells and whistles added on over time. One embellishment was the practice of the two wing-forwards dropping back to help defend the opposition puckout, giving Kilkenny seven players in the neighbourhood of a delivery aimed down the centre and ample bodies on hand to snaffle the breakdown. Another was the sleight of Aidan Fogarty and Eddie Brennan crossing to the other man's vacated corner to latch onto deliveries from out the field and shoot points. The gaps were now being filled.

The training regime was tweaked too. Cody overdid it in Nowlan Park coming up to both the 2003 and the 2004 All Ireland finals. Kilkenny got away with it the first time but not the second. The error was not repeated. Less on the training field became more. One of the few insightful admissions to emerge from the masonic secrecy of the camp in later years was Martin Fogarty's revelation that the management had agreed that if Kilkenny lost games it would be because they'd done "too little rather than too much" in training. Tommy Maher's "light training methods" of 1957 all over again.

The caricature of the manager as the pitiless Mr Gradgrind of Sheestown was precisely that. A caricature, a lazy consensus. Had he been as unfeeling as popular opinion had it, Cody could never have kept so many of his players inside the tent. Had he been as inflexible, he would never have learned from his mistakes. Yet he did, time and again.

Putting all the scoring eggs in the one basket seemed the obvious course of action prior to the 2001 All Ireland semi-final. *Too* obvious. Galway succeeded in choking off the supply to Charlie Carter, DJ Carey and Henry Shefflin, the upshot being that a half-forward line of John Hoyne, John Power and Stephen Grehan were never going to pick up the slack in scoring terms. It was an error that would not be repeated. Shefflin, up to then the sorcerer's apprentice, was moved to centre-forward in 2002. There he took over the orchestration from Carey. Conductor, creator, finisher.

One trait of the Kilkenny management that passed largely unacknowledged was their ability to diagnose opposition weaknesses – or strengths – and plan accordingly. Easier to do when you possess heavier ordnance, granted, but the possession of heavier ordnance is no excuse for not engaging in lateral thinking. John Hoyne was placed at left-half forward to do a stopper job on Brian Whelahan in the 2000 All Ireland final. Shefflin was instructed to go straight down the centre against Seánie McMahon two years later. In 2007 the Kilkenny management concluded that Shefflin had the beating of Limerick's Stephen Lucey in the air and decreed that Seamus Hickey must be prevented from coming out of his corner with the ball with the same youthful abandon he'd shown in the semi-final versus Waterford. In 2008 the influence of Ken McGrath, arguably the most joyously, sweepingly gifted hurler of his generation, was negated by the expedient of having Martin Comerford first-time the ball away from him and Declan Prendergast's weakness in the air at full-back exploited by supplying Richie Power with a stream of head-high deliveries which the full-forward could either take on himself or lay off to a runner from deep. Those late nights Cody spent at 'his' table in Langton's, in the corner just beyond the door to the kitchen, were not spent regaling Fogarty and Dempsey with old war stories about himself and Fan.

Still, for all the tactical curlicues, first principles remained inviolate. Herewith Cody at a Leinster Council coaching day held in St Kieran's College in 2008.

"A fella playing half-back must stop the ball. That's the first and foremost business he has to do. He can decorate the game in other ways later on if he can, but if he taps over a couple of points and doesn't do the basics of stopping the ball he shouldn't be playing half-back. No way. The defender's job is to defend.

Stop, stop, stop, stop. You're holding up the ball. You must have defenders who can do that. Defenders defend. Some fellas love to see these beautiful wing-backs, beautiful stylists. That's why we have wing-backs without beautiful style. [Laughter.] First to the ball should be always in your head."

Cody, being Cody, would have taken as much pleasure from the grit of the 2008 All Ireland final as from the multitude of pearls. Moments after hitting his second goal, Eddie Brennan was out in midfield getting wired into Waterford players. TJ Reid announced his entry into the lists by hooking Jack Kennedy before he got around to shooting the first of his four points. JJ Delaney's shot that came back off the upright in the closing minutes was the result of the one and only sally upfield by a Kilkenny defender all afternoon. Having the match long won, in other words, was no excuse for self-indulgence or abandonment of basic defensive duties. Cody's men alright. Hard, honest work on the training field remained the first requirement, the last requirement, the only requirement.

He was not operating in a vacuum. The coach of one of the 2009 Kilkenny under-age teams had the cones set out for a training session one evening only for the manager to announce that they wouldn't be doing drills, they'd be playing a match instead and they wouldn't be holding back. It was a page lifted straight from Chairman Brian's Little Red Book. Ten days before the 2008 All Ireland final, the managers of the under-14 and under-16 teams contesting the national tournaments in those grades were informed by county board officials that Kilkenny intended to win each of the six All Irelands they were contesting over the course of the next fortnight and that they'd better not let the side down. Michael Walsh's All Ireland-winning under-21s of that year set up the same way as the seniors, dropping their midfielders and wing-forwards back on the opposition puckout and constructing barriers in the middle third of the field. Richie Mulrooney's All Ireland-winning minors had a four-point standard operating procedure cribbed from the seniors. First to the ball; move the ball; support each other; fight like dogs.

Not the least of Cody's accomplishments – indeed the most pleasurable of the lot of them for Kilkenny supporters of an older vintage, not all of them resident on or around the county's western border – was the creation of an entirely new narrative vis a vis Tipperary. That Cody was visibly excited at the end of the 2002 All Ireland semi-final, in which Kilkenny had made heavy weather of it to beat Tipp by four points, their first championship victory against their neighbours since the 1967 All Ireland final, was understandable. Some degree of inherited existential hangover, however nebulous, in whatever abyss it was lodged in the county's psyche, had to have been roiling in the deep.

Admittedly the counties had met only twice in the intervening 35 years, but in the way of these things Tipperary supporters would have been more inclined to mention the 35 years rather than the two meetings therein. The sides met at the same stage of the competition the following year and Kilkenny, no longer locked in subliminal combat with the hand of history, won by 12 points. The sweets of life would become sweeter still. Fast forward to the end of 2011, by which point Cody's Kilkenny had faced Tipperary five times in the championship and beaten them on four occasions, with the extra-time 2009 National League triumph thrown in for good measure.

Eaten trophies were soon forgotten. Kilkenny players were only as good as not their last game but their next game. The dark days were recalled more often, and with more feeling, than the sunny days. The Galway defeat in 2001 the manager ascribed in part to his own dropping of personal standards. Nothing major, nothing obvious, just little things here and there. Something like good timekeeping is important, he once stressed, because "if you're sloppy and careless with players it's a guarantee that you'll get sloppiness and carelessness back". The little things. The simple things. Very Tommy Maher.

Never once did Cody lose sight of his place in the greater scheme of things or of the honour that came with the job. "What I'm doing is managing the Kilkenny team," he announced at one pre-All Ireland fundraising dinner in Langton's. "That's a phenomenal honour, first of all. It's challenging, it's hugely enjoyable and it's an honour to work with the people I work with. The selectors. The backroom team. The county board. The respect that's there between everybody. The whole hurling set-up in the county. Under-age. Schools. The Kilkenny hurlers represent all of those. All the players represent that system. They are started by the people here tonight, the people who really matter."

The whole hurling set-up in the county: that was it. The garlands showered on Kilkenny's development squad system obscured the reality that these squads were not an end in themselves. Rather they were complementary to, and supplementary to, the work being done in every parish, far away from the bright lights. "The big thing about the development squads is that they bring young lads together from around the county, they give everyone an equal chance and they make no distinction between big clubs and small clubs," Brendan O'Sullivan points out. "But the development squads only meet seven nights in the year. The groundwork is being done in the clubs and schools. That's where it's coming from."

On those seven nights the players are coached. No weight training, no gym work. Coaching. Fr Maher could not but have approved. The raft of Kilkenny under-16 and under-17 squads that went to the national tournaments in August 2011 were highly competitive in their respective grades without bringing home silverware. That was fine with everyone too.

Earlier the same year a delegation from Kilkenny travelled to London Colney to study the youth set-up at Arsenal FC, in accordance with the Maher injunction about "learning from other people". To their surprise and encouragement, what they discovered from Steve Bould, head coach of Arsenal's under-18 academy team, and Pat Rice, Arsene Wenger's assistant, was how uncomplicated the training was: basic one-touch and two-touch drills repeated over and over again, a simplicity not natural in an era where every fresh championship season comes charged its own new-age voodoo (Nutron diets, warm-weather training, wristbands, elaborate pre-match warm-ups and so on ad tedium). Fundamentally, Arsenal's youth coaching was little different from the coaching at juvenile level in Kilkenny. Fr Maher would have approved mightily of that as well.

And yet. For all the tributes paid to the joined-up coherence of the underage structures on Noreside, for all the wealth of talent seeping upwards from the grassroots, much of what the county achieved in the noughties was due to one man and one man only. Kilkenny could not have been such consistent performers, such serial winners, such multiple champions, but for Brian Cody.

But no manager is an island, and Kilkenny would not have set out from their starting point under Cody – a county with 12 All Ireland victories in the previous 42 years – had it not been for Fr Tommy Maher. Two geniuses. Geniuses in entirely different registers.

What is done, and not done, in one generation echoes in the next, and in the generation after that also: the shoulders of giants and all that. Tommy Maher's real gift to his county was not what Kilkenny won when he was there, considerable as that was, but what they won after he was gone. Here was a light that did not go out.

You seek his monument? Look around you. It's not today's men and managers who have made Kilkenny famous.

CHAPTER 26

Technique

Tactics in hurling boils down to passing – passing to a loose comrade or passing to an open space. M formations, W formations, screen plays, etc, are unknown
Tony Wall, *Hurling*, 1965

Tommy Maher was not a tactical revolutionary. He was scarcely even a tactics man. For him the only tactic was technique, worked on endlessly and burnished to a high sheen. After that came specific instruction: a certain player coached to do a certain job on a certain day. After that again came whatever tactical adornments the selectors saw fit to plan and enact in any given game. But technique came first, and the tactical cart could never precede the skills horse.

It was only in the final quarter of the first 100 years of the GAA that the word 'coach' came into vogue, he wrote in an unpublished article around the time of the organisation's Centenary Year. "Back in the days of 'the giants' the word was never used. There was always somebody – be he chairman, county secretary or trainer – designated as such to 'look after' the team, who saw to it that at least some practice was done before big games. The training was, to say the least, haphazard and totally lacking in any coordinated effort on the part of the team or the officials involved.

"The players of that era had marvellous individual skills. These skills they performed purely as individual skills without executing them to the greatest possible advantage to their team. It was in discerning and admitting a lack of scientific approach and executive finesse that the first coaches felt the need for the thinking approach. Hence in this last quarter we have coaches in Gaelic games, as in all other types of modern and progressive games, whose job it is to perfect the skills of players and in so doing to improve team performance."

No individual did more to introduce that "scientific approach and executive finesse" to hurling than Fr Tommy Maher. He opened the door to a new kind of game and he led his county with him. In due course the rest of the hurling nation followed, some of its tribes more quickly than others.

Three questions arise. Exactly how good was the hurling in the age of "the giants" he mentioned? To what degree has the game evolved post-Maher? And is it for better or for worse?

"Old football was rubbish, old football/just wasn't very good," sang Frank Skinner and David Baddiel on the BBC's *Fantasy Football* programme during the mid-1990s. Old hurling, as Ger Loughnane and Eamonn Cregan among others were honest enough to concede when TG4's repeats of matches from the 1970s and '80s did much to banish the rosy glow that surrounded the game of yesteryear, frequently wasn't up to all that much either.

Putting together a lowlights reel from, say, the 1978 All Ireland final wouldn't take very long. We might subtitle it 'When Good Hurlers Go Bad'.

Paddy Prendergast hits a lineball straight to an unmarked Ray Cummins who despatches the sliotar between the uprights, no Kilkenny defender having found it appropriate to be in Cummins's precinct in the event of a mishit. Cummins subsequently driving another chance wide from in front of the posts, 30 yards out on the run and under no pressure. Joe Hennessy attempting to deposit a 70 in the Cork danger area and falling well short. Dermot McCurtain throwing up the ball and catching it again (and getting away with it). Denis Coughlan killing an incoming delivery on his stick with his first touch and spooning it barely two yards with his second, out over the sideline for an opposition lineball. And the nadir, a Keystone Cops sequence shortly before half-time that features a clutch of players from both sides striking mishitting, spilling, being blocked, muffing handpasses and losing control of the ball. It ends with Frank Cummins picking it up off the ground. In the unlikely event this series of misadventures is ever shown on television again, it will surely be accompanied by the music from the *Benny Hill Show*.

But here's the thing. This is not an All Ireland final from the mists of time but one that, viewed from the perspective of early in the 21st century, occurred relatively recently. And the players involved were household names. Prendergast was a defensive powerhouse, Ray Cummins the full-forward on the Team of the Millennium and the man credited with redefining the role of the number 14, Hennessy and McCurtain and Coughlan ballplaying defenders and Frank Cummins the winner of seven All Irelands on the field of play.

If we cannot trust our own memory, how seriously can we take the hurling hagiography, the whole "stern naked grandeur" routine, of the first half of the 20th century? An account of the 1929 Munster semi-final meeting of Cork and Tipperary waxed lyrical about "men crashing into one another: one, two, three, four men went down in sequence. Virile manhood was manifested in all its power and glory." Or, if you prefer, communal oafishness was enabled by light-touch regulation.

The style, such as it was, of the Tipperary team of the 1930s was described by one of its number as the practice of all the players moving in unison up the field in a spirited and determined attack, throwing everything at the opposition in an attempt to score. As Seamus King noted in *A History of Hurling*, this smacks more of rugby; 'scientific', that stamp of approbation beloved of hurling writers of the age, it categorically was not. And strip away the mythology that was piled on it and Cork/Wexford in 1954 sounds like a pig of an All Ireland final.

No sport fetishises its past the way hurling does. It wraps its exponents of old in clouds of glory like mythical figures from a pre-Celtic dawn of time. It anoints them and it sanctifies them. The finest hurler ever to emerge from east Cork? Many a long-departed inhabitant of the area who grew up going to matches in the early part of the 20th century swore in their later years that that young Ring lad from Cloyne couldn't hold a candle to the mighty Jamesie Kelleher of Dungourney. So it goes.

It is no tangent to wonder how incumbent upon themselves the media of the day felt it to present the native games in the brightest light possible. In *Over The Bar*, his GAA memoir written to coincide with Centenary Year, Breandán Ó hEithir mentioned being driven to the verge of apoplexy by Micheál O'Hehir's radio commentary on the 1946 All Ireland football semi-final, a game in which Kerry horsed a skilful but light Antrim forward line out of it. The crowd booed at the persistent fouling of the Kerry defence; O'Hehir, determined to see no evil, still less broadcast it, affected not to know "for the life of him" the source of their displeasure. That John D Hickey's pent-up frustration at years of being told what was good for him erupted in fury over the events of the 1968 league final comes as little surprise.

How far, therefore, can we trust the GAA reportage of the past? Do we honestly believe "the giants" did not possess feet of clay from time to time? In the closing stages of the 1948 Munster final, with Waterford leading Cork by a point, Vin Baston vacated his position to take a sideline cut that was turned over by Cork and worked upfield. One of the Cork forwards essayed the levelling point from about 40 yards out. The sliotar went narrowly wide and the day was lost. The Cork forward? Christy Ring. If nothing else, it is an incident that should serve to bring it home to impressionable Cork folk that not even Ring did everything perfectly all of the time.

Pa Dillon is one man not tempted to hark back to a golden past. "In the 1960s there were very exciting games. Referees weren't as strict. Hard knocks were given and taken. I know there should have been a lot more frees. When you're younger maybe these things look more exciting – dust flying in the square and all that. The Kilkenny team under Brian Cody, any of them would have made any Kilkenny team of the past. *All* of them would have.

"Obviously the game is faster and more intensive now, and teams have more players to choose from. Back then there weren't panels of 30 or full-scale matches in training, so training was just games of backs and forwards. Another big difference is that nowadays a player will get possession and run at the opposition defence and try to either win a free or to open it up for his teammates. Back then everybody stayed stationary. Everybody waited for the big high ball in."

On his annual summer visits to Urlingford from Sacramento, Monsignor Ned Kavanagh could see "a tremendous change" gradually taking place in the matches he attended. A new game, a faster game, a less individually combative game. He had no doubt as to the man to whom some of the credit could be ascribed. "Did the fact that Tommy Maher was a mathematician help? It didn't hurt. The shortest distance between two points is a straight line."

If a tenuous comparison could be made between Kilkenny's 1957 team and any contemporary soccer outfit, it would be with Arthur Rowe's Push and Run championship-winning Tottenham side of 1950-51. Rowe's catchphrase? "Make it short, make it simple, make it quick." Tommy Maher's insistence that the skills were there to be cultivated, moreover, flew in the face of the prevailing orthodoxy in English soccer which insisted that players be starved of the ball in training during the week on the basis they'd be hungry for it when Saturday came.

He'd have loved Pep Guardiola's FC Barcelona, a collection of gifted players who made the game look easy because, Lionel Messi apart, they rarely attempted the difficult, their daily bread being the simple pass played over and over again. Talking of Messi, one Alf Galustian, a pioneer of soccer skills coaching, has declared: "Messi is a one-off. But I'm certain everything he does can be taught. He's not simply 'blessed by God'. Messi has developed his skills."

Christy Ring, not one to genuflect to the gods of tradition, declared that the hurlers of his day were good but that there were better to come. Justin McCarthy asserted in 2007 that "the best hurlers are now". Is that too convenient?

"The best hurlers of the past would have achieved as much in the modern era," Liam Griffin argues. "Imagine Christy Ring if went through today's strength and conditioning regimes." Paddy Downey has a different take on it. His belief is that today's *hurling* is better but yesterday's *hurlers* were better. You pays your money...

The game of the 21st century is inarguably more precise. Kilkenny hit 19 wides and Limerick 17 wides in the 1974 All Ireland final; advance a generation and Kilkenny and Tipperary drove five wides each when victorious in 2009 and '10 respectively. Clare and Wexford hit 14 scores apiece when winning the 1995 and '96 All Ireland finals respectively; Kilkenny hit 24 scores when winning in 2009. A faster game and a game far less forgiving of sloppiness and solecisms. Every ball weighted and shotted and calibrated.

Paudie Butler, the national director of hurling, hailed the opening 20 minutes of the 2008 All Ireland semi-final between Kilkenny and Cork as "the best hurling ever played". It was a comment rendered obsolete by the full 70 minutes of the following season's final. On which point, irrespective of how classical the 1947 All Ireland decider may have been, it didn't come within an ass's roar of the 2009 renewal for intensity, controlled ferocity and the sustained deployment of the skills under pressure. It couldn't have. But was it the same sport?

Speaking 50 years after he played in the 1961 All Ireland final, Des Ferguson described modern hurling as being simultaneously more physical and less dirty, which isn't a contradiction. More disciplined too, which it has to be because it's more physical. "Players get the ball into their hand, power out with it, get belts and take them. Mind you, small fellas like meself would be in trouble now. You have guys getting the ball into their hand and powering out. And they're great at catching the ball, a skill that didn't exist in my day. It was too dangerous."

The biggest change of all, according to Paddy Buggy, has been the sliotar. "It was leather, it was stitched all the way around and it had a big rim. If you didn't hit it on the sweet spot of the hurl it wouldn't be accurate. And freetaking was much more difficult. Scoring a 70 was a terrific feat." Quite; when Billy Rackard split the uprights with a mortar shell from 95 yards in the 1955 All Ireland semi-final against Limerick, Dermot Kelly, his marker, walked over and shook hands.

Two pucks – the puckout and an overhead connection at midfield – brought the ball from one square to the other in those days. Like Buggy, Donie Nealon laments the death of overhead striking. It was one of his few areas of disagreement with Tommy Maher, who professed overhead striking to be unnecessarily inexact: "I hit the ball and God directs it," he was fond of groaning.

If Nealon were a corner-forward in the 21st century, he says, he'd go mad. "So much picking and passing out the field. When are they going to hit it into me? These days you have to stop and rise the ball. You have to get possession. You have to solo. You have to handpass. The upshot is that the ball is moving a lot slower than it used to. And half-forwards who are being outfielded by half-backs who are good under the dropping ball, they have to learn to get in under the ball and double on it. This is one skill that's not being coached."

Tommy Maher recognised which way the wind was blowing as early as 1971. That year's All Ireland colleges final, a 13-a-side game, saw St Kieran's, coached by Dermot Healy, beat St Finbarr's of Farranferris by 8-6 to 5-8. The winners had Brian Cody at centre-back, Nickey Brennan in the middle of the field and four-goal Billy Fitzpatrick up front, which wasn't a bad start. But they also had a clear conception of the kind of game they were playing.

"It was a win for the modern game," Fr Maher told reporters in the dressing room afterwards. "Fr Maher's concept of the modern game is clear cut," *The Irish Times* explained, "use of the crisp short pass and emphasis on creating space and the overlap up front." It was the only way to prise open the defence in this 13-a-side game, the great man amplified.

It is important at this juncture to revisit the Maheresque philosophy of the handpass. To his way of thinking, and it *was* a way of thinking, it was a device to be employed when a player was in difficulty, surrounded by two or three opponents, or used to link the play. It was a tactic rather than a strategy, a device that sought to speed up the game instead of slowing it down. Tommy Maher did not build a philosophy around the handpass; he built it into his philosophy. Cyril Farrell's Galway brought the handpass into territory its original champion had never envisaged, and the shark was well and truly jumped in the opening seconds of the 2011 All Ireland quarter-final when the Limerick full-back ran the ball across his own goalmouth before palming it, indifferently, to a colleague. "It was only to be used when in difficulty and passed to a player in a better position," Dermot Healy stresses. "Those were the golden rules. It wasn't for soloing up the field with players handpassing the ball one to the other."

In view of their belief that 'little' of combination play could be worked out beforehand, what would Gormanston's founding fathers – and, come to that, Tony Wall – have made of the Cork forward line of the noughties, with their structured and painstakingly choreographed running off the ball and creation of space? "The first requirement of a forward is to be able to shoot hard and accurately"? Not with this crowd, where the first requirement of a forward was to be able to get himself into a position to give a telling pass to a colleague similarly able to get himself into a position to receive it. This was hurling reinvented as high-speed chess.

Cork's possession game – Donal O'Grady, one of its midwives, bridled at the term "running game" – was founded on the mobility of Jerry O'Connor and Tom Kenny, 400-metre runners doubling as midfielders. When Cork defended they defended in numbers, with one of the midfielders tracking backwards towards the point of breakdown and acting both as an auxiliary defender and as the outlet for the pass that would initiate the next attack. When they attacked they attacked in numbers. The shirt numbers Kenny and O'Connor wore represented only nominally their domain. The midfielders of the past played their position; this duo played every position.

The pair had the freedom to go where they liked. "We were never told not to go anywhere," Tom Kenny reveals. "The only rule was that if one of us went somewhere, the other had to stay back to provide a presence at midfield. But Jerry had such a great engine that if he went up to the corner-forward position he could get back in seconds. Our game was all about possession, about holding onto the ball and not hitting it away."

The Cork team of 2004-06 created scores that had never been scored before. Two such efforts provided snapshots of the new game.

The first half of the 2005 Munster final at Páirc Uí Chaoimh. Cork versus Tipperary. Donal Óg Cusack saves an Eoin Kelly penalty. The sliotar breaks to Pat Mulcahy, who plays a short stick pass to John Gardiner. He takes possession deep in his own defence and solos as far as the 45-metre line. Handpass to Kieran Murphy, who solos to nearly as far as the Tipp 45 without a hand being laid on him, then strikes a point off the hurley on his left.

The first half of the 2006 Munster final at Semple Stadium. Cork and Tipp again. Brian Murphy gathers possession at left-corner back at the Town End. Does a 360-degree turn to survey his options and pick out a colleague. Plays a stick pass to Ronan Curran inside the Cork 20-metre line. Curran steps away from a Tipp player and plays a diagonal pass to Ben O'Connor, who takes possession on the halfway line under the New Stand. O'Connor turns his man and plays a short stick pass to Timmy McCarthy. McCarthy turns and handpasses to Tom Kenny, up supplementing the attack. Kenny advances for a few strides before playing a long handpass to O'Connor, who has continued his run and is all alone in space. The handpass hits the ground, but O'Connor gathers after a couple of strides and shoots for goal, beating Brendan Cummins at his near post.

Joined-up hurling. Heads-up hurling. Tommy Maher would have thrilled to the watchmaker exactitude and precision teamwork of it.

The death of ground hurling was no mystery to Eamon O'Shea, the mouldbreaking coach of Tipperary's 2010 All Ireland winners. "It's impossible to get fellas to do ground hurling now because if you do it well you're still giving the ball away, and when you give the ball away it's hard to get it back. That was a great feature of the game and the crowd loved it, but if it went to someone 30 yards away who snapped it over the bar you had a problem. So you have to bring in new skills such as bringing the ball down out of the air with the hurley, which all teams do now."

The game Kilkenny played in 2007 was different to the one they'd played in 1957. The game Cork played in 2004-06 was even more markedly different to the one that county played half a century earlier. And today's boys of Callan CBS do not play what one of their predecessors, Tony O'Malley, described as "the Christian Brothers style of hurling – pulling on the ball first time. Rising the ball only held the game up." Nor will they ever do so again.

Cork and Kilkenny took hurling into new realms in the noughties. What was lost on the journey?

Let us start with Ned Byrne, All Ireland-winning hurler and Irish international rugby player. "Rugby is now over-coached," he pronounces. "In all sports these days it's about possession and the fear of losing the ball. Hurling included."

Hurling most certainly included. Ponder the following sequence from the first half of the 2009 All Ireland final.

Kilkenny are attacking the Davin Stand end. Henry Shefflin wins a puckout from PJ Ryan but can't get past Conor O'Mahony, so he turns and plays the sliotar back to Tommy Walsh. Walsh loops it down the tramline to Richie Hogan, who turns Paul Curran but is chased by him, hooked by Lar Corbett and shouldered by James Woodlock. Hogan gets it to Eoin Larkin, who goes forward and is set upon from all angles. He manages to fight off Declan Fanning and Shane McGrath, has his handpass blocked by Brendan Maher but manages at the second attempt to process the ball forward to Derek Lyng. Lyng now has to see off the joint attentions of McGrath, who's tracked back, and Pádraic Maher before getting his shot in. Reports that the sliotar was heard to scream for mercy as it crept over the crossbar were never fully confirmed. Douglas Haig took ground at the Somme with less attrition.

One doesn't have to be a dreamy-eyed traditionalist for the better bits of the 1978 All Ireland final, specifically the best of the first-time striking, to prompt a sigh for what has been lost. Compare a cleansing, flensing ground ball struck by one of the Cork half-backs or midfielders that afternoon with the tedious bump 'n' grind of today. The ball taken into the hand and into contact. Hurling aping rugby. The war of the monster trucks.

By the same token, one does not have to be an octogenarian to yearn for the second coming of Enniscorthy's Adrian Fenlon, that one-man clearing house for fast midfield ball for Wexford for a decade. One touch to kill the sliotar, another touch to send it 40 metres. "If I were a corner-forward that's the kind of ball I'd like to be getting," Fenlon once said. He and Donie Nealon should get together and form a new political party.

Mickey Harte did not demur when the similarities between Brian Cody's Kilkenny and the Tyrone footballers were raised. "Sport is about observing what's going on, taking what you believe is useful and applying it to your own team and your own resources," he avers. "I think Kilkenny saw the way we played when we came on the scene in 2003. Some people who didn't like it described what we were doing as 'total defence', but I'd describe it as total honesty. You're asking players to enlarge their repertoire of skills. It was every player's duty to regain possession and help defend." Sound like any hurling team you know?

Modern hurling resembles its rugby equivalent in another way. Each game has become a sport for athletes first and artists second. Barry John and Gareth Edwards constituted a half-back pairing for the ages on the Welsh team of the early 1970s by dint of their genius, not their girth; John measured 5'10 and weighed 11'11, Edwards 5'8 and 12'8. The half-back pairing on Wales's Grand Slam winners of 2012 comprised Mike Phillips, a scrum-half measuring, astoundingly, 6'4 and weighing 16'5, and his partner Rhys Priestland, 6'1 and 14'9.

As with the oval ball, so too with the rimmed ball. The Kilkenny team that won the 1957 All Ireland had, whatever the social diarist of the *Evening Press* seemed to think, only one six-footer, John Sutton. The Kilkenny team that won the 2011 All Ireland had ten, including one man who measured 6'4, another 6'3 and three of 6'2.

Liam Sheedy was a player in an All Ireland final in 1997 and a manager in one 12 years later. Different eras and, to a degree, different sports. Would Sheedy have got his place at right-half back with Tipperary in 2009? "Probably not." Why not? "Pace. Although I might have been the first name on the team sheet in the 1970s... Pace. That's what it became all about. If Hell's Kitchen can't run they're fecked." *Citius, altius, fortius.*

Asked whether a ground-hurling approach could defeat a team playing a possession game, John Considine, multiple championship-winning coach with UCC and under-age Cork sides, agrees that it might. The problem, he warns, is the length of time it would take to coach a team to be fully comfortable with first-time striking. This is a clock that will not be turned back.

Liam Griffin among others is disturbed by the increase in what he calls "manufactured hurlers". Counties are "taking guys who are big, because big counts in the modern game, and putting work into them and making players of them". Contrast these cyborgs with, *mar shampla*, Joe Deane. Deane was one of the most popular, one of the most admirable, one of the most *natural* hurlers of the noughties. He wasn't big, he wasn't strong, he wasn't speedy and he had the kind of grip they warned about it Gormanston. But Deane was infinitely more than the sum of his parts because what he had in his legs was infinitely less important than what he had between his ears.

Are the days of the Joe Deanes numbered? "There's still room for one Joe Deane on every team," Griffin believes. "There's not room for four or five of them."

What about the 10,000-hour rule, as posited by Malcolm Gladwell in *Outliers*? The Beatles ruled the world, Gladwell suggested, not as a result of innate musical genius but as a result of hard work: playing 270 nights in the space of a year and a half during their Hamburg period, for five hours, six hours, frequently eight hours a night. In the warp-speed world of the 21st century, will the hurlers of the next generation be able to master the skills of the game in the way their predecessors were? I wanna hold my hurley, yes. But where will I find the time to do so?

"When and where does coaching begin?" asks Eamon O'Shea. "Should one have to coach players in the skills when they come into a senior intercounty setup? What should our expectations of these players be? How useful are current coaching structures at club and intercounty level? What about specialist coaching?"

That last question is not rhetorical. O'Shea spent much of his three years with Tipperary working with the goalkeepers on the panel. To a degree he was extemporising; he had no goalkeeping coaching template to work off. Shortly after the 2010 All Ireland final, he attended a college basketball game while in New York on business and was struck by the sight of no fewer than eight besuited coaches materialising during the timeouts to advise and encourage and cajole. *Eight*. And a basketball team has only five players on court at any one time.

"Who decides which skills are lost and found? What is the evolutionary process?" To get players hitting the ball from any distance to any other player so as to have Tipperary play "a long accurate game rather than a short game", O'Shea went as far as reading books on tennis in order to help his troops think about the sound of the sliotar being struck. At the end of 2010 he called for the appointment of a director of hurling in every county. "If you're the manager of a county minor team and I'm that county's director of hurling I could say, 'You're doing great but we need to consider this skill or that skill.' There's a need for some overview."

O'Shea's goalkeeping coaching did not fall on stony ground. Thus Brendan Cummins in 2011: "If you told me ten years ago that I'd be flicking the ball out to a left-corner back standing 20 yards from me and that he was going to round the corner-forward I'd say you were absolutely off your head. That's progression, that's development, that's the game moving on. If I stand still the game passes me by."

But some elements of hurling have not changed and will not. Tommy Maher had it correct from the beginning. Do the simple thing, do it properly and do it all the time.

Injury time in the 2011 All Ireland colleges final at Semple Stadium. Having just conceded the goal that put St Kieran's a point in front, the Árd Scoil Rís goalkeeper presents the puckout straight to the opposition centre-forward, who promptly sends it over the bar. Handed an even later opportunity to save the day from a close-range free, the Árd Scoil Rís freetaker fails with the first and most important part of the process, the rise, and has to pull on the sliotar on the ground. The ball is cleared to safety. St Kieran's win by two points. Man for man they may not be any more talented than their opponents, but their grasp of the basics holds up under pressure. Such are the margins on which All Irelands are won and lost.

"No apologies need be made to any player about insisting on repetitious performance of skills," Fr Maher wrote in the aforementioned unpublished article around the time of Centenary Year. "After all, you can say that if John McEnroe and Muhammad Ali have need of coaching, surely Johnny Hurler is not above the use of a coach."

Much in hurling has changed, even since those words were written. But the primacy of skill never will.

CHAPTER 27

Winter

He's in our thoughts. He always will be
Chunky O'Brien

After surviving his brush with death, Monsignor Maher spent some time in hospital in Thomastown before returning to Mullinavat, where his parishioners looked after him on a rota basis. Christina Brennan-Murphy, his old friend from Sion Hill, drove from Sligo to visit him one day.

"You're very good to him," she said to one of the ladies minding him.

"He has it well earned," the lady replied.

His next port of call was Aut Even Hospital in Kilkenny, where he was a patient for two years. His final residence was Archersrath nursing home on the outskirts of the city, fittingly not far from Nowlan Park. It was there that he spent most of his 80s and it was there that on April 25th 2012 his 90th birthday was marked with a small party for fellow patients and staff.

Throughout his long, slow decline he would have his good days and his bad. On the good days the spark of the old Tommy Maher still flamed. On hearing that Eddie Keher and Fr Tom Murphy were coming to visit him in Archersrath he announced, "These are two very important men." On discovering in early 2012 from his nephew Tomás that the Eucharistic Congress would be held in Dublin during the summer, and being reminded that Tomás's father Johnny had cycled to the 1932 Congress, he mused, "It doesn't be long coming around."

In sporting terms he was not the founder of a dynasty in the way that other men in other codes were. Dick Fitzgerald and JP O'Sullivan with Kerry football, Matt Busby and Herbert Chapman in English soccer, Vince Lombardi and Tom Landry in American football. But he took a crumbling empire, restored it and laid the foundations for even greater glories.

Kilkenny have been beaten 80 times or more in the championship. They were the first county to be beaten twice in the same championship. They've been beaten in successive All Ireland finals more than once, more than twice, more than three times. They managed the sum total of 0-9 – a bad football team's score – in not one but two All Ireland finals at the close of the 20th century.

Time after time they've lost and gone home with their tail between their legs. Sometimes they've sulked for a while and sometimes they've sulked for ages. Sometimes they've learned their lesson quickly and sometimes they've taken years to learn it. But in the end they've always looked in the mirror and they've always burned to bounce back and they continue to nourish a tradition that allows them to do nothing less. Consequently they've never ever let defeat go unavenged, no matter how long it has taken them, and under Brian Cody they learned to cope with winning as naturally as they'd been accustomed to coping with losing. And much of that was due to Tommy Maher.

A quarter of a century ago, half of the youths of Kilkenny city went around bearing scowls and Jesus and Mary Chain t-shirts. These days half of them seem to bear hurleys. Tommy Maher had something to do with that too.

"A man before his time." The phrase occurs again and again, from students, players, selectors, politicians past and present. Someone who had no reason to ask questions reimagined the game and rewrote the playbook. A man before his time, of his time and for all time.

He won silverware and plenty of it. He also won hearts. Consider the parishioners who looked after him in Mullinavat when he fell ill and made regular trips to visit him in Thomastown and Archersrath.

Or Noel Skehan, who visited him there out of a sense of duty: "I felt I owed it to him. He spent so much time coaching me."

Or John Hanley, a man Tommy Maher encountered in passing along life's journey: "It's great that a book is being written about him."

Or Seán Clohosey, a member of his first All Ireland-winning team: "He had the height of respect for us and we for him. If he had anything to say to you he'd take you aside and say it. The right way for a trainer to operate."

Or Justin McCarthy, a man who walked to nobody's drumbeat but his own yet who revered Fr Maher.

Perhaps Tom Walsh, the man whose career ended on the afternoon of Tommy Maher's greatest triumph, sums it up best. "Humility. Integrity. Wit. Common sense. Christian goodness." Would that more of us were deserving of such a simple, heartfelt tribute.

And he and his knowledge and his credo and his curiosity and his imagination and his common sense and his humanity shall reign forever and ever. Hurling's messiah.

CHAPTER 28

Deireadh

Comes out as far as Tommy Walsh once again. Again very clever use of possession. Flicking it out now to Michael Rice. Nothing hurried at all, everything's measured. And Colin Fennelly races forward, slipping a little handpass into a determined Eddie Brennan. Off he goes, like he's running in Shelbourne Park! Handpass across to Hogan. What a goal! That is quite superb! That's hurling for you! Hurling at its very best!
Ger Canning, 4.41pm September 4th 2011

A move that began on the Kilkenny endline and finished up in the Tipperary rigging. Two sculpted passes off the stick, the first aimed waist-high for the recipient to flick up into his hand and turn with, the second raked down the Cusack Stand sideline to a forward coming out to meet it and catch. One high, tumbling handpass inside timed neatly for a player charging through from deep. A 40-metre burst into the enemy barbican and then, with a point for the taking, a decision to go for the jugular. The sliotar caught a second time before being tossed out to the man in space on the left. The sliotar killed on the hurley and the option of taking it to hand eschewed in favour of a volleyed finish across the goalkeeper and into the far top corner of the net.

Tommy Walsh, Tullaroan and St Kieran's, to Michael Rice, Carrickshock and St Kieran's, to Colin Fennelly, Ballyhale Shamrocks and Scoil Aireagail, to Eddie Brennan, Graigue-Ballycallan and St Kieran's, to Richie Hogan, Danesfort and St Kieran's. A score that embodied everything Tommy Maher believed in and had taught, to boys in black and white hoops and men in black and amber stripes. A score that won an All Ireland 54 years on from the afternoon that hurling changed forever.

Not a ground stroke therein, admittedly, but that would have been a throwback not natural in an age like this, and Walsh's short pass to Rice was as near to a ground ball as made no difference.

The handpass, employed as a tactic rather than a strategy, slung to a man on the run. This wasn't a pointless pat-a-cake handpass to a colleague on one's shoulder. It was a stiletto of a handpass to the enemy's heart.

The man on the run hitting the gap – fill all spaces – and making it a canyon all his own. The ball goes faster than a man. Except when the man is Fast Eddie.

The same man thinking slowly while running quickly, surveying his options and catching a second time before offloading. Heads-up hurling

The man inside him possessed of a sufficiently sinuous first touch to stun the sliotar on his stick, with his second touch wrongfooting Brendan Cummins and struck in the knowledge that angling it back across the goal would pose an extra difficulty for a goalie with his left hand on top.

And into that shot was poured all the craft, all the wristiness, all the power, all the venom, all the mistakes, all the bad days, all the lessons taught and learned, of half a century of Kilkenny hurling.

It was as though everything Tommy Maher had imparted had been placed in aged oak in 1957, left to mature for decades and emerged as a pure drop, clean and fresh and invigorating. Into this moment went the Kilkenny handpassing of the 1970s and the Offaly astringency of the 1980s. Into this moment went Eddie Keher and Tom Walsh and Chunky O'Brien and Billy Fitzpatrick and DJ Carey and all the rest of the Noreside communion of saints. Into this moment went Tommy Maher and everything he'd taught.

A simple game, yes, yet simultaneously a game so potentially complicated, with so many discrete skills, that the only course of action for the thinking man is to strip it down and start from scratch. Play with your eyes open and look for a colleague to pick out. Don't take five steps when two will do. Don't risk getting hooked when a well directed handpass can open up a defence. Don't give the defender the chance to hook, block or bottle you up when you can kill the ball dead with one touch and redirect it with a second touch.

It was a Hallelujah Chorus of a goal, composed by Tommy Maher with trumpets by GF Handel. It is not great feats that win All Irelands but the basics performed well, over and over again.

Occam's Razor raised to its highest power. Journey's end.

ACKNOWLEDGEMENTS

This book could not have been written without the blessing and active assistance of the Maher family, in particular Tommy's niece Stacy Herlihy and his nephew Tomás Maher. Another niece, Anne Maher in California, was very helpful on the family history.

Thanks also go to Eddie Keher, the Kilkenny GAA Supporters Club and the St Kieran's College Past Pupils Union for their encouragement. And to PJ and Rosemary Cunningham in Ballpoint Press. And to Tom Brett for his cover photograph. He has many more where this one came from.

Many thanks to June Grennan for permission to quote from 'A Hero's Life', her wonderful college project on Monsignor Maher. It was an invaluable work of reference.

I didn't starve on my travels. Catriona Downey gave me sandwiches and cake. Maura Ferguson had a fine salmon dinner ready. Peggy Buggy gave me sweets for the train journey home. Judy Byrne served a mean cup of coffee.

Monsignor Ned Kavanagh took time off, and on a Sunday too, to drive from Sacramento to San Francisco. Michael Ryan, the manager of the Mount Sion GAA complex, got me to Plunkett Station on time. Walter Purcell chauffeured me in and out to Windgap. Charlie Cullen came in one afternoon to open up the library in Rothe House. Dominic Williams played a blinder on the Wexford end of things. Dermot Kavanagh furnished me with the script of a talk he gave on hurling in Kilkenny in the 1940s and '50s. Thanks to one and all.

Thanks to Breda and Dan McEvoy for obvious reasons. To Elizabeth McEvoy of the National Archives of Ireland for pointers about the wonderful magic that is archives today. To Edward and Frances Kennedy. And, seeing as I'd better not leave them out, to Mary, Lisa, Clodagh McEvoy Johnston, the best juvenile camogie player in Bronxville, and her brother Conal, who watched his first All Ireland final on September 4th 2011 in Newport, Rhode Island, at the age of seven months, resplendent in a black and amber jersey autographed by the four in a row-winning captains.

Hanging out in the front bar in Langton's on a Sunday night, and lending an ear to tales of matches long ago, is a hurling education in itself. Thanks for their continued company to Tony Deegan, Tommy O'Connell and Bill Sullivan, and in affectionate memory of Andy Heffernan.

Brian O'Neill has been a constant presence since that far-off first Monday in St Kieran's. I'd thank him for the idea for the preface except that it had already occurred to me by the time he suggested it – further proof, were it needed, of how alarmingly similarly we think.

Thanks to Dan and Paul Butler for all those Sundays. *Ad multos annos.*

Thanks to the *Sunday Tribune* mob as, alas, was, a group of young men whose sense of fun was matched only by their talent and imagination. Step forward Malachy Clerkin, Joe Coyle, Ciaran Cronin, Miguel Delaney, John Foley, Dave Hannigan, Patrick Horan, Ewan MacKenna, Pat Nugent and Kieran Shannon. Mr Nugent, the finest *Tribune* sports editor that never will be, did much to bring clarity to a number of chapters. Malachy and John are splendid manuscript-readers and can be thoroughly recommended to anyone writing a book; they don't charge much either. And Joe Coyle is, simply, the Henry Shefflin of design and layout. Thanks also to Ger Siggins.

Thanks to Frank Roche for his guidance on Chapter 26. *Audere est* etc.

Gratitude to the usual crew of helpers, statisticians and general knowalls: Jim Fogarty, Leo McGough, Seamus "Sultan of Statistics" O'Doherty and PM O'Sullivan. I trust the latter will not be unduly discombobulated by my erratic hyphenation, his endless patient tutorials notwithstanding.

Denis Bergin and Fr Fearghus Ó Fearghail, scholars and classicists both, were a mine of information on all matters related to St Kieran's College. They each boast a prose style Tommy Maher, not to mention Peter Birch, would have been proud of. Also helpful on college affairs were Art Anglin, Seamus Daly, Adrian Finan, Tommy Lanigan, Dick McEvoy, Micheál Ó Diarmada and Michael O'Dwyer.

Colette O'Flaherty, the director of the National Library of Ireland, and John O'Sullivan went well above and beyond the call of duty. James Leyden at the Department of the Taoiseach helped too, as did Damien Brett in Kilkenny County Library, Amanda Fennelly and Vicky Moran in RTE, Eddie Gray in Gray's TV, Mac Dara Mac Donncha of Nemeton and Martin Walsh in A to Z Computers. Likewise two exceptional county GAA PROs, Conor Denieffe in Kilkenny and Ger Ryan in Tipperary.

Other acknowledgements are best done on a chapter by chapter basis. So...

Chapter 1: Paddy Buggy, Seán Clohosey, Eoghan Corry, Paddy Downey, Eamon Dunphy, Liam Griffin, the late Mick Kelly, Johnny McGovern, Jim Murphy, Senator Pat O'Neill, Marian Rackard, Dick Rockett, Matt Ruth, John Stapleton, Jim Walsh, Tom Walsh (Callan), Kevin Whelan and Tom Williams.

Chapter 2: Bridget Brennan, JJ Kavanagh, Paul Kavanagh, Benjy Lawlor and Mick O'Neill.

Chapter 3: Joe Dunphy, Mick Heffernan and Liam Ó Donnchu.

Chapter 4: Carol Herbert, Tony Herbert, Christina Murphy and Liam Ryan.

Chapter 5: Maurice Aylward, Mick Carroll, Martin Costello, Dick Dowling,

Liam Hinphey, the late Martin Lanigan, Philip Lanigan, Paschal McCann, the late Fr John Nyhan, Ollie Ryan, Dick Walsh, Irene Walsh, Martin Walsh and Tony Walsh.

Chapter 6: Tony Doyle, Kevin Heffernan, Dan Hogan, Dermot Kavanagh, Seán Moran, Jane O'Malley, Breda Walton and Tom Walton junior.

Chapter 7: Liam Cleere, Ned Fenlon, Austin Flynn, Denis Heaslip, Billy Hoare and Eugene McGuinness.

Chapter 8: Phil Fanning, Jimmy Grey, John O'Connor, Jamie O'Keeffe, Declan O'Meara, Frankie Walsh, Hugh Walsh and Mickey Walsh.

Chapter 9: Senan Cooke, Fr Tom Murphy, Noel Skehan and Tom Walsh.

Chapter 10: Dr Johnny Cuddihy, Pa Dillon, Pat Henderson, Aoife Teehan and John Teehan.

Chapter 11: Joan Cleere, Seamus Cleere, Seamus Leahy, Martin Maher, Paddy Moran and Donie Nealon.

Chapter 13: Eddie Gray, John Harrington, James O'Reilly (the consultant opthalmic surgeon, not the politician) and Tony Wall.

Chapter 14: Geoff Drea, Henry Drea, Michael Fitzgerald, Pat Fitzgerald, Mick Lanigan, Tom McGarry, Joe Millea and Michael Walsh.

Chapter 15: Johnny Callinan, Jarlath Cloonan, Tom Cloonan, Tim Crowe, Anthony Daly, Cyril Farrell, Des Ferguson, John Hanley, Brendan O'Sullivan and Conor Power.

Chapter 16: Donie Butler, Shem Downey, Edwina Grace, Frankie Grace-Walsh, Paddy Grace junior, John Knox, John O'Shea and Jim Rhatigan.

Chapter 17: Martin Coogan, John Kinsella, Georgie Leahy, Rita Leahy, Michael Moynihan, Brian Murphy, Liam O'Brien, Kieran Purcell, Tomás Ryan and Jim Treacy.

Chapter 18: Nickey Brennan, Eamonn Cregan, Mick Crotty, Billy Fitzpatrick, Seán Foley, Bernie Hartigan, Pat Lawlor, Tom McCormack, Willie Moore, Michael O'Grady and Ned Rea.

Chapter 19: Ultan Macken.

Chapter 20: Mick Crotty junior, Joe McDonagh, Cian O'Connell, Seán Silke, David Smith and Seán Walsh.

Chapter 21: Gerry Buckley, Michael Fortune and Dr Con Murphy

Chapter 22: Chris Dooley, Seamus Dooley, Johnny Flaherty, Pat Fleury, Andy Gallagher, Diarmuid Healy, Liam Hogan, Pádraig Horan, Seán Mac Connell, Damien Martin, Sheila Molony, Pat Nolan and Paul Rouse.

Chapter 23: Elaine Aylward, Michael Brennan, Brendan Conway, Jim Conway, Tommy Duggan, Mossy Murphy and Dan Power.

Chapter 25: DJ Carey, Mick Dempsey, Adrian Fenlon, Derek Lyng, Richie Mulrooney, Briain Ryan and Henry Shefflin.

Chapter 26: Ned Byrne, John Considine, Brendan Cummins, Mickey Harte, Tom Kenny, Seamus King, Noel McGrath, Eamon O'Shea, Liam Sheedy and Denis Walsh.

Further thanks are due to Liam Burke, Peter Carbery, Michael Carey, Pat Carroll, Micheál Clifford, Chris Comerford, Dermot Crowe, Mary Dooley, Ned Doyle, Donie Duggan, Mick Duggan, Regina Fitzpatrick, Barrie Henriques, Richie Hogan, Liam Horan, Brian Jaffray, John Kilroy, John Kirwan, Dominic McCormick, Mac Dara Mac Donncha, Siobhan Maher, Val Malone, Henry Martin, Alan Milton, Ned Moran, Fleur Muldowney, Niall Murphy, Kevin Nolan, Michelle Nolan, James O'Neill, Fr Troy Powers, Aileen Shanahan, Nicky Teehan and Dick "the Village" Walsh in Tullaroan.

Gratitude is also due to Anita Coogan, Martin Coogan, Madeleine Cummins, John Murphy in Crumlin, Fr Harry Ryan in Hexham and Michael Shortall.

So many people in so many ways helped to make it an armchair ride. The pleasure, the privilege, was all mine.

Birch, Peter, *St Kieran's College Kilkenny* (Gill, 1951)

Burke, Frank, *All Ireland Glory* (2004)

De Búrca, Marcus, *The GAA – A History* (Gill & Macmillan, 1999)

Dundon, Michael and the Byrne Family, *The Rattler – Mickey Byrne, Tipperary Hurling Legend* (2010)

Codd, Martin, *The Way I Saw It* (Corrigeentee Publishing, 2005)

Cody, Brian with Martin Breheny, *Cody – The Autobiography* (Irish Sports Publishing, 2009)

Cody, Joe, *The Stripy Men* (Mac Óda Publishing, 2009)

Cronin, Mike, Duncan, Mark and Rouse, Paul, *The GAA: A People's History* (Collins Press, 2009)

Cronin, Mike, Duncan, Mark and Rouse, Paul, *The GAA: County by County* (Collins Press, 2011)

Cusack, Donal Óg, *Come What May* (Penguin Ireland, 2009)

Dorgan, Val, *Christy Ring* (Ward River Press, 1980)

Duggan, Keith, *The Lifelong Season* (TownHouse, 2004)

English, Nicky with Vincent Hogan, *Beyond the Tunnel* (MedMedia, 1996)

Flood, Tim with Andy Doyle, *My Best Shot – The Life and Times of a Hurling Legend* (Blackwater Press, 2007)

Fullam, Brendan, *Giants of the Ash* (Wolfhound Press, 1991)

Furlong, Nicky, *The Greatest Hurling Decade* (Wolfhound Press, 1993)

Gladwell, Malcolm, *Outliers* (Little, Brown, 2008)

Harrington, John, *Doyle – The Greatest Hurling Story Ever Told* (Irish Sports Publishing, 2011)

Horgan, Tim, *Christy Ring – Hurling's Greatest* (Collins Press, 2008)

Horgan, Tim, *Cork's Hurling Story* (Collins Press, 2010)

Jaworski, Ron, with Greg Cosell and David Plaut, *The Games That Changed the Game* (Ballantine Books/ESPN Books, 2010)

Kavanagh, Dermot, *A History – Kilkenny Senior Hurling County Finals* (2004)

Kavanagh, Dermot, *Ollie – The Hurling Life and Times of Ollie Walsh* (Blackwater Press, 2006)

Keating, Babs with Donal Keenan, *Babs – A Legend in Irish Sport* (Storm Books, 1996)

Keegan, Charlie, *The Year of the Cats* (St John Publishing, 2008)

Keegan, Charlie, *The Four by the Nore* (St John Publishing, 2009)

King, Seamus J, *A History of Hurling* (Gill & Macmillan, 1996)

King, Seamus J, *Tipperary's GAA Story 1935-1984* (1988)

King, Seamus J, *Tipperary's GAA Story 1985-2004* (2005)

Leahy, Seamus, *The Tipp Revival* (Gill and Macmillan, 1995)

Looney, Tom, *King in a Kingdom of Kings* (Currach Press, 2008)

McCarthy, Justin, *Hooked: A Hurling Life* (Gill & Macmillan, 2002)

McEvoy, Enda, *Fennessy's Field* (Red Lion Press, 1998)

Macken, Ultan, *Eddie Keher's Hurling Life* (Mercier, 1978)

Martin, Henry, *Mick Mackey: Hurling Legend in a Troubled County* (Collins Press, 2011)

Martin, Henry, *Unlimited Heartbreak: The Inside Story of Limerick Hurling* (Collins Press, 2009)

Morrison, Tom, *For the Record* (Collins Press, 2005)

Moynihan, Michael, *Rebels: Cork GAA Since 1950* (Gill & Macmillan, 2010)

Murphy, James, *The Poetry and Songs of Black and Amber Glory* (2002)

Ó Fearghail, Fearghus, *St Kieran's College Kilkenny 1782-1982* (St Kieran's College, Kilkenny, 1982)

O'Flynn, Diarmuid, *Hurling – The Warrior Game* (Collins Press, 2008)

Ó hEithir, Breandán, *Over the Bar* (Ward River Press, 1984)

O'Neill, Gerry, *The Kilkenny GAA Bible* (2005)

Power, Conor, *My Father: A Hurling Revolutionary* (Three Good Boys, 2009)

Puirséal, Pádraig, *The GAA in Its Time* (Purcell, 1982)

Rackard, Billy *No Hurling at the Dairy Door* (Blackwater Press, 1996)

Ryall, Tom, *Kilkenny: The GAA Story 1884-1984* (1984)

Smith, David, *The Unconquerable Keane* (Original Writing, 2010)

Smith, Raymond, *The Clash of the Ash* (Aherlow Publishers, 1981)

Wall, Tony, *Hurling* (Cityview Press, 1965)

Walsh, Denis, *Hurling: The Revolution Years* (Penguin Ireland, 2005)

Walsh, Jim, *Sliabh Rua* (2001)

Williams, Dominic, *The Wexford Hurling & Football Bible 1887-2008* (2008)

Williams, Tom, *Cuchulainn's Son* (Blackwater Press, 2006)

Wilson, Jonathan, *Inverting the Pyramid* (Orion, 2008)

Kilkenny: History and Society – Interdisciplinary Essays on the History of an Irish County
Editors: William Nolan, Kevin Whelan (Geography Publications, 1990)

Offaly: History and Society – Interdisciplinary Essays on the History of an Irish County
Editors: William Nolan, Timothy P O'Neill (Geography Publications, 1998)

Kilkenny GAA Yearbook, 1972–
St Kieran's College Record, 1956–

Kilkenny GAA club histories
The Continent Abú: A History of the GAA in St John's Parish, Kilkenny (1999)
Famous Tullaroan (1984)
Fenian Lore (1999)
A Field of Dreams: Graignamanagh GAA Club Golden Jubilee (2003)
The Gowran GAA Story (2000)
Mullinavat GAA History (1984)
Up the 'Boro: Dicksboro GAA Club 1909-2009 (2009)
100 Years of the Village (1988)

INDEX